VOICES
FROM THE
GATHERING
STORM

VOICES
FROM THE
GATHERING
STORM

The Coming of the American Civil War

GLENN M. LINDEN

A Scholarly Resources Inc. Imprint
Wilmington, Delaware

Scholarly Resources Inc.
104 Greenhill Avenue
Wilmington, DE 19805-1897
www.scholarly.com

Library of Congress Cataloging-in-Publication Data

Voices from the gathering storm : the coming of the American Civil
   War / [compiled by] Glenn M. Linden.
        p. cm.
   Includes bibliographical references.
   ISBN 0-8420-2998-2 (alk. paper) — ISBN 0-8420-2999-0 (pbk :
alk. paper)
        1. United States—Politics and government—1849–1861—
Sources. 2. United States—History—1849–1877—Sources.
3. United States—History—Civil War, 1861–1865—Causes—
Sources. I. Linden, Glenn M., 1928–

E415.7 .V65 2001
973.7'11—dc21   2001020989

Acknowledgments

The editor wishes to thank a number of individuals for their assistance in the making of this book. Thomas J. Pressly read early versions of the manuscript and helped in the identification of the historical persons who were used. Ed Countryman also offered valuable comments in early stages and supported its publication. The support of Stephen Woodworth, editor of the American Crisis Series, was invaluable in the final shaping of the book. Thanks is also due to my recent Civil War classes that patiently received portions of the manuscript and offered constructive criticism. Two members of the Scholarly Resources staff, Matthew Hershey and Michelle Slavin, gave critical aid in the advanced stages of the completed manuscript. Additional thanks is due to James McPherson and Eric Foner for their support of the idea of studying the past through a careful study of the writings of those who lived in the past. I am grateful to my wife, Virginia Linden, for her tireless work in typing the many versions of the book and for her help in finding the seventeen photographs, and, finally, I am grateful to Scholarly Resources for their willingness to publish *Voices from the Gathering Storm*.

About the Author

Glenn Linden is associate professor of history at Southern Methodist University, where he has taught since 1968. He received his Ph.D. from the University of Washington. He is the author of two textbooks on the Civil War period—*Voices from the House Divided, 1861–1865* and *Voices from the Reconstruction Years, 1865–1877*—and two other books, *Desegregating Schools in Dallas: Four Decades in the Federal Courts* and *Politics or Principle: Congressional Voting on the Civil War Amendments and Pro-Negro Measures, 1837–1869*. He has been active in a number of historical associations, including the American Historical Association, the Southern Historical Association, and the Organization of American Historians.

Contents

Preface

*M*ost Americans in 1846 believed in a perpetual and inviolable Union. Daniel Webster stated this article of faith eloquently in 1830 when he said: "When my eyes shall be turned to behold for the last time the sun in heaven, may I not see him shining on the broken and dishonored fragments of a once glorious Union . . . let her last feeble and lingering gleams rather behold the gorgeous ensign of the republic, now known and honored throughout the earth, still full high advanced . . . liberty *and* Union, now and forever, one and inseparable!" Thus, when the war with Mexico broke out in 1846, sixty thousand Americans answered the call to arms. They came from both North and South prepared to fight for their country. Though outnumbered, U.S. forces won every battle and the final victory in 1847. Especially remarkable was the major role played by both Northern and Southern junior officers trained at West Point: Robert E. Lee, Ulysses S. Grant, Jefferson Davis, George B. McClellan, Thomas J. Jackson, George Thomas, and Pierre G. T. Beauregard. They did not know that they were rehearsing for a larger conflict fifteen years later. In 1846 the country was still united and confident of its future.

In 1861, however, the United States was a divided and disintegrating nation. The election of Abraham Lincoln as the first Republican president in November 1860 led to the secession of seven Southern states by February 1861 and the setting up of a Confederate government in Montgomery, Alabama. Lincoln's election and his opposition to the expansion of slavery into the western territories were viewed as a dangerous threat to the South and its way of life. Six weeks after his inauguration the new Confederacy fired on the Union forces at Fort Sumter in Charleston, South Carolina, and the Civil War began.

How did this dramatic change in thinking come about? What happened in those fifteen years that caused Southerners to question the value of the Union, begin to think about the possibility of secession, and then secede from the Union? Why was the Northern response so different? For years the North and South had talked to each other and had been able to find common ground. Slowly, however, the conversation began to become more heated and emotional; the discussions turned into arguments and then into bitter disputes. Before long, each side was talking but no longer hearing the other. Positions hardened, and there was less room for concessions. Only in the last months before the war did many recognize the seriousness of the situation. Senator John J. Crittenden pleaded for his compromise: "Unless something be done, you will have disunion or anarchy and war will follow." But his last-ditch efforts were unsuccessful. Neither side was willing to compromise.

In order to better understand what happened in those years, the writer has selected seventeen individuals who left firsthand accounts of their lives and then followed them through the fifteen-year period. These seventeen persons include six Southern white men, two Southern white women, four Northern white men, two Northern white women, one Northern black man, and two Northern black women. The reader will be transported back into the past and begin to think like those who lived before the Civil War. He or she will be able to see how those persons' ideas were changed by the great events of the pre-Civil War period. When this happens, the reader will have a greater awareness of the problems and the efforts to find satisfactory solutions and feel a new appreciation and empathy for the participants.

The readings have been arranged chronologically, beginning with the Wilmot Proviso in 1846 and ending with the first shots on Fort Sumter on April 12, 1861. There are three periods: 1846–1854, the Wilmot Proviso to the Kansas-Nebraska Act; 1854–1857, the Kansas-Nebraska Act to the Dred Scott decision; and finally, 1857–1861, the Dred Scott decision to the outbreak of the war at Fort Sumter. As the reader examines these firsthand accounts, two major themes become apparent. One is the growing rivalry between the North and South over the expansion of slavery into the western territories. Each section viewed the conflict with increasing seriousness. Slowly each side began to believe that if the issue was not resolved, it could lead to disunion. The other theme is a reexamination of the nature and value of the Union. Some began to question whether it still served their own interests, while others became even more firmly committed to the idea of an indivisible nation. The reader will also see that slavery became stronger in those years, and Southerners ceased to be apologetic about its existence and its importance to the nation. At the same time, there was growing willingness in the North to stop the expansion of slavery and to assert the inviolability of the Union. Efforts to find a compromise proved unsuccessful, and the most tragic war in American history began with the firing on Fort Sumter in April 1861.

Please note that the spelling and punctuation found in the diaries, letters, documents, and other accounts presented in this book, such as salutations with periods instead of commas or colons and ampersands ("&") instead of "and," have for the most part been maintained.

Cast of Characters (in order of appearance)

Collections of the New York Public Library, Astor, Lenox, and Tilden Foundations

CHARLES SUMNER was born in Boston, Massachusetts, on January 6, 1811. He was educated at the Boston Latin School and at Harvard, graduating from the college in 1830 and from the law school in 1833. The next year he was admitted to the bar and formed a partnership with G. S. Hilliard. After practicing law for several years, he spent three years in France, England, Italy, and Germany traveling, continuing his studies, and making new friends. His first public appearance of note was an address on July 4, 1845, entitled "The True Grandeur of Nations," in which he denounced war. A month later he attacked slavery at the Whig convention in Massachusetts. In the following years, Sumner continued to be an articulate spokesman for those who opposed slavery.

Charles Sumner became chairman of the Senate Committee on Foreign Affairs and took an active part in the Civil War, urging immediate emancipation, employment of black soldiers, and confiscation of Confederate property. After the war he urged a severe Reconstruction policy toward the South, took part in the impeachment of Andrew Johnson, and continued to feud with President Ulysses S. Grant throughout his presidency. In 1872 he broke with the Republican Party and supported Horace Greeley, the Democratic nominee for president. His efforts to have the Senate accept a comprehensive Civil Rights Bill failed, but after his death on March 14, 1874, the bill was passed as a tribute to his efforts in behalf of civil rights for freedmen.

Southern Historical Collection, Wilson Library, The University of North Carolina at Chapel Hill

ABRAHAM LINCOLN was born in Hardin County, Kentucky, on February 12, 1809, the son of Thomas and Nancy Hanks Lincoln. His early education was uneven and scanty. In 1816 the family moved to Spencer County, Indiana. Two years later his mother died; the next year his father married Sara Bush Johnston, who helped young Abraham improve his reading and writing. After a trip to New Orleans in which Lincoln had his first glimpse of the outside world, the family moved to Illinois. In the next few years he worked as a clerk, a surveyor, and a postmaster. He began to take an interest in politics, running for the state legislature but failed the first time. He was elected in his next attempt and reelected the following year. He became a lawyer, forming his first partnership with Stephen Logan in 1837 and a second one in 1843 with William Herndon, which lasted until his death. In 1842 he married Mary Todd and subsequently they had four children—Robert, Edward, William, and Thomas.

As president of the United States, Lincoln was determined to preserve the Union at all costs. At first he hoped for a short war, sixty to ninety days, but within a year he knew it would be much longer and would have to involve the ending of slavery. His efforts to provide federal money to induce border states to voluntarily end slavery proved unsuccessful. This lack of success freed him to consider a more extreme solution—to broaden the war aims to include the end of slavery in all states in rebellion on January 1, 1863. The Confederacy refused his offer, and soon the war became a total one upon the Southern way of life. For two years, Lincoln searched for a general who could win the war. Finally, in the winter of 1863–1864 he settled on Ulysses S. Grant, who planned a campaign of simultaneous massive attacks on the Confederate heartland. The end came with General William Tecumseh Sherman's march through Georgia to the sea, Robert E. Lee's surrender at Appomattox, and Joseph E. Johnston's surrender to Sherman.

Lincoln had been thinking about the Reconstruction of the South for several years. His early efforts in Louisiana and Arkansas seemed promising but met strong resistance from Congress. In the last days before his death, Lincoln took a more flexible and pragmatic approach, and in his last speech on April 11, 1865, he promised "some new announcement" on Reconstruction in the near future. Three days later he was assassinated by John Wilkes Booth. He was fifty-six years old.

Courtesy of International Publishers Co., Inc.

FREDERICK DOUGLASS was born a slave in February 1817 to Captain Anthony in Talbot County, Maryland, and named Frederick Augustus Washington Bailey. His father was white and his mother, Harriet Bailey, of brown complexion. In 1838 he escaped to the North and took the name of Douglass. He married a free black woman, Anna Murray, and went to New Bedford to live. Because of his color, he was not able to take up his trade as a caulker; instead he worked as a common laborer. During his stay in New Bedford he spoke at meetings where matters of race were being discussed. His speeches attracted the attention of abolitionists, and in August 1841 he was persuaded to devote his time and talents to the abolition movement. Soon he was traveling with the Massachusetts, Rhode Island, and American Anti-Slavery Societies. In 1844 he wrote a narrative of his life in order to remove doubts that he had been a slave. In the account he revealed his master's name and residence, thus exposing himself to the danger of being returned to slavery. In December 1847 he began to edit and publish a weekly newspaper in Rochester, New York, called *The North Star*, which he continued until President Lincoln issued the Emancipation Proclamation in 1863, making further agitation unnecessary.

When the war began, Douglass advocated arming the slaves. He assisted in raising the 54th and 55th Black Regiments in Massachusetts in which two of his sons, Lewis and Blake, served as noncommissioned officers. At the end of the war he urged instant and complete enfranchisement of the freedmen in the South.

Douglass moved to Washington, DC, in 1872 and held a number of government positions in the next two decades—the secretary of the Santo Domingo Commission, marshal (1877–1881) and recorder of deeds (1881–1886) of the District of Columbia, and minister to Haiti (1889–1891). He fought for black rights until his death in Washington on February 20, 1895. He was seventy-eight years old.

Antiochiana Collection, Antioch College

HORACE MANN was born in Franklin, Norfolk County, Massachusetts, on May 4, 1796. Until the age of fifteen he had never been to school more than eight to ten weeks in a year. He studied the few books then available in a local city library until he came in contact with an eccentric but brilliant scholar who opened up a school in his neighborhood. Mann made the most of the opportunity, learning Greek and Latin and studying the Bible. When his teacher left, he went to Providence and entered the sophomore class at Brown University and graduated in 1819. He completed his law studies, passed the bar examination in 1823, and practiced law until 1837.

Mann moved to Boston in 1833 and formed a partnership with Edward Loring. The same year he entered politics, was elected to the state senate, and continued to be elected for four more years, being president the last year. In 1837, Mann retired from politics in order to work in the field of education. In the next decade he established in Massachusetts the best public school system in the United States. He visited European schools and incorporated his findings in a number of reports that forever changed the face of American education. With the retirement of John Quincy Adams in 1848, Mann was elected to Congress as a Whig. His first speech in the House was on the right of Congress to restrict slavery in the territories. His was a powerful voice for the ending of slavery.

SOJOURNER TRUTH, first named Isabella, was born in 1797 in the village of Hurley in Ulster County, New York. Her parents were James and Elizabeth, the slaves of Johannis Hardenburgh, a Revolutionary War colonel. She was the youngest of ten or twelve children. After her master died, she was sold three times, the last time to John Dumont, where she remained for the next twelve years. During that time she married Thomas, one of Dumont's slaves, in 1815 and had five children.

Courtesy of Library of Congress

The state of New York passed a law providing for gradual emancipation beginning on July 4, 1827. The year before, she had heard God's voice and prepared herself to be free. However, Dumont sold her youngest son, Peter, and it took Isabella several years to get back Peter and then to move to New York City, where both were able to live free. There she found religion, became a preacher, and for a time was a disciple of John Newland Moffit, a charismatic preacher. Then on June 1, 1843, she decided to leave New York and named herself Sojourner Truth. She had become a follower of William Miller and expected the day of judgment to come soon. For the next three years, Truth became part of a cooperative community in Northampton, Massachusetts, where she was led into the feminist antislavery movement. Her stories and speeches on slavery proved irresistible to white reformers, and within a few years she was a well-known antislavery proponent.

Truth was an active supporter of the Union cause during the Civil War. In the early months she spoke at meetings and pro-Union rallies. At one meeting she was arrested because African Americans were by law denied entry into the state of Indiana. Undeterred she continued antislavery work in volunteer services in support of black troops; for example, Truth went from door to door collecting Thanksgiving Day food for a black regiment in Detroit. In October 1864 she met President Lincoln, who signed her autograph book and accepted her thanks for his conduct of the war. In later years she met two more presidents,

Andrew Johnson and Ulysses S. Grant. After the war, Truth worked in refugee relief, women's suffrage, and the colonization of freedmen into the West. For the last three years of her life she lived in Harmonia and Battle Creek, Michigan. She died on November 26, 1883, at the age of eighty-six.

Courtesy of South Caroliniana Library, University of South Carolina, Columbia

WILLIAM GILMORE SIMMS was born in 1806 in Charleston, South Carolina, the son of a poor immigrant tradesman. With little formal schooling, he served as an apprentice to an apothecary and in later years read law. In 1830 he purchased the *Charleston City Gazette* and supported the Union in the Nullification Controversy of 1832. He began to write poems and novels in this period; his best and most popular novel was *The Yemassee*, published in 1835. In the following years, down to the Civil War, he edited ten periodicals as well as wrote seven Revolutionary War romantic novels of crime, colonial history, and Spanish history; seventy short stories; and seventeen volumes of verse and criticism.

Simms was a vigorous supporter of slavery and an early leader in the secession movement. After witnessing the firing on Fort Sumter, he consistently supported the Confederate cause. In letters to James Henry Hammond and others, he discussed the military and economic potentials of the North and South and offered ideas about strategy. During the early years of the war he was certain that the South would win and wrote letters to his Northern friends boasting about Southern victories and the inevitable final triumph. However, 1863 was a bad year for him; his wife and a child died and his beloved plantation burned down. By the end of the war, Simms had lost everything—every building of value, his 10,000-volume library; moreover, he was supporting nine persons on ten dollars per week.

After the restoration of peace, Simms renewed his contacts with friends in the North. He went to New York in the fall of 1861 and was pleased with the warm reception accorded him. Upon his return to Charleston, Simms became associate editor of the *Daily South Carolinian*, where his editorials complained of Northern military rule, a lack of food, and continuing high prices. He also wrote a serial for a magazine, the *Old Guard*, completed a volume of war poetry, and had three romance novels published. In his last months he declared that he had few objects of importance left but to provide for his children. Exhausted and in poor health, he died on June 11, 1870, at the age of sixty-four.

Southern Historical Collection, Wilson Library, The University of North Carolina at Chapel Hill

JEFFERSON DAVIS was born on June 3, 1808, in Fairfield, Kentucky. His family moved to Wilkinson, Mississippi, when he was an infant. After attending the county academy, Davis entered Transylvania College at the age of sixteen and advanced to the senior class when he was appointed to the U.S. Military Academy at West Point. He entered in September 1824, graduated in 1828, and became an officer of infantry on the frontier for several years. After a successful campaign against the Indians, he resigned from the army in order to marry the daughter of Zachary Taylor. In Warren County he purchased a plantation from his brother and settled down to plant cotton and study. However, after his wife died, he went into seclusion for several years. In 1843, Davis began to take part in political activities, and the next year he was chosen presidential elector at large. The following year he was elected to the House of Representatives and took his seat in December 1845. When the Mexican War broke out, he was chosen to be colonel of a group of volunteers.

Davis served as president of the Confederacy until the end of the war. As the conflict progressed, he assumed more control of the government, which angered many Southerners who believed in states' rights. A military man by training, he was nevertheless a successful politician who found it increasingly difficult to satisfy everyone. Still he maintained an unshakable conviction that the Confederacy would win. As late as May 1864, Davis stated: "The armies in Northern Virginia and Tennessee still pose, with unshakable front, a formidable barrier to the progress of the invader." In the next eleven months, Davis tried desperately to end the war, but in April 1865 Confederate forces retreated from Richmond and Petersburg and surrendered at Appomattox. General Sherman marched through Georgia into North Carolina, where Joseph Johnston surrendered.

At the conclusion of the war, Davis was placed in prison at Fortress Monroe where he remained for two years. There was talk of putting him on trial, but, due mainly to the efforts of his wife and Horace Greeley, Davis was finally released. The last years of his life were brightened by the admiration of the Southern people for the man who had come to symbolize the lost cause. He gave numerous speeches for Confederate reunions and at the laying of cornerstones at Confederate monuments. The public response was an outpouring of emotion unlike any that the South had witnessed in recent memory. Then, while on a trip, he caught cold and died in New Orleans on December 9, 1889. He was eighty-one years old.

Chicago Historical Society, ICHi-30458

JOHN JORDAN CRITTENDEN was born near Versailles, Woodford County, Kentucky, on September 10, 1781, the son of Major John and Judith Harris Crittenden. His father, a Revolutionary War soldier, was a farmer of moderate means. John J. graduated from the College of William and Mary in 1807 and, after studying law, became a lawyer in Russell, Kentucky. He was attorney general of the Territory of Illinois in 1809–1810, served in the War of 1812, and was on the staff of Governor Isaac Shelby in Canada at the battle of the Thames, October 5, 1813. He served in the U.S. Senate from 1817 to 1819 and again from 1835 to 1841, when he was appointed attorney general by President William

Henry Harrison. After Harrison's death he resigned the position and was again elected U.S. Senator and served from 1842 to 1848, when he was elected governor of Kentucky on the Whig ticket.

In the last two years of his life, Crittenden worked tirelessly to keep Kentucky neutral in the Civil War. Strong pressures from the Confederacy were resisted, and, by the time of his death on July 26, 1863, Crittenden was instrumental in the transition of Kentucky from neutrality to cooperation with the Union. James G. Blaine thought that he "more than . . . any other man saved Kentucky from rebellion." President Lincoln believed that he was entitled to "the admiration and gratitude" of all loyal Unionists. He died at Frankfort, Kentucky, on July 26, 1863.

GEORGE TEMPLETON STRONG was born on January 26, 1820, in New York City. His father, a successful lawyer, enrolled him in the grammar school attached to Columbia College, where later he would graduate second in his class. He was admitted to the bar and began work in the firm of Strong and Bidwell in 1844; the next year the firm was renamed Strong, Bidwell, and Strong. George T. Strong became a trustee of the college (later university), a patron of the arts, and a supporter of the Whig Party. Widely read, he was an astute observer of politics and human nature in the 1840s and 1850s. In 1848 he married Ellen Ruggles after a three-month courtship.

Collection of The New-York Historical Society

Strong supported Union efforts to suppress the Southern secession. As treasurer of the United States Sanitary Commission he had opportunities to meet and visit with President Lincoln on two occasions. After the victory at Antietam he wrote that Lincoln was now an effective leader. The victory at Gettysburg was "priceless," but he cautioned that the war was not over. As the conflict entered its last year, Strong actively supported Lincoln and considered his election as "the most momentous popular election ever held since ballots were invented."

After the war, Strong continued his diary, which he had begun in 1835 when he was fifteen years old, commenting on the political and economic events of the time. He maintained his interest in Columbia College. He supported efforts to reconstruct the South but in later years became disillusioned with their results. Strong did not live to see the end of Reconstruction, dying on July 21, 1875, at the age of fifty-five.

Courtesy of Nicholas H. Cobbs and St. Paul's Episcopal Church, Greensboro, Alabama

AUGUSTUS BENNERS was born in New Bern, North Carolina, on December 25, 1818. His father was Lucas Jacob Benners IV, a state senator, church warden, and treasurer of Christ Episcopal Church in New Bern; his mother was Frances Batchelor Benners. Augustus Benners graduated from Chapel Hill, North Carolina, and moved to Alabama where he practiced law from 1840 to 1885. He married Jane Hatch in 1846, became a plantation owner in 1850, and began to keep a journal.

In the early years of the war, Benners was optimistic about the future. The "glorious news" of the Southern victory at Manassas filled him with pride, but as the war continued, he began to have misgivings. The federal blockade cut off supplies, prices began to rise, and military victories were fewer and more costly. By the end of 1864 he had little hope of victory, and in the last days of the war he prayed, "God of Heaven, send us reconciliation and peace."

During the Reconstruction years, Benners wrote of his frustration with postwar conditions: "The sadness of these times can scarcely be described." Freedmen worked slowly, and it was difficult to bring in a crop. His economic situation did not improve, and political conditions troubled him. His interest in politics was revived by the election of 1872, when he thought that Ulysses S. Grant could be beaten, but Grant won easily.

Benners reentered politics and became a delegate to the state convention in 1876. He closely followed the presidential contest between Rutherford B. Hayes, the Republican, and Samuel Tilden, the Democrat, expecting Tilden to win. However, the dispute over delegate count led to the appointment of a special commission to resolve the differences. In late January, Benners received a telegram to appear in Washington before the Senate Subcommittee on Elections. He testified on February 13, 1877, that there had been no intimidation of black voters and no bribery in the election in Alabama. Despite his testimony the Commission decided to confirm Hayes as president. Benners was furious: "the vote on the Commission was a party one from first to last & disgraceful to them."

He continued his journal until August 7, 1885, the day he died. Benners was sixty-six years of age.

HARRIET BEECHER STOWE was born in Litchfield, Connecticut, on June 14, 1811, the daughter of the famous preacher, Dr. Lyman Beecher, and Roxanna Foote Beecher. She had an older sister, Catherine, and a famous younger brother, Henry Ward Beecher. Her mother died when she was four years old, and she was taken by relatives to Guilford, Connecticut, where she was trained in the catechism and needlework. Later she attended Litchfield Academy and her sister's school in Hartford, where she prepared students in

Courtesy of Ohio Historical Society

drawing and painting. In 1832 the family moved to Cincinnati where Lyman Beecher became president of Lane Theological Seminary. The next year the subject of slavery was brought to her notice upon a trip across the river to Kentucky when she visited an estate that afterward she described as Colonel Shelby's in *Uncle Tom's Cabin*. In January 1836, Harriet married Calvin Stowe, a professor of sacred literature at Lane Seminary. She continued to write short stories and essays and assisted her brother, who was editor of the Cincinnati *Daily Journal*. When the issue of slavery gained more attention, Harriet wrote letters in an effort to find a solution. In 1839 she received into her family a slave girl who had left Kentucky. The master tried to take her back, but Calvin Stowe and Henry Ward Beecher drove the fugitive away and left her with a Quaker family. Later Harriet wrote about the episode in *Uncle Tom's Cabin*. The next years were those of extreme trial to the family— poverty, sickness, and separation from her husband, who went East to recover his health.

In her writings, Stowe urged her readers to support the Civil War and prepare for "a long pull." She praised abolitionists Wendell Phillips and William Lloyd Garrison for not mixing the slavery question with the present crisis. Her son, Fred, volunteered and was accepted into the 1st Massachusetts Regiment.

On September 22, 1862, President Lincoln issued the preliminary Emancipation Proclamation, which he intended to make final on January 1, 1863. This act encouraged Stowe to write a letter to the women of Great Britain explaining his decision and asking for their help in the effort to end slavery. After all, the president was only following their example of abolishing slavery. She met Lincoln on December 2 and attended a celebration at the Boston Music Hall for those who worked to end slavery. The crowd chanted her name until she stood up and acknowledged the tribute. In the summer of 1863 she visited the camp of the all-black 54th Massachusetts Regiment and was impressed with the soldiers' dignity and deportment.

After the war, Stowe bought property in Florida, where she had a house built. She continued to write and lecture for the next fifteen years. While she took an interest in women's rights, corresponding regularly with Elizabeth Cady Stanton and Susan B. Anthony, she was never an active speaker for feminist ideas. During the 1880s, Stowe wrote little except occasional notes to friends. Her health declined in the 1890s, and on July 1, 1896, surrounded by her family, she died. It was two weeks after her eighty-fifth birthday.

CHARLOTTE FORTEN GRIMKÉ was born in Philadelphia in 1837 to Robert Bridges Forten and Mary Virginia Woods Forten. She was an only child. Her immediate family had several wealthy members including James Forten, Sr., the owner of a sail-making company in Philadelphia. Her mother, a mulatto member of a prominent abolitionist family, died when Charlotte was three years old. Family members raised her with an awareness of the need to end slavery and to work to secure equal rights for blacks. When she was sixteen, Charlotte went to live with

Courtesy of Moorland-Spingarn Library at Howard University

an abolitionist family in Salem, Massachusetts, and received a good education in a nonsegregated school system.

Charlotte remained active in the abolitionist cause throughout the war. In October 1862, at the suggestion of John Greenleaf Whittier, she went south to teach escaped slaves who had fled to Union camps. For eighteen months she taught in the Port Royal, South Carolina, area. She visited the camp of the 54th Regiment in June 1863, where she met Colonel Shaw. Later, shocked by his death and the deaths of nearly one-half of his regiment at the Battle of Fort Wagner, she decided to serve as a nurse at the local army hospital to the wounded members of Shaw's regiment who returned after the engagement.

After the war, Charlotte continued teaching the freed slaves. She then moved to Massachusetts, where she lived until 1871. The next year she taught in Charleston, South Carolina, after which she moved to Washington, DC. There she met and married Francis Grimké, a mulatto graduate student, twelve years her junior, who had graduated from Princeton Theological Seminary in 1878 and become pastor of a Presbyterian church. They had one child, a girl, who died in 1880. They resided in Washington for the remainder of their lives. In 1913, Charlotte became ill and, after thirteen months in bed, died in July 1914 at the age of seventy-six.

THE JONES FAMILY includes Rev. Charles Colcock Jones, Sr., the father (1804–1863); Mary Jane Jones, the mother (1808–1869); and Charles Colcock Jones, Jr., the son (1831–1893).

Charles Colcock Jones, Sr., attended schools in Northern cities; he received his bachelor's degree and license to preach from Princeton College in 1830. A minister to blacks in his county, he published several books on their religious education. Jones was a professor at the Presbyterian Theological Seminary in Columbia, South Carolina, in the 1830s

Rev. Charles Colcock Jones, Sr.
Special Collections, Tulane University Library, New Orleans, Louisiana

and 1840s; lived in Philadelphia from 1850 to 1853; and served as corresponding secretary of the missions program of the Presbyterian Church.

When the war began, Jones, Sr., remained loyal to the Confederate cause. He was pleased with the early victory at Bull Run, believing that God was on the Confederate side. During the second year of the war, Jones worried about the loyalty of the slaves "who may pilot an enemy into your bed chamber." He died on March 16, 1863, at Arcadia plantation in Georgia.

Mary Jane Jones
Special Collections, Tulane University Library, New Orleans, Lousiana

Mary Jane Jones and her husband owned three plantations of 3,500 acres in Liberty County, Georgia. The U.S. Census lists them with 167 slaves in 1850 and 129 in 1860. As a teenager she had attended McIntosh Academy at Barsden's Bluff (1820–1823) and the academy of Abiel Carter in Savannah (1823–1827) and then married Rev. Charles Jones in 1830. Three of their children, including Charles, Jr., lived to maturity.

"Our hearts are filled with gratitude to God," she rejoiced, over the victory at Manassas. Mary worried over the losses at Forts Henry and Donelson but was cheered in the spring of 1862 by Robert E. Lee's victory in Virginia. When her husband died in March 1863, she was forced to run the three plantations alone. As General Sherman's troops marched through Georgia, she fled to her brother's plantation in Baker County. Mary returned home in the fall of 1865 and tried unsuccessfully to run the plantation at Montevideo. In January 1868 she moved to New Orleans to live with her daughter and her family. Her health began to decline and she died in April 1869 at the age of sixty-one.

Charles Colcock Jones, Jr., was tutored privately in Georgia, studied at South Carolina College in Columbia, and graduated from Princeton College in 1852. He studied law at Harvard and received his law degree in 1855, when he became a lawyer in Savannah.

Jones served as an officer in the Confederate Army, rising in rank from lieutenant to lieutenant colonel by the end of the war. He was so gratified with his duties as a colonel of the artillery that he declined to accept a commission as brigadier general. He surrendered with Johnston in

Charles Colcock Jones, Jr.
Georgia Historical Society, Savannah, Georgia

April 1865. Earlier in the war, in 1861, Jones's wife had died, leaving an infant girl who was cared for by his parents. He married again in 1863.

After the war, Jones lived in Savannah for six months managing a cotton plantation. Tiring of the work, he accepted an offer from a New York City law firm and practiced law there until the spring of 1877, when he returned to Georgia with his family. He bought an antebellum mansion, practiced law, and devoted his leisure time to literature and to research in the historical lore of his native state. He was president of the Confederate Survivors Association of Augusta from 1879 to 1887. He died in Augusta on July 19, 1893.

Courtesy of Caroline Birchett, Jackson, Mississippi

TRYPHENA BLANCHE HOLDER FOX was born in Massachusetts in 1834, educated at the Maplewood Young Ladies Institute in Pittsfield, and moved in 1852 to Mississippi to tutor the adopted daughter of George Messinger, a planter. Four years later she married David Fox, a physician who practiced in Plaquemines Parish, Louisiana. After "marrying up," she wrote, "I am so glad that I am no longer dependent upon this one or that one for shelter." Wanting protection from the "hardships and trials" of the life of a tutor, she became instead a plantation mistress with its own set of trials and tribulations. In the years from 1852 to 1862 she wrote eighty-three letters, mostly to her mother in Massachusetts. Unfortunately the letters she received were lost; however, her letters from 1856 to 1861 provide considerable information on her life and attitudes in those years.

Despite living much of her life in the North, Tryphena was firmly convinced that the Confederacy would win the war because "one Southerner could whip ten Yankees." She also stated that "Southerners can *never* be conquered; they may all be killed, but conquered, never." The family moved to Woodborne plantation in Mississippi near Vicksburg just before the fall of New Orleans on April 25, 1862. Conditions worsened and she could not send money to her mother in the North. Her hatred of Yankees grew as Northern soldiers ravaged her husband's family home. The loss at Vicksburg was especially painful. Dr. Fox joined the Confederacy as a surgeon and medical examiner in northern Mississippi.

After the war ended, Tryphena had difficulty accepting the outcome. The South was "not subdued, only overpowered." Readmission to the Union was worse than defeat. Their original house, Hygiene, was burned down in early 1866; it was rebuilt one year later. Her husband lost his fortune for the third time in 1873; "I bear it resignedly though I feel it is *hard*." Tryphena continued to write to her mother in an effort to maintain the family tie between Mississippi and Massachusetts. Upon her husband's death in 1893, Tryphena left Hygiene and made her home in Warren County, Mississippi, with her daughter, Blanche Cleveland. As she had done forty years earlier, she left behind her beloved home and possessions. She died in 1912 at the age of seventy-eight.

KEZIAH GOODWYN HOPKINS BREVAD was born in 1803. She studied at Minervaville Academy and Columbia Female Academy in South Carolina. She married Alexander Joseph Brevard in April 1827. He began to drink heavily, ending up as a patient in the South Carolina State Hospital, and died on June 1, 1842. Brevard inherited his modest estate and two years later her father's estate. Thus, she now owned 2,600 acres. By 1860 she had doubled her holdings, had 209 slaves, and maintained regular outputs of cotton, corn, wool, and sweet potatoes.

Courtesy of Dr. Edward Hopkins, Columbia, South Carolina

In 1860, Keziah Brevard was a fifty-seven-year-old widow running her own plantation in the heart of South Carolina—the Richland District. She started a diary on July 27, 1860, and continued to record her experiences until April 15, 1861, when the war broke out.

She continued to manage her plantation throughout the Civil War. However, Sherman's men burned at least two of her homes, Cabin Branch and Mill Place; another home, Alwehar, was vandalized but not burned. Her slaves were set free and her railroad stock was valueless. Adding to her troubles, her half-sister Sarah Hall had mental problems but lived with her until her death in 1867.

Brevard continued to lease her lands to tenants and used the income to pay her taxes. Tradition has it that she never sold a slave or a tree. That may be true, but she did exchange 14 acres of land for a family cemetery where she and her husband were buried. By the end of her life she had an estate of 6,710 acres. She died in 1886.

Part I

A Growing Rivalry between the North and South, 1846–1854

The successful waging of the Mexican War added vast new territories to the United States. Soon a rivalry developed between the North and South over the introduction of slavery into these territories. Most Southerners opposed any restriction of slavery even if the territories to the west were unsuited to the "peculiar institution." However, a growing number of Northerners were becoming Free Soilers and did not want slavery extended into the new areas. They opposed the admission of new slave states but were willing to leave slavery where it presently existed.

The question of slavery in the new territories needed to be discussed in Congress before any of them could be admitted to the Union. When President James K. Polk asked for $2 million to purchase land from Mexico, the question of slavery expansion was raised by David Wilmot, a congressman from Pennsylvania, who introduced an amendment to the appropriation bill forbidding slavery in any territory that might be acquired by treaty from Mexico. In the next few years the proviso was debated but not passed by both houses of Congress. The votes clearly showed the deep differences in the nation over the issue of slavery in the territories.

In the election of 1848 both major parties tried to ignore the slavery issue, but the newly created Free Soil Party raised it by opposing any extension of slavery into the new territories. The issue so divided the Democratic Party that it led to the election of a Whig president, Zachary Taylor. Ten percent of the New York voters cast their ballots for the Free Soil candidate, former president Martin Van Buren, resulting in Taylor's carrying New York and enough other states to win the election. Slavery was now an important part of the political struggle.

In 1850, Congress made a serious attempt to resolve the issue of slavery and its extension into the West. The major effort to draw up a compromise was made by Henry Clay. He proposed the admission of California as a free state, the setting up of New Mexico and Utah without regard to slavery but allowing each to make its own decision and then seek admittance as a state, the prohibition of the slave trade in the District of Columbia, compensation for Texas for an adjustment in its boundary and land area, and a more effective fugitive slave law. After eight months of debate the Compromise of 1850 was passed, largely due to the efforts of Illinois's Senator Stephen A. Douglas. The menace of disruption of the Union was averted, but the fundamental differences were not resolved.

Of major concern to the North in the next few years was the return of fugitive slaves to the South. Many in the North refused to obey the new law and, with the assistance of the Underground Railroad, helped slaves to escape to Canada. Harriet Beecher Stowe's *Uncle Tom's Cabin* in 1852 gave dramatic expression to Northern passions and anxieties and would shape a whole generation's view of slavery. In that same year the Know-Nothing Party was formed and stressed the dangers of the massive invasion of more than three million Irish and Germans into the American political system. Rapid social and economic changes increased anti-Catholic fears among many Protestants as well as created hostility toward politicians and a desire to change the political system.

As a result, Franklin Pierce was elected president of the United States. His victory was due to the strength of the Know-Nothing Party and the weakness of the Whigs, who were divided over the issue of slavery. In the next two years the Whig Party collapsed, leaving the field open for a new second political party. The Know-Nothings had several years of experience and a clear message for the voters. The soon-to-be formed Republican Party had greater difficulty but coalesced around the need to stop the expansion of slavery into the territories. Only time would tell which party would ultimately be successful.

1

The Mexican War, the Wilmot Proviso, and the Election of 1848

NORTHERNERS

Charles Sumner

Sumner was an active reformer in the 1840s. At first he was involved in prison reform and the building of normal schools, but by the mid-1840s he was drawn into the debate over slavery during the Mexican War. Always fiercely antislavery, he began to agitate for the end of hostilities in Mexico, as can be seen in his letters to family and friends in the next few years.

> To George Sumner [his brother]
> Boston Dec 31st '46
> My dear George,
> . . . The affairs of our country are now in a deplorable condition. The Mexican War & Slavery will derange all party calculations. The Anti-Slavery principle has acquired such force as to be felt by all politicians. In most of the Free States it will hold the balance between the two parties, so that neither can succeed without yielding to it in a greater or less degree. The Abolitionists have at last got their lever upon a *fulcrum*, where it can operate. It will detach large sections from each of the other parties.
> Both parties are not controlled in their conduct, even on the Mexican War, by a reference to the next Presidential election. The Whigs shrink from opposing it, for fear of unpopularity at the South & West; & the leaders of both parties act mainly with a view to maintain the force of their party.—The question of Slavery advances upon the country with great strides. . . .
>
> Ever Thine,
> *Charles*

Several months later, he rejoiced in the rapid change in attitude toward slavery in the North. Perhaps it would be the "grand issue" in the next presidential contest.

To Francis Lieber
Boston March 22nd '47
My dear Lieber,
. . . The Mexican War has hastened by 20 or 30 years the question of Slavery. The issue is now made. It will continue, until Slavery no longer has any recognition under the Constitution of the U.S. I tell you—what you already know—that preparations are now maturing to make the *grand issue* in the next Presidential contest on slavery. The chief part of the Ohio & Massachusetts Whigs are ready for this. I do not think it possible to stave this off. Clay, Webster & Taylor *cannot* be the candidates of the *united* Whig party. Secret efforts have been made by Webster's friends in the Mass. Legislat. within a few weeks to have him nominated for the Presidency; but it was ascertained *that the nomination could not be made.* This has caused disappointment in some quarters. . . .

I think we may now see *le commencement du fin* [the beginning of the end] of the Slavery contest. Massachusetts is fast becoming, if she be not now, a thorough uncompromising Anti-Slavery State. . . .

Ever yrs,
Charles Sumner

During the summer of 1848 a foundation was laid for the Free Soil convention to meet in Buffalo in August. At that convention, compromises were made between the members of the Liberty Party, the Barnburner Democrats, and Whigs who opposed Zachary Taylor on the issue of slavery. A strong antislavery platform and the nomination of Martin Van Buren as the presidential candidate were the results. The new Free Soil Party's slogan was "Free Soil, Free Speech, Free Labor, and Free Men."

In a letter to a friend on November 8, Sumner expressed cautious optimism over the coming election.

To Henry Gilpin
Boston Nov. 8th '48
My dear Mr Gilpin,
. . . The urn has been shaken, & our fates have come forth. The papers will tell you what we have done in Massachusetts. I am inclined

to think this has been the scene of the closest contest—that there has been more force in the field on both sides, or rather on all sides—more speakers—& more money spent here than in any other state. . . .

Next Monday we choose Governor, State officers & members of Congress. You kindly refer to me as candidate. I am put up as a mark; for there is no chance for us here in Boston. I am exposed, perhaps, to as strong a pressure as can be encountered in the whole country.

If Taylor is elected, as seems probable now, we must rally our forces on the basis of the Northern Democracy. We must plant ourselfs on the Declaration of Independence & the Constitution of the United States, & insist upon bringing back the Govt. to the true spirit of these instruments, so that it shall be administered, not in the spirit of Slavery, but of Freedom. Here is something truly conservative & reforming. We shall be the party of Conservative Reform.

It seems to me that our friends ought to hold a consultation speedily in order to mark out our future course, which should be developed in an address to the people of the U.S.

It is supposed here that Pennsylvania has gone for Taylor. Believe me, my dear Sir,

very faithfully Yours,

Charles Sumner

Despite the best efforts of the Free Soil Party, Taylor was elected president. Van Buren received 14 percent of the Northern vote and was a key factor in the elections of New York and Ohio. Still, Sumner was not discouraged. In a letter to Salmon P. Chase, he expressed satisfaction over the efforts and looked forward to the future.

To Salmon P. Chase
Boston Nov. 16th 1848
My dear Sir,

Our contest is at last closed—for the present. I have been so deeply engaged in it, that I have had no time for correspondence. You also have been constantly occupied.

Looking over the field now, I feel that we have cause for high satisfaction. We have found a large number of men through all the Free States, who are willing to leave the old parties & join in a new alliance of principle. The public mind has been stirred on the subject of slavery to depths never before reached; & much information with regard to the Slave-Power has been diffused in quarters heretofore ignorant of this enormous tyranny.

What shall we do in future? Here in Mass. the old Democratic party is not merely defeated—but, as it seems to me, irretrievably broken. Is it not in the same state throughout the country? In Ohio & the Western States, it has a numerical superiority,—but it has no *principles* on which it can rally. It must seek safety upon our Buffalo platform. The only opposition that can be formed to Taylor's Administration will be upon our platform.

It seems to me that an Address to the People of the U.S. should be issued as soon as possible, summing up the results of this contest, & rallying our friends to continue firm in their new organization. Unfortunately we have no National Committee. It might be prepared by delegates from the State Committees or by our friends at Washington on the opening of Congress. . . .

Charles Sumner

Sumner was surprised and delighted by news of the election of Chase to the U.S. Senate on February 22, 1849. Chase had managed to put together a coalition of Ohio Democrats and Free Soilers in order to gain the position. Sumner considered it a major victory for those who opposed slavery.

To Salmon P. Chase
Boston Feb. 27th '49
My dear Sir,

It is then all true! I can hardly believe it. Ignorant as I am of the details of yr local politics I can only imperfectly comprehend the movement which has given our cause so triumphant a triumph in yr election.

It does seem to me that this is "the beginning of the end." Yr election must influence all the Great West. Still more yr presence in the Senate will give an unprecedented impulse to the discussion of our cause. It will confirm the irresolute, quicken the indolent, & confound the trimmers. I know you will grapple at once with John C. Calhoun on any issue that he shall venture to make. . . .

In the fall, on September 18, 1849, Sumner wrote a letter to his friend Chase in which he again urged the need for all who opposed slavery to remain together.

To Salmon P. Chase
Boston Sept. 18th '49
My dear Chase,

Many thanks for yr letter of Sept. 15th from New Haven, & especially for the words of sympathy. And yet I am unwilling to pass into the limbo of mere theorists. A student of the *ideal*, I trust never to lose sight of the *practical*.

Our Convention was very large & respectable. Persons older in political wars than myself said that it was the best political convention they had ever attended. Certainly, it was most enthusiastic & harmonious. In the course of the day you were more than once called for, & I was gratified once by the report that you had been seen in Worcester. Judge Allen read to the Convention yr note, by way of excuse. . . .

. . . let us stand together. We in Massachusetts shall keep to our Ancient Anti-Slavery ways, & shall try to consolidate our party. I think you must do the same in Ohio. I doubt if you can throw yourself so completely as you hope on the old democracy. Our party is composite, & you must try to harmonize all sections. With us the fusion is complete. . . .

Ever sincerely Yours,
Charles Sumner

Abraham Lincoln

Lincoln, the new Whig congressman from Illinois, arrived in Washington, DC, just as the fighting in the Mexican War was ending. He had said little about the conflict during the congressional campaign. However, when President Polk claimed victory in a war initiated by Mexico's "invading the territory of the State of Texas, striking the first blow, and shedding the blood of our citizens on our own soil" and asked for additional funds to end the conflict, the response of Lincoln and his Whig colleagues was a series of attacks upon the president, his administration, and the Democratic Party.

On December 22, Lincoln introduced the "Spot" Resolutions asking for an immediate response from the president. These resolutions alleged that the war began with an unprovoked attack on Mexican citizens in their own country.

"Spot" Resolutions in the United States House of Representatives
December 22, 1847

Whereas the President of the United States, in his message of May 11th. 1846, has declared that "The Mexican Government not only refused to receive him" (the envoy of the U.S.) "or listen to his propositions, but, after a long continued series of menaces, have at last invaded *our teritory*, and shed the blood of our fellow *citizens* on *our own soil*"

And again, in his message of December 8, 1846 that "We had ample cause of war against Mexico, long before the breaking out of hostilities. But even then we forbore to take redress into our own hands, until Mexico herself became the aggressor by invading *our soil* in hostile array, and shedding the blood of our *citizens*"

And yet again, in his message of December 7, 1847 that "The Mexican Government refused even to hear the terms of adjustment which he" (our minister of peace) "was authorized to propose; and finally, under wholly unjustifiable pretexts, involved the two countries in war, by invading the teritory of the State of Texas, striking the first blow, and shedding the blood of our *citizens* on *our own soil*"

And whereas this House desires to obtain a full knowledge of all the facts which go to establish whether the particular spot of soil on which the blood of our *citizens* was so shed, was, or was not, *our own soil*, at that time; therefore

Resolved by the House of Representatives, that the President of the United States be respectfully requested to inform this House—

First: Whether the spot of soil on which the blood of our *citizens* was shed, as in his messages declared, was, or was not, within the teritories of Spain, at least from the treaty of 1819 until the Mexican revolution.

Second: Whether that spot is, or is not, within the teritory which was wrested from Spain, by the Mexican revolution.

Third: Whether that spot is, or is not, within a settlement of people, which settlement had existed ever since long before the Texas revolution, until its inhabitants fled from the approach of the U.S. Army.

Fourth: Whether that settlement is, or is not, isolated from any and all other settlements, by the Gulf of Mexico, and the Rio Grande, on the South and West, and by wide uninhabited regions on the North and East.

Fifth: Whether the *People* of that settlement, or a *majority* of them, or *any* of them, had ever, previous to the bloodshed, mentioned in his messages, submitted themselves to the government or laws of Texas, or of the United States, by *consent*, or by *compulsion*, either by accepting office, or voting at elections, or paying taxes, or serving on juries, or having process served upon them, or in *any other way*.

SIXTH: Whether the People of that settlement, did, or did not, flee from the approach of the United States Army, leaving unprotected their homes and their growing crops, *before* the blood was shed, as in his messages stated; and whether the first blood so shed, was, or was not shed, within the *inclosure* of the People, or some of them, who had thus fled from it.

SEVENTH: Whether our *citizens*, whose blood was shed, as in his messages declared, were, or were not, at that time, *armed* officers, and *soldiers*, sent into that settlement, by the military order of the President through the Secretary of War—and

EIGHTH: Whether the military force of the United States, including those *citizens*, was, or was not, so sent into that settlement, after Genl. Taylor had, more than once, intimated to the War Department that, in his opinion, no such movement was necessary to the defence or protection of Texas.

The attack continued when George Ashmun of Massachusetts proposed a resolution condemning the war as unnecessary and unconstitutional. It was supported by eighty-five Whig congressmen, including Lincoln.

On January 12, Lincoln made the longest speech of his congressional career, bitterly attacking President Polk and demanding a response to a series of questions. If the president chose not to respond, then "I shall be firmly convinced . . . that he is deeply conscious of being in the wrong—that he feels the blood of this war, like the blood of Abel, is crying to Heaven against him."

Now sir, for the purpose of obtaining the very best evidence, as to whether Texas had actually carried her revolution, to the place where the hostilities of the present war commenced, let the President answer the interrogatories, I proposed, as before mentioned, or some other similar ones. Let him answer, fully, fairly, and candidly. Let him answer with *facts*, and not with arguments. Let him remember he sits where Washington sat, and so remembering, let him answer, as Washington would answer. As a nation *should* not, and the Almighty *will* not, be evaded, so let him attempt no evasion—no equivocation. And if, so answering, he can show that the soil was ours, where the first blood of the war was shed—that it was not within an inhabited country, or, if within such, that the inhabitants had submitted themselves to the civil authority of Texas, or of the United States, and that the same is true of the site of Fort Brown, then I am with him for his justification. In that case I, shall be most happy to reverse the vote I gave the other day. I have a selfish motive for desiring that the President may do this. I expect to give some votes, in connection with the war, which, without his so doing, will be of doubtful propriety in my own judgment, but which will be free from the doubt if he does so. But if he *can* not, or *will* not do this—if on any pretence, or no pretence, he shall refuse or omit it, then I shall be fully convinced, of what I more than suspect already, that he is deeply conscious of being in the wrong—that he feels the blood of this war, like the blood of Abel, is crying to Heaven against him. . . .

Again, it is a singular omission in this message, that it, nowhere intimates *when* the President expects the war to terminate. At its beginning, Genl. [Winfield] Scott was, by this same President, driven into disfavor, if not disgrace, for intimating that peace could not be conquered in less than three or four months. But now, at the end of about twenty months, during which time our arms have given us the most splendid successes—every department, and every part, land and water, officers and privates, regulars and volunteers, doing all that men *could* do, and hundreds of things which it had ever before been thought men could *not* do,—after all this, this same President gives us a long message, without showing us, that, *as to the end*, he himself, has, even an immaginary conception. As I have before said, he knows not where he is. He is a bewildered, confounded, and miserably perplexed man. God grant he may be able to show, there is not something about his conscience, more painful than all his mental perplexity!

Pleased with his speech, Lincoln hoped it would make him one of the leaders in Congress. Instead little attention was paid to the resolutions—they were never voted on—and the president ignored his questions. In fact, many of Lincoln's constituents criticized his opposition to the war since he had not made clear his position during the political campaign. They believed that he opposed the conduct of the war and viewed his actions as a lack of patriotism.

During the last months of his term in Congress, Lincoln tried to find an answer to the bitter arguments over slavery in the District of Columbia. Antislavery congressmen continued to present petitions for the ending of slavery while Southerners opposed all such efforts. Lincoln met with representatives of both sides and developed a compromise that gained broad support. On January 10, 1849, he proposed that the Committee on the District of Columbia report out "a bill for an act to abolish slavery in the District of Columbia, by the consent of the free white people of said District, and with compensation to owners."

SECTION 1. Be it enacted by the Senate and House of Representatives of the United States of America, in Congress assembled: That no person not now within the District of Columbia, nor now owned by any person or persons now resident within it, nor hereafter born within it, shall ever be held in slavery within said District.

SECTION 2. That no person now within said District, or now owned by any person, or persons now resident within the same, or hereafter born within it, shall ever be held in slavery without the limits of said District: *Provided*, that officers of the government of the United States, being citizens of the slave-holding states, coming into said District on public business, and remaining only so long as may be reasonably necessary for that object, may be attended into, and out of, said District, and while there, by the necessary servants of themselves and their families, without their right to hold such servants in service, being thereby impaired.

SECTION 3. That all children born of slave mothers within said District on, or after the first day of January in the year of our Lord one thousand, eight hundred and fifty shall be free; but shall be reasonably supported and educated, by the respective owners of their mothers or by their heirs or representatives, and shall owe reasonable service, as apprentices, to such owners, heirs and representatives until they respectively arrive at the age of - years when they shall be entirely free; and the municipal authorities of Washington and Georgetown, within their respective jurisdictional limits, are hereby empowered and required to make all suitable and necessary provisions for enforcing obedience to this section, on the part of both masters and apprentices.

SECTION 4. That all persons now within said District lawfully held as slaves, or now owned by any person or persons now resident within said District, shall remain such, at the will of their respective owners, their heirs and legal representatives: *Provided* that any such owner, or his legal representative, may at any time receive from the treasury of the United States the full value of his or her slave, of the class in this section mentioned, upon which such slave shall be forthwith and forever free: and *provided further* that the President of the United States, the Secretary of State, and the Secretary of the Treasury shall be a board for determining the value of such slaves as their owners may desire to emancipate under this section; and whose duty it shall be to hold a session for the purpose, on the first monday of each calendar month; to receive all applications; and, on satisfactory evidence in each case, that the person presented for valuation, is a slave, and of the class in this section mentioned, and is owned by the applicant, shall value such slave at his or her full cash value, and give to the applicant an order on the treasury for the amount; and also to such slave a certificate of freedom.

SECTION 5. That the municipal authorities of Washington and Georgetown, within their respective jurisdictional limits, are hereby empowered and required to provide active and efficient means to arrest, and deliver up to their owners, all fugitive slaves escaping into said District.

SECTION 6. That the election officers within said District of Columbia, are hereby empowered and required to open polls at all the usual places of holding elections, on the first monday of April next, and receive the vote of every free white male citizen above the age of twenty one years, having resided within said District for the period of one year or more next preceding the time of such voting, for, or against this act; to proceed, in taking said votes, in all respects not herein specified, as at elections under the municipal laws; and, with as little delay as possible, to transmit correct statements of the votes so cast to the President of the United States. And it shall be the duty of the President to canvass said votes immediately, and, if a majority of them be found to be for this act, to forthwith issue his proclamation giving notice of the fact; and this act shall only be in full force and effect on, and after the day of such proclamation. . . .

Mr. LINCOLN then said, that he was authorized to say, that of about fifteen of the leading citizens of the District of Columbia to whom this proposition had been submitted, there was not one but who approved of the adoption of such a proposition. He did not wish to be misunderstood. He did not know whether or not they would vote for this bill on the first Monday of April; but he repeated, that out of fifteen persons to whom it had been submitted, he had authority to say that every one of them desired that some proposition like this should pass.

Three days later, on January 13, Congressman Lincoln announced that he would introduce the bill himself, since his earlier attempt had been unsuccessful. However, he never followed up on the announcement because he had lost the support of most of his backers. Many Northern congressmen objected to paying slave owners for their slaves, while Southerners saw the effort as a first step toward ending slavery across the country. So Lincoln dropped the matter, knowing that "it was useless to prosecute the business at that time." It would be thirteen years before Lincoln, as president of the United States, would be in a position to free slaves in the District of Columbia, at which time he succeeded.

Frederick Douglass

In the summer of 1846, Douglass, a former slave in Maryland who had escaped at the age of twenty-one, afraid now of being arrested and sent back into slavery, was traveling in the British Isles. The news reports of the Mexican War greatly upset him. Writing to friends in Massachusetts, he vented his frustration and considered the possibility of dissolving the Union.

> To the Lynn Anti-Slavery Sewing Circle
> London, August 18, 1846
> My Dear Friends:
> . . . I confess I feel sad, and sick at heart, by the present posture of political affairs in the United States. The spirit of slavery reigns triumphant throughout all the land. Every step in the onward march of political events is marked with blood—innocent blood; shed, too, in the cause of slavery. The war with Mexico rages; the green earth is drenched with warm blood, oozing out from human hearts; the air is darkened with smoke; the heavens are shaken by the terrible roar of the cannon; the groans and cries of the wounded and dying disturb the ear of God. . . . I am sad; I am sick; the whole land is cursed, if not given over to destruction. Massachusetts, the brightest of every other state, is now but the tool of Texas. . . .
> The American Anti-Slavery Society has the right on this question. Her ground is the true one. I believe that the salvation of the country depends, under God, upon the effort of that society. The Union must be dissolved, or New England is lost and swallowed up by the slave-power of the country. Work on, dear friends, work on! walk by faith, and not by sight. Come good, or come evil—prosperity or adversity—work on! See that all which can be done by patriotic and humane women for the salvation of millions groaning in chains, is done; and whoever else may approve, you shall have the approbation of a good conscience, and the tear of grateful hearts, for your reward.
> *Frederick Douglass*

In August and September 1847, Douglass and William Lloyd Garrison toured the states of Pennsylvania, Ohio, and New York. At first there was brutal opposition to their appearances. Their efforts to preach antislavery ideas were not well received.

To Sidney Howard Gay
[August, 1847]
My dear Gay:

. . . We were last night confronted by a most brutal and disgraceful mob—the first fruits of our Western tour, a sort of foretaste of what may await us further West. To the everlasting shame and infamy of the people of Harrisburg, I record the fact that they are at this moment under the domination of mob law; that the freedom of speech and the right of peaceably assembling is cloven down; and that the officers appointed to preserve order and to protect the rights and privileges of the people, have basely, by their indifference, consented to this sacrifice to the Moloch of Slavery. . . .

A meeting was convened in the court house of this town last night, to hear addresses on Slavery by Mr. Garrison and myself. At the time appointed Mr. Garrison was present, and commenced the meeting by a calm statement of facts respecting the character of Slavery and the slave power, showing in how many ways it was a matter deeply affecting the rights and interests of the Northern people. He spoke with little or no interruption for the space of an hour, and then introduced me to the audience. I spoke only for a few moments when through the windows was poured a volley of unmerchantable eggs, scattering the contents on the desk on which I stood, and upon the wall behind me, and filling the room with the most disgusting and stifling stench. . . . One struck friend Garrison on the back, sprinkling its *essence* all over his honoured head. At this point a general tumult ensued, the people in the house became much disturbed and alarmed, and there was a press toward the doorway, which was completely wedged with people. The mob was now howling with fiendish rage. I could occasionally hear amid the tumult, fierce and bloody cries, *"throw out the n - - - - - r,* THROW OUT THE N - - - - - R." Here friend Garrison rose, with that calm and tranquil dignity, altogether peculiar to himself, and said— (speaking for himself and me). Our mission to Harrisburg is ended. If there be not sufficient love of liberty, and self respect in this place, to protect the right of assembling, and the freedom of speech, he would not degrade himself by attempting to speak under such circumstances and he would therefore recall the appointment for Sunday night, and go where he could be heard. . . .

> In great haste, very sincerely yours,
> *Frederick Douglass*. . . .

In December 1847, Douglass founded The North Star, *an abolitionist journal that favored legal and political methods for ending slavery. Funds were made available for the purchase of a printing press and printing materials. Under his leadership* The North Star *became the voice of black men and women across the country.*

Three months later, on March 17, 1848, Douglass published "The North and the Presidency" in The North Star. *Expressing serious doubts about the ability of the political process to find an answer to slavery, he criticized the two major parties for their unwillingness to directly face the issue. Little good would come out of the election of 1848, he prophesied.*

Congress has, within the last few days, voted down the only principle upon which the North has made the slightest show of independence. The only foundation of the North is gone, and while the South stands firm, bold and united, in favor of the complete preservation and extension of slavery, and the permanent supremacy of the slave power, the North lies disjointed, scattered, and confused, with no great and commanding interest or principle to maintain or defend. . . . A threat of dissolving the Union makes them shiver in their shoes with terror. . . . The Wilmot Proviso was an issue, and one of much consequence; and we have no doubt that many at the North supposed that now would come a noble struggle on the part of Northern freemen against Southern slaveholders; nor can we doubt that many, in both the Whig and the Democratic party, meant to stand by the principles of that Proviso at all hazards; but they little understood the base metal of which they were made.—Large numbers, in both the Whig and Democratic party, at the very first word of their Southern masters, meanly deserted their principles, the Whigs dropping entirely the offensive word "No more *slave* territory," and adopting the soulless one of "No more territory"; and the Democrats, repudiating the idea of making the Wilmot Proviso a test in the coming Presidential contest, thus yielding up to their masters everything which they have ever demanded. What respect can the South have for such servile dough-faces? —They have but to shake the rod, and they are down upon their knees at once, suing for pardon. . . .

We are glad to believe that there are yet a few in each political party who would be pleased to have the coming contest waged on the principle of the Wilmot Proviso, but they are the youthful, and not the influential of the parties. They are the weak against the strong. Could John Van Buren rally a few as noble as himself, a stand might possibly be made by at least New York and New England for freedom. He, however, is unsupported, and we wait to see him crushed, though we will ever yet hope for the triumph of his movement.

Douglass was referring to John Van Buren, the son of the former president and an organizer of the Barnburners. He had persuaded his father to run as the presidential candidate of the Free Soil Party. However, Zachary Taylor won the election, with Lewis Cass coming in a close second. This victory was a bitter pill for Douglass to swallow. A great opportunity to change the political situation was lost.

In his editorial entitled "The Blood of the Slave on the Skirts of the Northern People," Douglass poured out his anger and disappointment.

As a people, you claim for yourselves a higher civilization—a purer morality—a deeper religious faith—a larger love of liberty, and a broader philanthropy, than any other nation on the globe. In a word, you claim yours to be a model Republic, and promise, by the force and excellence of your institutions, and the purity and brightness of your example, to overthrow the thrones and despotisms of the old world, and substitute your own in their stead. Your missionaries are found in the remotest parts of the globe, while our land swarms with churches and religious institutions. In words of Religion and Liberty, you are abundant and pre-eminent. You have long desired to get rid of the odium of being regarded as pro-slavery, and have even insisted that the charge of pro-slavery made against you was a slander and that those who made it were animated by a wild and fanatical spirit. To make your innocence apparent, you have now had a fair opportunity. The issue for freedom or slavery has been clearly submitted to you, and you have deliberately chosen slavery.

General Taylor and General [Lewis] Cass were the chosen and admitted Southern and slavery candidates for the Presidency. Martin Van Buren, though far from being an abolitionist, yet in some sort represented the Anti-Slavery idea of the North, in a political form—him you have rejected, and elected a slaveholder to rule over you in his stead. . . . While General Taylor is the well-known robber of three hundred human beings of all their hard earnings, and is coining their hard earnings into gold, you have conferred upon him an office worth twenty-five thousand dollars a year, and the highest honor within your power. . . .

You may imagine that you have now silenced the annoying cry of abolition—that you have sealed the doom of the slave—that abolition is stabbed and dead; but you will find your mistake. You have stabbed, but the cause is not dead. Though down and bleeding at your feet, she shall rise again, and going before you, shall give you no rest till you break every yoke and let the oppressed go free. The Anti-Slavery Societies of the land will rise up and spring to action again, sending forth from the press and on the voice of the living speaker, words of burning truth, to alarm the guilty, to unmask the hypocrite, to expose the frauds of political parties, and rebuke the spirit of a corrupt and sin-sustaining church and clergy. Slavery will be attacked in its stronghold—the compromises of the Constitution, and the cry of disunion shall be more fearlessly proclaimed, till slavery be abolished, the Union dissolved, or the sun of this guilty nation must go down in blood.—

F. D.

The North Star, November 17, 1848

Horace Mann

In 1848, Mann's passion for education was replaced by a desire to end the institution of slavery. He accepted the nomination for the unexpired term of Congressman John Quincy Adams, who died on February 21, 1848. In a letter to the Whig Party, Mann explained why he was willing to return to politics.

I must add, in closing, that so far as personal preferences are concerned, I infinitely prefer remaining in my present position, with all its labor and its thanklessness, to any office in the gift of the people. I had hoped and intended, either in a public or private capacity, to spend my life in advancing the great cause of the people's education. . . .

However, there were two considerations that tempted him to leave education for politics. "The first is important."

The enactment of laws which shall cover waste territory, to be applied to the myriads of human beings who are hereafter to occupy that territory, is a work which seems to precede and outrank even education itself. Whether a wide expanse of country shall be filled with beings to whom education is permitted, or with those to whom it is denied,—with those whom humanity and the law make it a duty to teach, or with those whom inhumanity and the law make it a *legal* duty not to teach, seems preliminary to all questions respecting the best systems and methods for rendering education effective.

The second was that he had been committed by personal friends so that no option remained—"by persons whose judgment" he respected. Mann was easily elected and began his service in Congress in April 1848. The intensity of feeling over slavery and its extension into the territories surprised him. Southerners were full of anger over the Wilmot Proviso. They wanted no limitation to slavery's extension. Charles Sumner and Joshua Giddings kept prodding him to enter the debate with an antislavery speech. For two months he refused.

Finally, on the last day of June, Mann made his first speech in the House of Representatives. Members hurried to their seats eager to hear his remarks on slavery and its expansion into the West. Would he side with Daniel Webster or Charles Sumner? The Massachusetts delegates were divided down the middle.

First, Mann discussed the reasons why slavery should not be allowed into the territories.

Enslave a man, and you destroy his ambition, his enterprise, his capacity. In the constitution of human nature, the desire of bettering one's condition is the mainspring of effort. The first touch of slavery snaps this spring. The slave does not participate in the value of the wealth he creates. All he earns another seizes. A free man labors, not only to improve his own condition, but to better the condition of his children. The mighty impulse of parental affection repays for diligence, and makes exertion sweet. The slave's heart never beats with this high emotion. However industrious and frugal he may be, he has nothing to bequeath to his children, —or nothing save the sad bonds he himself has worn. Fear may make him work, but hope—never. When he moves his tardy limbs, it is because of the suffering that goads him from behind, and not from the bright prospects that beckon him forward in the race.

Of special importance was the effect of slavery on education.

But slavery makes the general education of the whites impossible. You cannot have general education without Common Schools. Common Schools cannot exist where the population is sparse. Where slaves till the soil, or do the principal part of whatever work is done, the free population must be sparse. Slavery, then, by an inexorable law, denies general education to the whites. The providence of God is just and retributive. Create a serf caste, and debar them from education, and you necessarily debar a great portion of the privileged class from education also. It is impossible, in the present state of things, or in any state of things which can be foreseen, to have free and universal education in a slave state. The difficulty is insurmountable.

Addressing himself to the notion that only "abolitionist rabble rousers" were against the extension of slavery, he argued that it was a matter of concern for men of reason everywhere.

Sir, how often, on this floor, have indignant remonstrances been addressed to the north, for agitating the subject of slavery? How often have we at the north been told that we were inciting insurrection, fomenting a servile war, putting the black man's knife to the white man's throat? The air of this hall has been filled, its walls have been, as it were, sculptured, by southern eloquence, with images of devastated towns, of murdered men and ravished women; and, as a defence against the iniquities of the institution, they have universally put in the plea that the calamity was entailed upon them by the mother country, that it made a part of the world they were born into, and therefore they could not help it. I have always been disposed to allow its full weight to this palliation. But if they now insist upon perpetrating against the whole western world, which happens at present to be under our control, the same wrongs which, in darker days, Great Britain perpetrated against them, they will forfeit every claim to sympathy. Sir, here is a test. Let not southern men, who would now force slavery upon new regions, ever deny that their slavery at home is a chosen, voluntary, beloved crime.

Mann closed with a passionate plea that he hoped would reach the hearts of Southerners.

Sir, on the continent of Europe, and in the Tower of London, I have seen the axes, the chains, and other horrid implements of death, by which the great defenders of freedom for the soul were brought to their final doom, —by which political and religious liberty was cloven down; but fairer and lovelier to the view were axe and chain, and all the ghastly implements of death ever invented by religious bigotry or civil despotism to wring and torture freedom out of the soul of man;— fairer and lovelier were they all than the parchment roll of this House on which shall be inscribed a law for profaning one additional foot of American soil with the curse of slavery.

He spoke for nearly an hour and received support from many in the North but "barely restrained anger from southern congressmen." "Well, Massachusetts has reason to be proud of her sons," one congressman whispered to another. Mann was a worthy successor to John Quincy Adams.

Sojourner Truth

In 1846, Truth began to dictate her autobiography to Olivia Gilbert, a fellow member of the Northampton (Massachusetts) Association. Completed three years later, it was entitled Narrative of Sojourner Truth, a Northern Slave. *It was a turning point in her life. With its publication, she became an important figure in antislavery circles.*

Truth's contact with William Lloyd Garrison and his friends opened up a new world for her—the world of antislavery with its many opportunities for her to speak. The following excerpts are from her biography by Nell Painter.

The evolution of the evangelist Sojourner Truth into the anti-slavery feminist Sojourner Truth had begun well before publication of the *Narrative*. In the fall of 1844, Truth gave her first antislavery speech in Northampton. In May 1845, she spoke to the annual meeting of the American Anti-Slavery Society in New York City, identified in the *National Anti-Slavery Standard* only as "a colored woman who had been a slave, but more recently resident of Northampton, Mass." Truth's remarks, according to the *Standard*, were full of "good sense and strong feeling."

I cannot track completely Truth's antislavery and women's rights appearances, for reporters did not invariably consider her worth iden-tifying by name, or even mentioning at all. She doubtless attended and addressed many meetings without notice between 1845 and 1850. I do know for certain that she attended and addressed a large women's rights meeting in Worcester, Massachusetts, in 1850—the first such meeting of national scope in the United States. This Worcester meeting was an immediate successor of the pioneering Seneca Falls, New York, women's convention of 1848 organized by Elizabeth Cady Stanton, Lucretia Mott, and others—including the Rochester abolitionist Amy Post, who would play so large a role in Truth's later life.

Garrison supported the meeting at Worcester, Massachusetts, and probably suggested that Frederick Douglass and Truth speak on the program.

According to a newspaper report, Truth "uttered some truths that told well," although her skin was dark and her outward appearance "uncomely." Truth spoke primarily as a preacher: "She said Woman set the world wrong by eating the forbidden fruit, and now she was going to set it right. She said Goodness never had any beginning; it was from everlasting, and could never die. But Evil had a beginning, and must have an end. She expressed great reverence for God, and faith that he will bring about his own purposes and plans."

In her concluding remarks, Lucretia Mott, a leader of the convention, mentioned Truth by name as "the poor woman who had grown up under the curse of Slavery," and repeated Truth's formulation of the finite nature of evil and the everlasting quality of good. Truth's other early reported antislavery speech in 1850, at the annual meeting of the Rhode Island Anti-Slavery Society in Providence, in November, was also vague on antislavery politics. While the men, Frederick Douglass, Charles C. Burleigh, and Charles Lenox Remond, damned the Fugitive Slave Act for hours and demanded Garrison's version of disunion—"No union with slaveholders!"—Truth was reported as brief and hesitant: "she had been a slave, and was not now entirely free. She did not know anything about politics—could not read the newspapers—but thanked God that the law was made—that the worst had come to worst; but the best must come to best."

SOUTHERNERS

The attitudes of Southerners on the Mexican War, the Wilmot Proviso, and the election of 1848 were different from those of people in the North. Southerners were in full support of the Mexican War, opposed to the Wilmot Proviso, and in favor of a Southerner for president in 1848. On the other hand, Northerners were more divided on the Mexican War, many supported the Wilmot Proviso, and were uncertain about the election of 1848. Furthermore, Southerners were increasingly concerned about Northern abolitionists and their attacks on the South.

William Gilmore Simms

In the spring of 1847, Simms, the Southern writer and editor, wrote a letter to John C. Calhoun concerning the lands to be acquired in the Mexican War. He worried that politicians might bargain away the Southern rights to those lands.

> To John Caldwell Calhoun
> Woodlands, Feb 10. 1847
> My dear Sir
> . . . We are all looking very anxiously to your course on the subject of our Mexican relations. That the South desires the territory we have gained—that the public mind everywhere is fully resolved that we shall keep it—I have little question; but the point with us is to make the conditions preliminary, by which our domestic institutions will be made secure. I think the popular greed will put down the abolitionist faction at the North, if once satisfied that the acquisition of territory cannot be made unless the South is pacified. How far the South, by a temporary coalition with the opponents of Government, can succeed in withholding supplies &c. is a question. . . .
>
> With great respect
> Your obt Servt &c
> W. Gilmore Simms

In the next month, Simms expressed his disdain to a friend, James Lawson, of Northern efforts to deprive the South of its right to expand slavery. In fact, he wanted "to press forward into the interior."

> I told Mr C. that while I was for sustaining the War and even for acquiring territories, I thought the South ought tenaciously to insist on certain preliminary securities—in other words that the action on the Wilmot Proviso should satisfy us—before we voted any more men & money. The Proviso I regarded as a *brutum fulmen* [literally, insen-

sible thunderbolt]—offensive rather than dangerous—for all abolition could not keep our people with their slaves from any *contiguous Southern* territory. They might enact what they pleased, we should take & keep what we could get. Once in, it would be in no power under the sun to dispossess us. Oregon was a different matter, but as in the case of Texas, so, beyond the Rio Grande, what we once acquired would enure to the South & to the South exclusively, and though I did not say this, I thought that it might ultimately help us to a sufficiently large republic of our own &c. I threw out the hint that the Anglo Norman race would never forgive the public man who should fling away territory.

By the summer of 1847, Simms believed that the "dissolution of the Union [was] inevitable." Until that happened, the Southern states must not compromise on the issue of slavery.

To James Henry Hammond
Woodlands. April 2. 1847
dear Hammond
. . . My notion is that the whole policy of our State [South Carolina] must be revised before we can be successful—that our feelings & opinions are destined to a rapid modification which alone can save us. I look upon it now, that Mexico is necessary to the Southern states— that a dissolution of the Union is inevitable—that for twenty years perhaps, Maryland will go with the South; but that, after that period, she with Virginia and the states south of her including the Carolinas & Georgia will have incorporated among themselves new interests, which will greatly change their characteristics. *At all events, the slave interest must be held intact without reference to the soil upon which it happens to labor now.* Remember that! It is one inevitable necessity with slavery that it must accommodate its habitation to its profits—in other words that slave labor will only be continued where it yields an adequate profit. Slavery will be the medium & great agent for rescuing and recovering to freedom and civilization all the vast tracts of Texas, Mexico &c., and our sons ought to be fitted out as fast as they are ready to take the field, with an adequate provision in slaves, and find their way in the yet un-opened regions. The interest is one which must be maintained without reference to places. In that is its hope. All the Wilmot Provisos in the world will never keep us from the possession of our Mexican

conquests whenever we desire to use them; and the necessity for the conquest which every politician must now acknowledge declares the time at hand which Providence has appointed for their use. It is a coincidence of no small signification, that these fields should be laid open to us, just at the time when our institutions, diminishing in their profits in the worn out states, are assailed by cupidity & fanaticism at home & abroad. The acquisition of Texas and Mexico secures the perpetuation of slavery for the next thousand years. . . .

By the spring of 1848, Simms believed that Zachary Taylor would be the next president. The future looked bright, as he wrote again to his close friend, James Henry Hammond.

. . . it strikes me that the necessity for Taylor's election grows more & more apparent. He, only, can now be elected *from the South*, and the vital matter is abolition. The Whig measures are really all gone by the Board, & not even Clay himself, unless an absolute fool, would attempt the restoration of the Protective System or the Bank, or would be willing to risk his administration on the Int. Imp. [International Improvement] System. So. Caro. [South Carolina] should come out decidedly for Taylor & secure, in this way, a claim upon his Govt. Will she? What a glorious opportunity is afforded us of South, security & progress, in the possession of Yucatan,—perhaps, next to Cuba the best key to the Gulf. You know my policy. To use Uncle Sam at large & all his resources, for those acquisitions, which in the event of a dissolution will enure wholly to the South. . . .

God bless you & Yours—

W. Gilmore Simms

After the election, Simms felt the need to gather several Southern states together in order to resist abolition. The election of Taylor, a Southern slaveholder, was not enough. More must be done.

Nov. 11. [1848]
dear Hammond.
. . . I sent you by yesterday's mail, a copy of a circular (prepared by myself) and a pamphlet copy of the last proceedings (political) in which I have been engaged in Charleston. The preamble was prepared by

[Andrew G.] Magrath with small alterations of my own. Two of the resolutions are mine—three are Calhoun's (Congress) and the rest by Magrath & others of the Committee. I trust that they will meet with your approbation. I think they embody your views generally. You will perhaps be better prepared to feel the importance of the course which we suggest, as already movements are in progress which have for their object an Independent State movement—a movement which places S. C. in the lead, from which & against which all our Sister States have revolted. Our only hope of successful resistance to abolition is by a concerted action of three or more States, and a resolved and earnest effort judiciously made, will, at this juncture, and particularly during the progress of the next session of Congress, be likely to attain this object. . . .

Jefferson Davis

While serving in the army in Mexico, Davis received a letter from a Mississippi friend asking for a clarification of his political views. On September 19, 1847, he responded with a long discussion of the growing conflict between the North and South.

To Charles J. Searles
Brierfield, 19th Sept. 1847.
My Dear Sir: . . .
The political information you communicate was entirely new to me, and it is only under the belief that the crisis renders important the views of every southern man, that I can account for any speculations having arisen about my opinions as to the next Presidency. I have never anticipated a separation upon this question from the Democracy of Mississippi, and if such intention or expectation has been attributed to me, it is not only unauthorised but erroneous.

That it might become necessary to unite as southern men, and to dissolve the ties which have connected us to the northern Democracy: the position recently assumed in a majority of the non-slave holding states has led me to fear. Yet, I am not of those who decry a national convention, but believe that present circumstances with more than usual force indicate the propriety of such a meeting. On the question of Southern institutions and southern rights, it is true that extensive defections have occurred among Northern democrats, but enough of good feeling is still exhibited to sustain the hope, that as a party they will show themselves worthy of their ancient appellation, the natural allies of the South, and will meet us upon just constitutional ground. At least I consider it due to former association that we should give them the fairest opportunity to do so, and furnish no cause for failure by seeming distrust or aversion.

I would say then, let our delegates meet those from the north, not as a paramount object to nominate candidates for the Presidency and Vice-Presidency, but before entering upon such selection, to demand of their political brethren of the north, a disavowal of the principles of the Wilmot Proviso; an admission of the equal right of the south with the north, to the territory held as the common property of the United States; and a declaration in favor of extending the Missouri compromise to all States to be hereafter admitted into our confederacy.

If these principles are recognized, we will happily avoid the worst of all political divisions, one made by geographical lines merely. The convention, representing every section of the Union, and elevated above local jealousy and factious strife, may proceed to select candidates, whose principles, patriotism, judgement, and decision, indicate men fit for the time and the occasion.

If on the other hand, that spirit of hostility to the south, that thirst for political dominion over us, which within two years past has displayed such increased power and systematic purpose, should prevail; it will only remain for our delegates to withdraw from the convention, and inform their fellow citizens of the failure of their mission. We shall then have reached a point at which all party measures sink into insignificance, under the necessity for self-preservation; and party divisions should be buried in union for defence.

But until then, let us do all which becomes us to avoid sectional division, that united we may go on to the perfection of Democratic measures, the practical exemplification of those great principles for which we have struggled, as promotive of the peace, the prosperity, and the perpetuity of our confederation.

. . . I am, as ever, truly your friend,

Jefferson Davis

After the Mexican War ended, Davis declined an appointment as brigadier general and was later appointed U.S. Senator from Mississippi. Subsequently he was elected and served until September 23, 1851, when he resigned. Earlier, on

*June 4, 1848, Davis had responded to a letter from a nephew in which he ex-
pressed concerns about the growth of antislavery sentiment in the North and the
dangers that it posed.*

To Hugh R. Davis
Washington 4th June 1848
My Dear Nephew, . . .
The anti-slavery feeling in the North and the Internal improvement policy of the West, were strong enough in the convention to
defeat any sound man. The Whigs are busyly engaged in combinations for their convention, the Clay, McLane [John McLean], and Scott
men are combining, they will unite if possible to defeat Genl. Taylor's
friends in the convention. I have rather avoided than sought information, and cannot pretend to judge of events connected with Whig
schemes. It is probable however if the northern men succeed that the
Taylor men, the southern whigs, will withdraw and present his name
to the south as a southern independent candidate. Then a *geographical*
division will occur, the event which I have always deprecated, and which
must be the precursor of *disunion.* The northern Democrats could relieve us from this danger if they would brave the abolitionists. . . .

Jeffn: Davis

*During the election campaign of 1848, Davis spoke often of the growing division
between the North and South. In a letter he repeated his belief that slavery cannot be "submitted to the congress and [be] preserved." It was a constitutional right
that must be maintained.*

To Woodville Citizens
Warren County. 23d Oct. 1848.
Gentlemen:— . . . The great principle which has divided the people
of the U. States into two political parties from the formation of the
confederacy, is strict, or latitudinous construction of the terms of compact. To the majority, strict construction is an obstacle, to the minority, it brings confidence, and security. As the representative strength of
the Southern States has relatively diminished in the growth of our
Union; so, to us, has the importance of this principle increased, until it
has reached a value which should make it the political Shibboleth of
the South. . . .

There is another opinion among northern politicians to which I refer, lest silence should be construed into acquiescence; it is that the territorial inhabitants have the power to decide upon the right of slaveholders to migrate with their property to the territories. This like the position that Congress may prohibit such migration, I hold to be absolutely wrong; and being neither the apologist or defender of either creed, will not here enter into an inquiry as to which is more or less tenable. The rights of the states not delegated to the federal government, are as absolutely their own as if no union existed . . .

If the South hesitates in the assertion of her rights, or gives rise to a doubt as to the unanimity with which she will maintain them, the days of "northern men with southern principles" will soon be numbered; and we shall have united to meet the evil which an earlier exhibition of unanimity might have prevented. . . .

I am very truly, Your friend,

Jefferson Davis

John J. Crittenden

A U.S. Senator from Kentucky, John J. Crittenden hoped that a Whig president would be elected in 1848. The likeliest possibility was Zachary Taylor, the hero of the Mexican War. In the spring of 1848, Crittenden wrote a letter to a friend who was one of Taylor's advisers. He cautioned Taylor to be careful how he spoke about the impending resolution of the Mexican War. A mistake could cost him the presidential nomination.

(Crittenden to Orlando Brown)
Senate Chamber, March 25, 1848.

Dear Orlando, —I was shown, this morning, a letter from a confidential friend of General Taylor, from which I infer that he was about to write to you a letter intended for publication, expressing, probably, some political opinions, and especially in respect to the policy which we ought to observe towards Mexico, and the indemnity we ought to insist upon. That letter states that he *would* have indemnity, and TERRITORY for indemnity. Though this is the manner in which the letter-writer expressed himself, I am persuaded that General Taylor *would not so* express himself. This is a point in our present politics of exceeding delicacy, and in regard to which there is a great deal of sensitiveness, particularly in the New England States. You will see

Mr. Webster's speech published in the *Intelligencer* of this morning, in which he takes such very decided ground against the *acquisition* of *territory*, or against such acquisition as might form *new States*. I may say that I almost *know* he would not be opposed to the establishment of the Rio Grande, up to New Mexico, as the *boundary of Texas*, and thence (excluding New Mexico) to such a parallel of latitude as would, when pursued to the Pacific, include the harbor of San Francisco. But if General Taylor was to say in general terms that "he *would have indemnity* and *territory* for indemnity," it might fairly be construed that he meant to include in that indemnity all the expenses of the war, and to *coerce* that indemnity in territory, *regardless* of its *extent*. Such a declaration, on his part, would put him, as you will perceive, into *direct conflict* with the opinions of Mr. Webster and the feelings and prejudices of the New England States, —a position much to be avoided at this crisis. I know that such is not General Taylor's true meaning, and I am persuaded that he has not and will not so express himself in his contemplated letter to you. . . . Whatever General Taylor may say in reference to public questions, ought to be, in general terms, relating to *principles* rather than to *measures* and *avoiding details*. His opinions (as I believe them to exist) in regard to a peace with Mexico, might be sufficiently expressed in some such manner as this: That peace between the two republics was greatly to be desired, that the honor of our country had been fully vindicated by our victories, that the fallen condition of Mexico ought to prompt us to magnanimous moderation and forbearance towards her, and make us careful to exact nothing beyond the just measure of her rightful claims, and a satisfactory establishment of a boundary for Texas; that for the satisfaction of those claims we ought to accept, *if* more convenient and suitable to Mexico, such limited cessions of territory as *might give us* a boundary, including the harbor of San Francisco, without incumbering us with a useless extent of territory, that might embroil us with disturbing questions at home. This would cover the whole case without entering into detail. . . .

Your friend,

J. J. Crittenden.

Several months later, Crittenden resigned his Senate seat and was elected governor of Kentucky in the fall of 1848. In his first message to the legislature, on December 30, he spoke about the need to preserve the Union. It was a matter of growing concern to him.

The union of the States is not only indispensable to our greatness, but it is a guarantee for our republican form of government. With the preservation of that Union and the Constitution by which it is established, and laws by which it is maintained, our dearest interests are indissolubly blended. An experience of near sixty years, while it has confirmed the most sanguine hopes of our patriotic fathers who framed it, has taught us its inestimable value. Its value will be above all price to us so long as we are fit for liberty, and it will fail only when we become unworthy of it. No form of government can secure liberty to a degenerate people. Kentucky, situated in the heart of the Union, must and will exercise a powerful influence on its destiny. Devotion to the Union is the common sentiment of her people. I do not know a man within the limits of the State who does not entertain it. We all feel that we can safely rely upon a Union which has sustained us so triumphantly in the trials of peace and war; and we entertain no fears from those who have a common interest in it with ourselves. The paternal feelings with which we regard them, and the filial reverence we ourselves have for the link that binds us together, give us strength in the faith that they cherish the same bonds of brotherhood, and will practice no intentional injustice towards us. We can have no better security for our rights than that Union and the kindred feelings that unite us with all the members of the Confederacy. If these sentiments ever cease to prevail, I trust that Kentucky will be the last spot from which they will be banished. Errors and even abuses may occasionally arise in the administration of the general government,—so they may in the administration of all governments, —and we must rely upon public opinion, the basis of all republican governments, for their correction. The dissolution of the Union can never be regarded—ought never to be regarded—as a *remedy*, but as the *consummation of the greatest evil that can befall us*.

2

The Compromise of 1850

NORTHERNERS

George Templeton Strong

A New York lawyer, Strong began to think seriously about the South and the possibility of the dissolution of the Union. In earlier years he had rarely mentioned the South in his diary, with one exception. On December 30, 1848, at the end of his remarks for the year, Strong noted among the events that might occur before December 1849 "the possible rupture between North and South on the slavery question." He did not want to speculate about the future. However, in the early months of 1850 he began to take notice of congressional debates over what was later called the Compromise of 1850.

January 26. . . . Mr. [Samuel B.] Ruggles back from Washington. He reports the South very rampant and a good deal in earnest. Probably they will go into convention, and there will be much fuss and many speeches more or less eloquent, and that will produce a panic and United States fives [five percent bonds] will fall like lead. But I think the convention will be a safety valve that will save us from an explosion, though things are not in a comfortable state, and it is not easy to see our way out of the complication we're in very distinctly. No doubt a small party at the South wants dissolution for its own sake, because they prefer being first in a Southern confederacy to being second-rate and insignificant in the Union. And the great body of slaveholders certainly have troubles and trials, grievances, perhaps, that may well make them restless and uneasy and may account for their being unreasonable, though it's not easy to see what they would gain by dissolution. All the slaves in the frontier states of the new confederation would run away the first night. Mr. Garrison and Abby Folsom would set up agencies for the seduction and reception of fugitive niggers all along the line. The bitterest feeling of hatred would arise between the two rival nations and the North would become enthusiastic in abolition—and frontier disputes would be followed by servile wars in the *outside* states that would compel them to abolish slavery for their own peace and quiet and to save their property and their lives, and so antislavery would gradually march towards the South. Nothing but rigid non-intercourse could save them.

In early March many Whigs, including Strong, took notice of the furious debate in the U.S. Senate. James Mason read the last written speech of John C. Calhoun, who was too old and ill to deliver it himself, in which he pleaded for equal rights for the South and its interests: "If you of the North will not do this, then our Southern states separate and depart in peace." Daniel Webster argued for the Union and the Constitution, pronouncing peaceful secession an impossibility.

March 9. Notabilities of the day. Calhoun's speech and Webster's are both clear, strong, and statesmanlike efforts. Calhoun's grand fallacy is the notion of an "equilibrium between North and South." Why should the Potomac be a recognized landmark rather than the Mississippi, and why should not Arkansas lift up her voice and lament that there is a want of equilibrium between the states east of the Father of Waters and those west thereof?

On July 4, President Taylor consumed large quantities of iced milk and cherries (it was a hot day). He died of gastroenteritis on July 9. His death was a severe blow to Strong.

July 9, Tuesday. . . . Very busy today. Tonight to Mr. Ruggles' and thence to Mr. [Robert] Ray's, where I spent a couple of hours. The President very ill—the indomitable Zachary is all but succumbing to cholera morbus with typhoid symptoms, and one telegraphic despatch announced that he was not likely to get through the day. I hope he may be spared, for his death would be a calamity at this time. . . .

July 11. At home again. The President died at half-past ten Tuesday evening. A very unhappy event, not only because he was a good and upright man, such as is uncommon in high office, but because everybody North and South had a vague sort of implicit confidence in him, which would have enabled him to guide us through our present complications much better than his "accidental" successor [Millard

Fillmore], of whom nobody knows much, and in whom no party puts any very special trust or faith.

Two months later, on September 9, Strong again referred to the actions of Congress on the "great Southern problem." He was particularly unhappy with South Carolina, "[t]hat preposterous little state."

September 9. . . . Congress has acted at last on the great Southern problem; passed the Texas and California bills, checked the Southern chivalry in the generation of gas, and blighted the hopes of Billy Seward [U.S. Senator from New York] and his gang of incendiaries, who wanted to set the country on fire with civil war that they might fill themselves with place and profit in the confusion. Extreme people on both sides much disgusted with the result, but the great majority satisfied and relieved. For there was some cause for anxiety. Texas and little South Carolina would probably have run into their holes when they found the general government was going to maintain its rights, and was prepared to substitute light artillery and mounted riflemen for proclamations and Congressional eloquence; but there might have been some sort of armed resistance got up among the lank loafers of the Texan frontier, and if a single horse-stealer had been knocked in the head by Uncle Sam's regulars, a serious breeze might have sprung up. I'm glad it's settled, though it would have been refreshing to see Texas snubbed and South Carolina spanked. That preposterous little state is utterly below the city of New York or Boston or Philadelphia in resources, civilization, importance, and everything else; but Goliath of Gath with all his war paint on was not a more obstreperous, intolerable braggart and bully. . . .

In the fall of 1850 the question of sending fugitive slaves back to the South became a major issue. The recently passed Fugitive Slave Law mandated the return of runaways, and Northerners began to enact legislation that made their return impossible. As the debate escalated, Strong became concerned; he was especially critical of abolitionists who resisted the federal law.

October 5, Saturday. . . . *Fugitive Slave Bill* much discussed in the city. Still more out of it. Seward-dom in great excitement, of course, and as for Garrison and Gerrit Smith and their tail, black and white, they exhausted the vocabulary of Billingsgate so thoroughly long ago that they can find no adequate expression of their wrath in that or any other dialect. They deserve to be scourged and pilloried for sedition or hanged for treason, but as the execution of justice upon them would do more harm than good and draw attention to their impotent efforts for evil, it is better to let them alone. The state must temper justice not only with mercy (which these people cannot claim), but with due regard to expediency, and must sometimes wink at projects of crime because they are despicable, and might be made dangerous if their authors were consecrated into martyrs by the gallows they deserve.

My creed on that question is: That slave-holding is no sin.

That the slaves of the Southern States are happier and better off than the niggers of the North, and are more kindly dealt with by their owners than servants are by Northern masters.

That the reasoning, the tone of feeling, the first principles, the practices, and the designs of Northern Abolitionists are very particularly false, foolish, wicked, and unchristian.

By late November, Strong was critical of certain Southerners despite the legitimacy of their demands to have fugitive slaves returned. Some of their claims were "preposterous" and "bombast."

November 3. . . . It is no doubt a fact that many sober-minded people at the South anticipate a dissolution of the Union within five years. The North laughs at them and proceeds to prove that the South would lose by the separation by way of shewing that it's not supposable that the South will separate. But people will do foolish things when they're in a passion, and the damage to the South won't lessen the damage to the North. And the South has reason *now* for getting into a state of indignant exaltation, for the law-loving citizens of Massachusetts have been nullifying law and treading on the verge of treason, and they have made it evident that legislation is inoperative, and that the South can look for no redress from anything Congress can do. . . .

November 25, Monday. . . . . South still clamorous, querulous, and absurd, *Quattlebum Rampans*, preventing people from seeing their just grounds of complaint by the preposterous vaporing, bombast, and brag wherewith they make themselves and their concerns ridiculous. . . . I'm beginning to think that Southern Ultraism may be let alone to cut its own throat and punish its own lunatics, without let or interference. Where will they divide the Mississippi?

Horace Mann

Mann resisted pressures to join the Free Soil Party in 1849; he was not ready for that change. However, the efforts of Henry Clay and others to effect a compromise in 1850 alarmed him. Especially distressing was the continued slave trade in Washington. Finally, on February 15, 1850, Mann took the floor in Congress to make a scathing attack on Boston slave masters who profited from the trade.

First he explained that Free Soil meant, to him, an advocacy of freedom for all the territorial possessions.

For myself, I will engage in any honorable measure most likely to secure freedom to the new territories. I will resist any and every measure that proposes to abandon them to slavery. The epithet "Free Soiler," therefore, when rightly understood and correctly applied, implies both political and moral worth; and I covet the honor of its application to myself. But what does its opposite mean? What does the term "Slave Soiler" signify? It signifies one who desires and designs that all soil should be made to bear slaves. Its dreadful significancy is, that, after Magna Charta and the Petition of Right, in Great Britain, and after the Declaration of Independence, in this country, we should cast aside with scorn, not only the teachings of Christianity, but the clearest principles of natural religion and of natural law, and should retrograde from our boasted civilization, into the Dark Ages,—ay, into periods that the dark ages might have called dark. It means that this *Republic*, as we call it, formed to establish freedom, should enlist in a crusade against freedom. . . .

Next, Mann answered attacks on abolitionists.

In my apprehension, sir, before we can decide upon the honor or the infamy of the term "Abolitionist," we must know what things they are which he proposes to abolish. We of the north, you say, are Abolitionist; but abolitionists of what? Are we abolitionists of the inalienable, indefeasible, indestructible rights of man? Are we abolitionists of knowledge, abolitionists of virtue, of education, and of human culture? Do we seek to abolish the glorious moral and intellectual attributes which God has given to his children, and thus, as far as it lies in our power, make the facts of slavery conform to the law of slavery, by obliterating the distinction between a man and a beast?

If we are abolitionists, then, we are abolitionists of human bondage; while those who oppose us are abolitionists of human liberty. We would prevent the extension of one of the greatest wrongs that man ever suffered upon earth; they would carry bodily chains and mental chains,—chains in a literal and chains in a figurative sense,—into realms where even the half-civilized descendants of the Spaniard and the Indian have silenced their clanking. We would avert the impending night of ignorance and superstition; they would abolish the glorious liberty wherewith God maketh his children free. In using this word, therefore, to calumniate us, they put darkness for light, and light for darkness; good for evil, and evil for good.

Then he expressed his alarm at the constant threats of secession by Southern legislators.

But gentlemen of the south not only argue the question of right and of honor; they go further, and they tell us what they will proceed to do if we do not yield to their demands. A large majority of the southern legislatures have solemnly "resolved" that if Congress prohibits slavery in the new territories, they will resist the law "at any and at every hazard." And yet they say they do not mean to threaten us. They desire to abstain from all language of menace, for threats and menaces are beneath the character of gentlemen. Sir, what is the meaning of the terms "threats" and "menaces"? . . .

And do those gentlemen who make these threats soberly consider how deeply they are pledging themselves and their constituents by them? Threats of dissolution, if executed, become rebellion and treason. The machinery of this government is now moving onward in its majestic course. Custom-houses, post-offices, land-offices, army, navy, are fulfilling their prescribed circle of duties. They will continue to fulfil them until arrested by violence. Should the hand of violence be laid upon them, then will come that exigency expressly provided for in the constitution and in the President's inaugural oath, "TO TAKE CARE THAT THE LAWS BE FAITHFULLY EXECUTED." Mr. Chairman, such collision would be *war*. Such forcible opposition to the government would be *treason*. Its agents and abettors would be *traitors*. Wherever this rebellion rears its crest, martial law will be proclaimed; and those found with hostile arms in their hands must prepare for the felon's doom.

Sir, I cannot contemplate this spectacle without a thrill of horror. If the two sections of this country ever marshal themselves against each other, and their squadrons rush to the conflict, it will be a war carried on by such powers of intellect, animated by such vehemence of passion, and sustained by such an abundance of resources, as the world has never before witnessed. "Ten foreign wars," it has been well said, "are a luxury compared with one civil war." But I turn from this scene with a shudder. If, in the retributive providence of God, the volcano of civil war should ever burst upon us, it will be amid thunderings above, and earthquakes below, and darkness around; and when that darkness is lifted up, we shall see this once glorious union,— this oneness of government, under which we have been prospered and blessed as Heaven never prospered and blessed any other people,—rifted in twain from east to west, with a gulf between us wide and profound, save that this gulf will be filled and heaped high with the slaughtered bodies of our countrymen; and when we reawaken to consciousness, we shall behold the garments and the hands of the survivors red with fratricidal blood. . . .

In conclusion, I have only to add, that such is my solemn and abiding conviction of the character of slavery, that under a full sense of my responsibility to my country and my God, I deliberately say, better disunion,—better a civil or a servile war,—better any thing that God in his providence shall send, than an extension of the bounds of slavery.

It was clear from this speech that Mann was not interested in any compromise that would allow slavery into the new territories. Only a united Whig Party could defeat such efforts. Unfortunately for Mann, Daniel Webster's speech on March 7 greatly changed the political situation. Webster decided to speak in support of the Compromise of 1850. For him, the Union had to be preserved regardless of the cost. Slavery would have to be tolerated in the territories if people voted for it. He hoped that a solution could be worked out. This decision split the Whig Party both in the country and in Massachusetts. Mann's response was highly critical of Webster, who singled out Mann for criticism. Webster insisted that Mann be denied Whig support for another term in office; he was replaced by a loyal Websterite.

Then the Free Soil Party and factions in the Whig Party offered to support Mann's reelection. He accepted, and in November he was reelected by a margin of forty-one votes out of thirteen thousand cast. It was a narrow victory. Mann was still in office but without Whig Party support.

Charles Sumner

Sumner was concerned that the political parties would refuse to take positions limiting the expansion of slavery. In a letter to Salmon P. Chase he spelled out his fears.

To Salmon P. Chase
Boston Jan. 24th '50
My dear Chase,
If I did not believe that Truth in the end must prevail, I should be disposed at the present moment to despair of our cause. Both the old parties are coming together on substantially the same principle—*non-action* or *non-intervention*. I trust to Calhoun's influence to drive them from this shelter. Can he do it?

Cass's speech will prevent for the present the Northern Democracy from joining with us. And yet his leading supporters in our legislature now in session said yesterday *in private* that they would not sustain him for the Presidency.

The course of the Democrats in Ohio is also disheartening. [The Democratic convention voted against endorsing the Wilmot Proviso.] I think even you must despair of them. . . .

Several months later, Sumner wrote to Horace Mann, congressman from Massachusetts, warning him that he represented the Free Soil Party and was accountable to it in his actions in Congress. Mann, in a letter stressing his political neutrality, said that he was "exclusively bound to none" of the existing parties.

To Horace Mann
Boston Sunday—April 28th 50
My dear Mann, . . .
I hope you will reconsider the first part of yr letter. Loyalty to you, & to a great cause compells me to call yr attention to this again.

You accepted a nomination for Congress from the Free Soilers, knowing their distinctive organization, & receiving from them at the time resolutions explaining it. You were chosen in part by their votes.

The first part of yr letter will be offensive to them in its tone, besides presenting an argt. against the *very organization* whose support you had accepted.

It will be offensive to all yr Free Soil associates in Congress.

The position you take, it seems to me, is unworthy of you, as a moralist. You seem to ignore the vital distinction between a question of morals, & of cotton. One may be compromised, & the other not. . . .

In July, Sumner responded to a letter from Richard Cobden, Member of Parliament in Great Britain, about the situation in the United States. His position continued to be "no more slave territory."

Our American politics, as you well know, have been in a perplexed state. The slave-holders are bent on securing the new territories for slavery; & they see, in perspective, an immense slave-nation, embracing the gulf of Mexico, & all its islands, & stretching from Maryland to Panama. For this they are now struggling; determined while in the union to govern it, & direct its energies; or, if obliged to quit, to build up a new nation, slave-holding throughout. They are fighting with desperation, & have been aided by traitors at the North. Webster's apostacy is the most bare-faced. . . . Not only the cause of true Anti-Slavery is connected with the over-throw of the slave-holding Propaganda, but also of Peace. As soon as it is distinctly established, as the unalterable policy of the Republic, that there shall be *no more Slave territory*, there will be little danger of War. My own earnest aim is to see Slavery abolished every where within the sphere of the National Govt, which is the District of Col. & on the high-seas in the domestic slave-trade; & beyond this, to have this Govt for Freedom, so far as it can exert an influence, & not for slavery. When this is accomplished, then Slavery will be taken out of the vortex of national politics & the influences of education, an improved civilization & of Christianity will be left free to act against it in the states where it exists.

It is difficult to say how the present contest at Washington will end. Nobody there can tell. Things look now as if Clay & his Compromise would be defeated.

Sumner declined to be a nominee as a Free Soil candidate in August 1850. He said that he wanted to remain in private life. In a letter to John Palfrey on October 15, Sumner lamented the lack of courage among politicians in Massachusetts.

My dear Dr,

. . . Oh! *back-bone—back-bone—back-bone*! This is what is needed; & not to be afraid of any names by which we may be called. For myself, I am neither Whig nor Democrat; but a Free Soiler.

And nothing seems clearer to me than our duty, in utter disregard of all state issues, & placing our Anti-Slavery above all other things— to try to obtain the *balance of power* in the Legislature, at least in the Senate, so that we may influence *potentially* the choice of a senator to Congress. This can be done only by thinning the Whigs. If I must vote for a Whig or a Democrat—I should be sorry to vote for either—let me vote for the Democrat, because in that way we may secure the *balance of power*. Mr [Samuel] Hoar would secure a Whig majority in the senate, & render us powerless; so that the nominee of the Whig caucus would walk over the course next winter. . . .

Ever Yrs,

Charles Sumner

Frederick Douglass

On March 11, 1850, Senator William Seward made a speech in opposition to Henry Clay's compromise plan in which he denounced the proposal for more stringent fugitive slave laws. Seward argued that "there is a higher law than the Constitution, which regulates our authority over this domain [that is, the territories not formed into states], and devotes it to the same noble purposes."

Douglass closely examined the speech and found it convincing. It helped him reach the conclusion that there was indeed a radical defect in the Constitution. It incorporated two separate and contradictory elements that could never be rendered consistent.

Liberty and Slavery—opposite as Heaven and Hell—are both in the Constitution; and the oath to support the latter, is an oath to perform that which God has made impossible. The man that swears to support it vows allegiance to two masters—so opposite, that fidelity to the one is, necessarily, treachery to the other. If we adopt the preamble, with Liberty and Justice, we must repudiate the enacting clauses, with Kidnapping and Slaveholding. It is this radical defect in this Constitution—this war of elements, which is now rocking the land. There is a deep reason for the singular attitude in which the straight forward opponents of slavery are now placed, contending as they are for the very measure as a means of preserving freedom, which the Slaveholders threaten to adopt as the last resort to uphold slavery. Garrison sees in the Constitution precisely what John C. Calhoun sees there—a compromise with Slavery—a bargain between the North and the South; the former to free his soul from the guilt of slaveholding, repudiates the bond; and the latter, seeing the weakness of mere parchment guarantees, when opposed to the moral scope of the parties to meet, seeks a dissociation of the Union as his only means of safety. This fundamental contradiction in the Constitution is the real cause of the present storm-tossed condition of the public mind. The South have looked to the Constitution, from the ramparts of Slavery, and have seen in it their highest power of defense. Slaveholders have sworn to support it as such, and have never sworn to support the whole Constitution. On the other hand, Northern men have recognised in the instrument the principles of liberty and justice; and have scarcely observed the proslavery principle cunningly wrought into the instrument. The opposite view, therefore, of the Constitution and its requirements, is the primary cause of the present agitation.

The question arises, as to who is right in this contest? We answer, so far as the Constitution is concerned, that all are wrong; and necessarily so; since neither party, North nor South, could, if they would be faithful to the requirements of the oath to support the Constitution of the United States. Every slaveholder in the land stands perjured in the sight of Heaven, when he swears his purpose to be, the establishment of justice—the providing for the general welfare, and the preservation of liberty to the people of this country; for every such slaveholder knows that his whole life gives an emphatic lie to his solemn vow. And how stands the case with our Free Soil friends, who swear to promote the Constitution? Why, they differ from the slaveholder only in motive. They swear to promote the Constitution, as a means of promoting beneficent measures; and under a certain system of reasoning, based on alleged necessity, they justify their oath. They have our sympathies, but not our judgment. They have a theory of human government, which makes it necessary to do evil, that good may come. We are not convinced that that theory is correct; and we must continue to hold, for the present, that the Constitution, being at war with itself, cannot be lived up to, and what we cannot do, we ought not to swear to do; and that, therefore, the platform for us to occupy, is outside that piece of parchment.

—*F. D.*

The North Star, April 5, 1850

His strong words and controversial behavior brought him praise by many but virulent criticism and insults by others. He was unbending in his response.

Never since the day I entered the field of public effort in the cause of my enslaved brethren, have I been called to endure persecution more bitter, insults more brutal, violence more fierce, scorn and contempt more malicious and demoniacal, than that heaped upon me in the city of New York, during the past three weeks. I have been made to feel keenly that I am in an enemy's land—surrounded on all sides by hardships, difficulties and dangers—that on the side of the oppressor there is power, and that there are few to take up the cause of my deeply injured and down-trodden people. These things grieve, but do not appall me. Not an inch will I retreat—not one jot of zeal will I abate— not one word will I retract; and, in the strength of God, while the red current of life flows through my veins, I will continue to labor for the downfall of slavery and the freedom of my race. . . . *My crime* is, that I have assumed to be a man, entitled to all the rights, privileges and dignity, which belong to human nature—that color is no crime, and that all men are brothers. I have acted on this presumption. The very "head and front of my offending hath this extent—no more." I have not merely talked of human brotherhood and human equality, but have reduced that talk to practice. This I have done in broad open day, scorning concealment. I have walked through the streets of New York, in company with white persons, not as a menial, but as an equal. This was done with no purpose to inflame the public mind; not to provoke popular violence; not to make a display of my contempt for public opinion; but simply as a matter of course, and because it was right so to do. The right to associate with my fellow worms of the dust, on terms of equality, without regard to color, is a right which I will yield only with my latest [last] breath.

—*F.D.*
The North Star, May 30, 1850

The Fugitive Slave Laws of 1850 signed on September 18 by President Millard Fillmore alarmed many blacks in the North. In Boston protest meetings were held by frightened and angry blacks and whites. A crowd of over five thousand rallied at Faneuil Hall on October 14. Douglass spoke several times and was interrupted by applause and cheering.

Mr. Chairman and friends . . . This law, as has been already known, has carried consternation and despair to many families in the Northern States, and even in this city has its dire effects been witnessed—aye, this very day. I have travelled within the last two days about 500 miles, for the purpose of attending this meeting, and during that time, I may say that I have met hundreds of my terror-stricken brethren, spread all along through this boasted land of liberty to the boundaries of Canada, all caused by the passage of this infamous Fugitive Slave Bill. And I am creditably informed that many in this city still feel greatly insecure; and numbers who have lately arrived have been obliged, through the want of means to support themselves here, to take their departure for the Canadas, there to spend a dreary winter, and perhaps a life. They are afraid that the man-hunters of the South will be here in the city of Boston,—here under the shadow of old Bunker Hill Monument, to reclaim them and carry them back to Slavery.

They know well, Mr. Chairman, what Slavery is, and dread to return to it, with a horror more piercing than the fear of death itself. For the highest crime that the slave can commit is an attempt on his part to escape from his master. This every slave well understands; and he knows that if he returns to bondage, he returns not merely to Slavery, not merely to labor for his master, but to gratify a deep-seated, malignant and deadly revenge. He who has once tasted the sweets of freedom, that man can never more be made a profitable slave, and his master will have a harder task to keep him than he would to whip him. (Cheers and laughter.) They therefore pursue the slaves in order to make examples of them; and the slave knows that, if returned, he will have to submit to excruciating torture. (Sensation.)

After a reference to recent efforts to take him back into slavery, Douglass concluded with a warning.

. . . we one and all,—without the slightest hope of making successful resistance,—are resolved rather to die than to go back. (Tremendous cheering, and cries of "that's the talk! Repeat it again!") If you are . . . prepared to see the streets of Boston flowing with innocent blood, if you are prepared to see sufferings such as perhaps no country ever before witnessed, just give in your adhesion to the fugitive slave bill—you, who live on the street where the blood first spouted in defence of freedom; and the slave-hunter will be here to bear the chained slave back, or he will be murdered in your streets. . . .

Abraham Lincoln

Lincoln dropped out of politics for several years after the completion of his congressional term in 1849, when he was readmitted to practice before the United States Supreme Court. Most of his work was in the circuit courts of Illinois. His main concern in the period was to rebuild his legal practice.

During these same years he maintained an interest in politics but did not seek office. As an "elder statesman" he was consulted on political matters and occasionally gave speeches or delivered eulogies upon the death of Whig politicians. He became active in national politics in the summer and fall of 1850.

On July 25, 1850, he delivered an address in Chicago eulogizing President Zachary Taylor. Near the end of the speech he expressed the view that Taylor's death could make it difficult to resolve "the one great question of the day"— slavery.

Upon the death of Gen. Taylor, as it would in the case of the death of any President, we are naturally led to consider what will be its effect, politically, upon the country. I will not pretend to believe that all the wisdom, or all the patriotism of the country, died with Gen. Taylor. But we know that *wisdom* and *patriotism*, in a public office, under institutions like ours, are wholly inefficient and worthless, unless they are sustained by the confidence and devotion of the people. And I confess my apprehensions, that in the death of the late President, we have lost a degree of that confidence and devotion, which will not soon again pertain to any successor. Between public measures regarded as antagonistic, there is often less real difference in its bearing on the public weal, than there is between the dispute being *kept up*, or being *settled* either way. I fear the one *great* question of the day, is not now so likely to be partially acquiesced in by the different sections of the Union, as it would have been, could Gen. Taylor have been spared to us. Yet, under all circumstances, trusting to our Maker, and through his wisdom and beneficence, to the great body of our people, we will not despair, nor despond.

In Gen. Taylor's general public relation to his country, what will strongly impress a close observer, was his unostentatious, self-sacrificing, long enduring devotion to his *duty*. He indulged in no recreations, he visited no public places, seeking applause; but quietly, as the earth in its orbit, he was always at his post. Along our whole Indian frontier, thro' summer and winter, in sunshine and storm, like a sleepless sentinel, *he* has *watched*, while *we* have *slept* for forty long years. How well might the dying hero say at last, "I have done my duty, I am ready to go."

Nor can I help thinking that the American people, in electing Gen. Taylor to the presidency, thereby showing their high appreciation, of his sterling, but unobtrusive qualities, did their *country* a service, and *themselves* an imperishable honor. It is *much* for the young to know, that treading the hard path of duty, as he trod it, *will* be noticed, and *will* lead to high places.

But he is gone. The conqueror at last is conquered. The fruits of his labor, his name, his memory and example, are all that is left us—his example, verifying the great truth, that "he that humbleth himself, shall be exalted" teaching, that to serve one's country with a singleness of purpose, gives assurance of that country's gratitude, secures its best honors, and makes "a dying bed, soft as downy pillows are."

SOUTHERNERS

There was serious concern among citizens of the South about the Compromise of 1850 and the possibility that "for the first time, we are about permanently to destroy the balance of power between the sections." If California were to be admitted as a free state, the existing balance of fifteen slave and fifteen free states would tip in favor of the North. No longer in control of the legislative process, Southerners worried about the passage of laws limiting or abolishing slavery. Thus, the call went out for a convention of Southern states to meet in Nashville in June 1850 "to devise and adopt some mode of resistance to Northern aggression."

William Gilmore Simms

By the early months of 1850, Simms believed that any compromise between the North and South was impossible. In fact, the formation of a separate Southern nation was inevitable.

To Nathaniel Beverley Tucker
Woodlands Jany. 30. 1850
My dear Sir:
. . . We greatly wished for your presence, and concluded with the congratulatory thought that the formation of the new republic would

bring us wonderfully nearer to one another. The idea grows upon us rapidly, and we are pleased to think upon the Southern people. I have long since regarded the separation as a now inevitable necessity. The Union depends wholly upon the sympathies of the contracting parties, and these are lost entirely. I have no hope, and no faith in compromises, of any kind; and am not willing to be gulled by them any longer. Any compromise now—the parties knowing thoroughly the temper of each—must originate in cowardice and a mean spirit of evasion on the part of the South,—and in a spirit of fraud and deliberately purposed wrong on that of the North. Yet you will see that Cass & Clay, still having the fleshpots in their eye, will equally aim at some miserable pottering to stave off the difficulty, & be called a Compromise, upon which they are [to] found their new claims to the Presidency. These scoundrelly professional politicians are at the bottom of all our troubles.—I forebore politics & the Southern Convention & Confederacy, while writing to you, as I did not desire, in the small space allowed me, to refer to subjects upon which the Southron [that is, Southerner] is apt to become diffuse, and which are now in course of discussion almost *ad nauseam*, all over the country. . . . I regard the Southern Convention, as, in fact, a Southern Confederacy. To secure the one it seems to me very certain is to secure the other. . . .

During the summer he expressed concern about the Nashville Convention, disputes over the boundaries of Texas, and the value of remaining in the Union.

To Nathaniel Beverley Tucker
Charleston, July 11, 1850
My dear Sir:
. . . I wished particularly to have had *your* account of the Convention—to have ascertained the degree of *hope* which *you* felt, and your views of the condition of affairs. The new element, that of the territorial jurisdiction of Texas which the U. S. disputes, will probably furnish a more conspicuous & fruitful issue than any other cause of quarrel. It is one which can be made intelligible to the people—which mere cunning partisans cannot torture into the equivocal or the innocent. In that is our hope; and the insolence of the military men may probably precipitate the events which we should conjure up with great delay & difficulty, by which we could bring on the one great conflict. It must be clear enough to every Southron & man of sense, that there is

no living with a people so utterly hostile & reckless as those of the North. Any adjustment must be a patch, and for the moment only, unless you could change by it their minds & moods & hearts. . . .

Yours lovingly

W. Gilmore Simms

At the end of the year, Simms spelled out the risks and dangers to be dealt with in the months to come. There would be great danger to the institution of slavery.

Woodlands Nov. 27. [1850]
Hon. Beverley Tucker.
My dear Sir:

. . . You have seen by this time that Georgia has for the nonce surrendered to the Submissionists. This I feared would be the case. Indeed, I have no hope of the South *until after* the next Presidential election. The two great national parties must make one more dying effort under their old organizations. The result will crowd the field with discontents, and all the success will enure to the abolitionists. They will push their success. They lack the wisdom which knows when to stop, and in their insolence they will push the South to extremities. In all probability the fugitive Slave Bill will be repealed this coming session. The abolition of slavery will follow, soon or late in the District of Columbia and in all places directly under the control of the Fed. Gov. Four years will certainly bring about all these things & probably interdict the slave trade between the States. Five years at the utmost—unless there be a great revolution in public sentiment at the north,—which is scarcely possible—will see the dissolution of the Union, since every pretext will then be set aside utterly, by which our trading politicians have succeeded in abusing the understanding of the people. That they should succeed—we need not wonder for the masses are very slow in general, particularly where the questions do not press directly & practically upon them, in detecting the treachery of old & long honored leaders. Were I to trust my feelings, I should say to S. C. [South Carolina] secede at once. Let our State move *per se*. . . . We must, at all hazards goad Geo. [Georgia] to extremities & give her no encouragement in her submission. With S. C. & Geo. moving for secession the effect would be conclusive upon all the South. British assistance could not be expected, unless they were shut out from *all* the cotton ports. Leave the majority of these open & they will encounter no contest with the U. S. for the trade of one or more of our Southern cities. Patience & shuffle the cards! Our emissaries must be at work. If we are to incur the imputation of rebellion, we must use all the arts of conspiracy. We must enter the field with the U. S. and hold out the proper lines to buyable politicians. We must show them that a confederacy of 13 South. States, must have the same foreign & domestic establishment now maintained by the 31 states; show them that we shall then have the same offices to distribute among 13 now distributed among 31, and thus be able to *bid* more highly for their support. We must select our men, and give them their price. Meanwhile, events *must* favor us. . . .

Jefferson Davis

In the midst of the prolonged struggle to choose a Speaker of the House of Representatives, Davis wrote a letter to a friend, Charles Searles. He had little confidence that a satisfactory answer would be found.

To Charles J. Searles
Washington, D. C., 20th Dec. 1849.
My Dear Sir:—We are yet in the prolonged struggle of the House for a Speaker, the end of which is still as much a matter of speculation as at first.

You will have seen the exposure of the disgraceful attempt to make a combination of the democrats and free-soilers. This, though painful, will be useful, and relieves me from one source of apprehension—such combination being to me far worse than a party defeat. There are besides the five southern Whigs, who have manfully burst party trammels, others of the same party, who, to secure the election of a *true* southern man, would unite with us; but the difficulty is, that as they come over, northern democrats will probably drop off from any man, who can get votes on the southern, as the paramount question. . . . For this, judgment has been properly suspended; and it would not be creditable to us to seek to force it to trial, upon the collateral question of removals and appointments. The delay which has occurred, however, has concentrated public attention upon the southern question as the cause of delay, and excited some feeling at the north against the South. Now we should persevere, until free-soilism becomes odious as the cause of defeat to the efforts for organization. We of the South have little to hope from federal legislation, in comparison to the much we have cause to fear. Not, therefore, with us, but at the North, will the first and loudest complaint be made against anything which defeats organization, and prevents legislation. They would soon abandon a movement against our negroes, which would deprive them of the benefit of appropriations.

I have little doubt now, of the passage of the Wilmot Proviso, or some equivalent measure. . . . But if my observations here have destroyed my hopes in Congress, they have on the other hand, created some confidence that the President will veto the bill. As I have often told you, his heart is with us; and if he believes the measure will be destructive to the Union, which he can now scarcely doubt, I am sure the honest old patriot will cast precedent and northern advice far from him, and meet the emergency as becomes his station and heroic fame. If he does so, it will be like his acts on the battle-field, the result of his own will, and not the fruit of his adviser's counsel and support. . . .

As ever, your friend.

Jefferson Davis.

Several months later, on May 15, Davis took the floor to prevent territorial legislatures from enacting laws against the citizens' right to own slaves in the territories. He suggested an amendment to the Compromise Bill of 1850.

The language of the bill, as it stands, would seem to exclude the idea of the right of property growing out of the institution of African slavery to receive the same protection from the territorial legislature as is accorded to all other species of property. As I now propose to amend the bill, it will prevent the territorial legislature from invading the rights of the inhabitants of the slaveholding States. I am willing to leave the question to be decided according to the great cardinal principles of the Democratic party; that the people inhabiting a territory, when they come to form a State constitution for themselves, can do as they please. It will leave to the territorial legislatures those rights and powers which are essentially necessary, not only to the preservation of property, but to the peace of the territory. It will leave the right to make such police regulations as are necessary to prevent disorder, and which will be absolutely necessary with such property as that, to secure its beneficial use to its owner.

Finally, he summarized his intentions with the amendment in order to prevent any further misunderstanding.

Now, sir, what is the amendment? It is to prevent the legislature of the territory from legislating so as to interfere with the right of property in slaves. It is not asking Congress to pass a law providing for the introduction of slaves into the territory, but it is asking Congress, while they are conferring the powers of legislation upon the inhabitants, to restrict them from legislating against our rights in slaves—to restrict them so that they shall not interfere with those rights of property which grow out of the institution of African slavery. That is the whole proposition. . . . I claim that territorial legislation shall not interfere with those rights of property which we have under the Constitution. That right I claim to be derived from the Constitution and nature of our Government.

After the passage of the Compromise of 1850, Davis returned home to explain the actions of Congress to his constituents. In a November 2 speech at Benton, Mississippi, reported in the Yazoo Democrat, *he expressed his deep disappointment with the final results.*

He [Davis] briefly reviewed the great questions, the settlement of which had grieved the South. He exposed their enormity & unconstitutionality. First in the series was Utah, to which Congress gave a territorial government without the Wilmot Proviso, but so hedged it in by free States and mountain barriers, that it is impossible to get slaves to it, even if its soil and climate should invite them. He then adverted to the admission of California; the dismemberment of Texas, and the abolition of the slave trade in the District of Columbia, all of which were aggressions upon the South by the North and indicated a disposition upon the part of the North to push aggression still farther. He also shewed our inability to protect our rights in the confederacy, and exhorted the South if she desired to preserve the Union, to make a manly and determined resistance now and demand new guards for her future security; to look to her rights, "and," to use his own language, "protect them in the Union if she can and out of it if she must." Her honor and safety, he presented as considerations of the first and highest importance. So clear and distinct did he portray the ills which the

South has suffered and the ruin now in prospect, that there was scarcely one in the assembly, who did not think and feel with him; and such was the complete control he had over the judgment and feelings of the multitude, that after stating the true and lamentable position of the South in the confederacy, and asking in view of "this state of facts what are we to do?" a murmur involuntarily ran throughout the audience, "that's it, that's the question." His answer was as satisfactory as it was distinct. He advised that each Southern State should call a convention, and that delegates should be elected from each State, to a general convention of all the Southern States, and let that convention, fresh from the people, point out the guarantees and safe guards, which the South is entitled to, and should exact. In this way every individual in the South, would have an opportunity to express his views, and a body thus chosen would carry with it a moral force, which the fierce abolitionist dare not oppose. If, however, its decision should be disregarded, as was that of the Nashville Convention, the South would have no alternative left and must therefore leave the Union.

He shewed that submission had only heretofore invited aggression and would do so again; and that by it we would inevitably lose all the advantages of the Union and our rights also.

Augustus Benners

Benners, a cotton planter and lawyer in Greensboro, Alabama, had moved there from Chapel Hill, North Carolina, in 1840. In the summer of 1850, Benners was raising cotton and keeping an eye on events in the national capital.

Friday 21 [June 1850]: Ther. 7 o.clock 72°—3 oclock 90°. News to day of very bad feeling in Congress on the slavery question. Mr. Clay & Mr. [Thomas Hart] Benton having come in collision. Mr. Webster it is said has promised to support Mr. Clay's adjustment bill. . . .

Friday July 12. T. 8. 76°. Went on yesterday to plantation. The morning was very warm. Thunder squall in evening. Found crops looking pretty well. Weed not large but a good many blooms & squares & some bolls. Best cotton on the upland. in the Bottom the stand bad and plant backward got home last night at 15 past 8 oclock very tired

Saturday July 13th 1850. Rainy & Hot. rec'd news to day of the death of President Taylor which occurred on Tuesday the 9th July at

11 oclock P.M. of chronic Diarrhea aggravated by Cholera Morbus— account being telegraphed is disbelieved by some—Rec'd letter from Pitts saying there are many worms in the cotton especially in the redland

Sunday July 14. Report of Gen Taylors death confirmed. Went to church. C. L. Stickney lay reader. sermon on love of riches. Hot & Rainy—Ther 84

Monday 15th. . . . . Public meeting held this day to pay a tribute of respect to Gen Taylor. . . .

[Aug] 12 Ther at 76° at 7 oclock A.M. 84° at 7 oclock. I saw extra from Montgomery paper in which it is stated Mr Fillmore has transmitted a message to Congress asserting his intention to maintain by force the authority of the W States in New Mexico from which a civil war may be apprehended. . . .

15th Ther at 88. very hot & dry—no rain yet. learned by telegraph that the Texas boundary question was settled in Congress.

John J. Crittenden

As governor of Kentucky from 1848 to 1850, Crittenden remained in contact with key figures in Washington. Letters from men such as Robert Toombs of Georgia kept him abreast of the growing division over slavery and the Wilmot Proviso. President Taylor was having difficulties, and Crittenden counselled patience and cooperation.

(Crittenden to Orlando Brown)
Frankfort, April 30, 1850.

Dear Orlando,—On my return, last Saturday, from Louisville, where I had been spending some days, I found your letter. I perused it with the most painful interest. My heart is troubled at the discord that seems to reign among our friends. [A. T.] Burnley will be in Washington when this reaches you, and with his good sense and his sincere devotion to General Taylor will be able to settle all difficulties about the *Republic*, and give to it a satisfactory and harmonious direction. The editors of that paper are the friends of General Taylor, and if his cabinet is not altogether what they could wish, they ought, for his sake and the sake of his cause, to waive all objections on that score. Concession among friends is no sacrifice of independence. The temper to do it is a virtue, and indispensable to that co-operation that is necessary to political success. I do not, of course, mean that any man, for any object, ought to surrender essential principles, or his honor; but in this instance nothing of that sort can be involved. The utmost differences of the parties must consist of personal feelings, or disagreements in opinion about expediencies. If even an old Roman could say, and that, too, with continued approbation of about twenty centuries, that he had rather *err* with Cato, etc., I think that we, his friends, one and all of us, ought to give to General Taylor the full benefit of that sentiment, and strengthen him thereby to bear the great responsibility we have placed upon him. Cato himself was not more just or illustrious than General Taylor, nor ever rendered greater services to his country. . . .

Near the end of the letter, Crittenden expressed his own view.

. . . Here, then, is a new case presented; and it seems to me that the grand *object* exhibited in the President's recommendation will be accomplished by the admission of California and the establishment of territorial governments without the Wilmot proviso. The prime object was to avoid that proviso and its excitements by inaction; but any course of action that gets rid of that proviso cannot be said to be inconsistent with the object in view. The only difference is in the means of attaining the same end, and that difference is the result of the altered state of the subject since the date of the President's message. In the attainment of so great an object as that in question, the peace and safety of the Union, it will, as it seems to me, be wise and magnanimous in the administration not to be tenacious of any particular plan but to give its active aid and support to any plan that can effect the purpose. I want the plan that does settle the great question, whatever it may be, or whosoever it may be, to have General Taylor's *Imprimatur* upon it.

I shall expect letters from you with impatience.

Your friend,

J. J. Crittenden.

Taylor died on July 9 and Vice President Millard Fillmore became president. Soon thereafter a letter was sent to Crittenden to determine his interest in becoming attorney general in the new administration. On July 19 he wrote to A. T. Burnley about his willingness to accept the position.

My relations with Mr. Fillmore have always been of the most agreeable and amicable character, and I hope they may continue so. It seems to me that if he pleased to desire my acceptance of the office of Attorney-General, the most proper course would be for him to tender it to me; and that the most proper and becoming course for me would be to wait till it was tendered.

Three days later, Crittenden joined Fillmore's cabinet as attorney general. He was then asked by President Fillmore to write an opinion on the constitutionality of the Fugitive Slave Law.

The whole effect of the law may be thus briefly stated: Congress has constituted a tribunal with exclusive jurisdiction to determine summarily and without appeal who are fugitives from service or labor under the second section of the fourth article of the Constitution, and to whom such service or labor is due. The judgment of every tribunal of exclusive jurisdiction where no appeal lies, is, of necessity, conclusive upon every other tribunal; and therefore the judgment of the tribunal created by this act is conclusive upon all tribunals. Wherever this judgment is made to appear, it is conclusive of the right of the owner to retain in his custody the fugitive from his service, and to remove him back to the place or State from which he escaped. If it is shown upon the application of the fugitive for a writ of *habeas corpus*, it prevents the issuing of the writ; if upon the return, it discharges the writ and restores or maintains the custody.

This view of the law of this case is fully sustained by the decision of the Supreme Court of the United States in the case of Tobias Watkins, where the court refused to discharge upon the ground that he was in custody under the sentence of a court of competent jurisdiction, and that that judgment was conclusive upon them. . . .

I conclude by repeating my conviction that there is nothing in the bill in question which conflicts with the Constitution or suspends, or was intended to suspend, the privilege of the writ of *habeas corpus*.

Crittenden's opinion that the Fugitive Slave Law was constitutional became the basis for its continuing enforcement. For the remaining years of the Fillmore administration, Crittenden served as attorney general and for a short time acting secretary of state while Daniel Webster recovered from an illness. He supported Fillmore's unsuccessful effort to be elected in 1852.

3

The Fugitive Slave Controversy, the Election of 1852, and Growing Sectionalism

NORTHERNERS

Harriet Beecher Stowe

In the summer of 1849, Cincinnati experienced a severe cholera epidemic. Cholera had been endemic in Cincinnati since its original outbreak in 1832. By the middle of June it was evident that it was worse than ever. Funerals were so numerous that there was a shortage of hearses and coffins. Then one of Harriet and Calvin Stowe's children, Charley, contracted the disease and, after days of suffering, died on July 26. His death was a terrible blow to Harriet. Years later she referred to that summer as a time of horror. In a letter to Calvin on July 26 she poured out her sorrow.

July 26. [1849]

My dear Husband,—At last it is over, and our dear little one is gone from us. He is now among the blessed. My Charley—my beautiful, loving, gladsome baby, so loving, so sweet, so full of life and hope and strength—now lies shrouded, pale and cold, in the room below. Never was he anything to me but a comfort. He has been my pride and joy. Many a heartache has he cured for me. Many an anxious night have I held him to my bosom and felt the sorrow and loneliness pass out of me with the touch of his little warm hands. Yet I have just seen him in his death agony, looked on his imploring face when I could not help nor soothe nor do one thing, not one, to mitigate his cruel suffering, do nothing but pray in my anguish that he might die soon. I write as though there were no sorrow like my sorrow, yet there has been in this city, as in the land of Egypt, scarce a house without its dead. This heart-break, this anguish, has been everywhere, and when it will end God alone knows.

Later in the year, Calvin received an invitation to teach at Bowdoin College in Brunswick, Maine, his alma mater. He was anxious to leave Cincinnati with its severe weather and unhealthy summers. He accepted the offer, and the next spring, Harriet took three of their children and traveled to Brunswick. Calvin was to come later with the other children when Lane Seminary found a replacement for him.

The last act passed by Congress in 1850 was the Fugitive Slave Law, which authorized the recapture of slaves who had fled to the North. Harriet began to receive letters from relatives and friends about the serious consequences of the new law. Slave hunters were going north to capture former slaves and take them back south; black families were broken up. Their plight filled Harriet with dismay. Then she received a letter from her sister-in-law, Mrs. Edward Beecher—"Now, Hattie, if I could use a pen as you can, I would write something that would make this whole nation feel what an accursed thing slavery is."

A member of Mrs. Stowe's family well remembers the scene in the little parlor in Brunswick when the letter alluded to was received. Mrs. Stowe herself read it aloud to the assembled family, and when she came to the passage, "I would write something that would make this whole nation feel what an accursed thing slavery is," Mrs. Stowe rose up from her chair, crushing the letter in her hand, and with an expression on her face that stamped itself on the mind of her child, said: "I will write something. I will if I live."

Another reason for Harriet's desire to write was the need for money. Calvin was earning a small salary, and more income was required to cover their expenses. Thus, pressed by fears about the return of fugitive slaves and by worries about money, she began to think about writing essays or a book about slavery. Then in February 1851, while sitting in church, she had a vision that had a profound effect on her.

For she was seeing a vision—seeing it as plain as if she were there, present, in the flesh, and the actors, too. There was an old slave, with white wool, clothed in rags—a gentle, Christian man, like Father Henson—being flogged to death by the white ruffian who owned him— such a man as the overseer Charles met on the New Orleans boat, the man with the fist hardened by knocking down niggers. This brute was too cowardly to do the murderous work himself but ordered two degraded slaves, ragged and dirty as their victim, to lay on the whips.

The lashes fell, the ebony skin broke, and blood as red as any white man's flowed from the stripes. And as he died, the black saint prayed the Lord's forgiveness for his torturers.

From far away Harriet heard the benediction pronounced and walked home in a trance, down Federal Street and across the track. At the dinnertable she was still deep in reverie, but the children were used to their mother's spiritual absences and chattered about their own concerns. Then Harriet went to her bedroom and wrote out the picture given her in the vision. She, who never held back in realism, made it almost unbearable. Even the names of the actors were coming to her now. The negro saint was Uncle Tom. The two slave executioners were Sambo and Quimbo. The name of the hairy, ape-like master was a sheer inspiration—Simon Legree. Few fictional names hold such sinister suggestion. Harriet elaborated the picture. The example of Christian steadfastness set by Uncle Tom in his agony touched even the savage hearts of the "imbruted blacks," Sambo and Quimbo. They saw the light and were brought to God.

When Harriet recovered her normal senses, she read to the children what she had written. They wept convulsively, and Henry cried out, "Oh, Mamma! slavery is the most cruel thing in the world!"

It was the beginning of her novel, Uncle Tom's Cabin. *At first she intended to write three or four installments. In a letter to Dr. Gamaliel Bailey, the editor of the* National Era *newspaper in Washington, DC, she explained her plans.*

Brunswick, March 9. [1851]

Mr. Bailey, Dear Sir: I am at present occupied upon a story which will be a much longer one than any I have ever written, embracing a series of sketches which give the lights and shadows of the "patriarchal institution," written either from observation, incidents which have occurred in the sphere of my personal knowledge, or in the knowledge of my friends. I shall show the *best side* of the thing, and something *faintly approaching the worst.*

Up to this year I have always felt that I had no particular call to meddle with this subject, and I dreaded to expose even my own mind to the full force of its exciting power. But I feel now that the time is come when even a woman or a child who can speak a word for freedom and humanity is bound to speak. The Carthagenian women in the last peril of their state cut off their hair for bow-strings to give to the defenders of their country; and such peril and shame as now hangs over this country is worse than Roman slavery, and I hope every woman who can write will not be silent. . . .

My vocation is simply that of *painter*, and my object will be to hold up in the most lifelike and graphic manner possible Slavery, its reverses, changes, and the negro character, which I have had ample opportunities for studying. There is no arguing with *pictures*, and everybody is impressed by them, whether they mean to be or not.

I wrote beforehand, because I know that you have much matter to arrange, and thought it might not be amiss to give you a hint. The thing may extend through three or four numbers. It will be ready in two or three weeks. . . . .

Yours with sincere esteem,

H. Stowe.

Dr. Bailey agreed to publish it for $300, but it took much longer than originally anticipated. Slowly the story unfolded. It was printed in installments for an eager public from June 5, 1851, until April 1, 1852. In 1852 it was published by John P. Jewett as a book. On the first day three thousand copies were sold; by the end of the year three hundred thousand copies had been sold. Later in 1852, Harriet responded to a request for information about herself from Sarah Josepha Hale, the editor of Godey's Lady's Book and Magazine.

December 16, 1852

My Dear Madam,

I hasten to reply to your letter, the more interesting that I have long been acquainted with you, and during all the nursery part of my life made daily use of your poems for my children.

So you want to know what sort of woman I am! Well, if this is any object, you shall have statistics free of charge. To begin, then, I am a little bit of a woman,—somewhat more than forty, about as thin and dry as a pinch of snuff—never very much to look at in my best days and looking like a used up article now.

I was married when I was twenty-five years old to a man rich in Greek and Hebrew and Latin and Arabic, and alas, rich in nothing else. . . . But then I was abundantly furnished with wealth of another sort. I had two little curly headed twin daughters to begin with and my stock in this line has gradually increased, till I have been the mother of seven children, the most beautiful and the most loved of whom lies buried near my Cincinnati residence. It was at his dying bed and at his grave that I learned what a poor slave mother may feel when her child is torn away from her. In those depths of sorrow which seemed to me immeasurable, it was my only prayer to God that such anguish might not be suffered in vain. There were circumstances about his death of such peculiar bitterness, of what seemed almost cruel suffering that I felt that I could never be consoled for it unless this crushing of my own heart might enable me to work out some great good to others.

I allude to this here because I have often felt that much that is in that book had its root in the awful scenes and bitter sorrow of that summer. It has left now, I trust, no trace on my mind except a deep compassion for the sorrowful, especially for mothers who are separated from their children. . . .

You ask with regard to the remuneration which I have received for my work here in America. Having been poor all my life, and expecting to be poor to the end of it, the idea of making anything by a book, which I wrote just because I could not help it never occurred to me. It was therefore an agreeable surprise to receive ten thousand dollars as the first fruits of three months sale and presume as much more is now due. . . .

I suffer exquisitely in writing these things. It may truly be said that I write with my heart's blood. Many times in writing "Uncle Tom's Cabin" I thought my health would fail utterly; but I prayed earnestly that God would help me till I got through, and still I am pressed beyond measure and above strength.

This horror, this nightmare abomination! can it be in my country! It lies like lead on my heart, it shadows my life with sorrow; the more so that I feel, as for my own brothers, for the South, and am pained by every horror I am obliged to write, as one who is forced by some awful oath to disclose in court some family disgrace. Many times I have thought that I must die, and yet I pray God that I may live to see something. . . .

Yours affectionately,

H. B. Stowe

Suddenly Harriet Beecher Stowe became one of the best-known women in the United States. Surprised by this turn of events she began to take on the duty of writing and speaking out for an end to slavery. Her book played a vital role in shaping the way Americans looked at slavery.

Charles Sumner

In the spring of 1851, Sumner was elected U.S. Senator from Massachusetts. The Massachusetts legislature, deadlocked for twenty-six ballots for a replacement for Daniel Webster after his death, finally voted Sumner into the prestigious position. Free Soilers and Democrats chose him over a Whig candidate. Suddenly, Sumner was in a position of power to push for the ending of slavery. With a new coalition—Democrats and Free Soilers in a majority—it was possible to align Massachusetts firmly in the antislavery camp. (This coalition would become the Republican Party within a few years.)

In a letter to Thomas Higginson, a Unitarian minister and antislavery advocate, he explained his hopes.

> To Thomas Wentworth Higginson
> Boston Sept. 5th '51
> Dear Mr. Higginson, . . .

It was only last evng that I returned to Boston after an absence from the state of several weeks. More than ever do I feel the importance to our cause of preventing the Cwlth [Commonwealth] from passing into the hands of Websterized Whiggery. This, of course, can be prevented only by a *combination*—I wish a complete community of principles would allow it to be a *union*—with the Democrats. Regretting that they are not more essentially with us, I feel that we shall throw our staff away, if we reject the opportunity, which seems offered, of their co-operation against the Whigs.

With a mutual understanding of each other, & with a real determination to carry the *combination* honestly through, in the hope of sustaining our great cause, I cannot doubt the result. . . . To accomplish this it is well worthy of our effort; & the only effort, practicable, is *combination* with the Democrats. If the latter will completely adopt our principles, then we hail them as brothers. If they fail to do this, then it seems to me that we should not fail to use them, wherever we can, to secure the balance of power in the Legislature, & to overturn the two W.W.'s [Webster and Senator Robert Charles Winthrop] of Massachusetts. For one, if they will help us in this two-fold purpose, I will welcome them & will "ask no questions. . . ."

When the Senate convened in December 1851, however, Sumner remained silent. Pressed to speak against the Compromise of 1850, he declined. Conscious of his lack of experience, he waited for the "right time" to give his first major ad-

dress. Several minor speeches, including one in support of a bill to grant Iowa a right-of-way for railway expansion, were well received.

Still he had not made the speech that his constituents expected. Then on August 26, 1852, Sumner delivered an address (just under four hours long) in which he vigorously attacked the Fugitive Slave Law. It was an assault upon a major part of the Compromise of 1850.

Sir, in the name of the Constitution which it violates; of my country which it dishonors; of humanity which it degrades; of Christianity which it offends, I arraign this enactment, and now hold it up to the judgment of the Senate and the world. Again I shrink from no responsibility. I may seem to stand alone; but all the patriots and martyrs of history, all the fathers of the Republic, are with me. Sir, there is no attribute of God which does not unite against this act.

But, I am to regard it now chiefly as an infringement of the Constitution. And here its outrages, flagrant as manifold, assume the deepest dye and broadest character only when we consider, that by its language it is not restrained to any special race or class, to the African or to the person with African blood; but that any inhabitant of the United States, of whatever complexion or condition, may be its victim. Without discrimination of color even, and in violation of every presumption of freedom, the act surrenders all, who may be claimed as "owing service or labor" to the same tyrannical proceedings. If there be any whose sympathies are not moved for the slave, who do not cherish the rights of the humble African, struggling for divine freedom, as warmly as the rights of the white man, let him consider well that the rights of all are equally assailed. "Nephew," said Algernon Sidney in prison, on the night before his execution, "I value not my own life a chip, but what concerns me is that *the law* which takes away my life may hang every one of you, whenever it is thought convenient." . . .

In conclusion, Sumner made a plea for the repeal of the act.

. . . Finally, Sir, for the sake of peace and tranquillity, cease to shock the public conscience; for the sake of the Constitution, cease to exercise the power which is nowhere granted, and which violates inviolable rights expressly secured. Leave this question where it was left by our fathers, at the formation of our National Government, in the absolute control of the States, the appointed guardians of personal liberty. Repeal this enactment. Let its terrors no longer rage through the land. Mindful of the lowly whom it pursues; mindful of the good men perplexed by its requirements; in the name of charity, in the name of the Constitution, repeal this enactment, totally and without delay. Be inspired by the example of Washington. Be admonished by those words of Oriental piety— "Beware of the groans of the wounded souls. Oppress not to the utmost a single heart; for a solitary sigh has power to overset a whole world."

The speech was widely hailed in the North. It was published everywhere, even in England. In Congress, Illinois's Senator James Shields considered it "the ablest speech ever made in the Senate on slavery." John H. Clarke of Rhode Island went even further: "It would be a text-book when they are dead and gone." Sumner had staked out his position clearly and convincingly.

After the election in November 1852, Sumner wrote a brief letter to William Seward, asking for a new political party. The election of Franklin Pierce over Winfield Scott by 1,601,474 to 1,386,580 votes sealed the fate of the Whig Party in the mind of Sumner.

To William H. Seward
Boston Nov. 6th '52
Dear Governor,
What say you of recent events?
It seems to me that you are the only Whig on his legs.

Now is the time for a new organization. Out of this chaos the party of Freedom must rise. . . .

Ever Yrs,
Charles Sumner . . .

Frederick Douglass

Douglass attended numerous meetings on the need to resist the return of fugitive slaves to the South. At the City Hall in Syracuse, New York, on January 7, 1851, he delivered a speech that urged resistance to "these bloodhounds."

We have come together to consult as to our duty in reference to the Fugitive Slave Law. This law has had pledged to its support the military and naval power of this Government. It is the only law which, for a long time, it has been deemed necessary, that the Executive should openly pledge for its support the whole power of the army and navy—aye, even to collusion with our citizens, whom he might have to slaughter in its execution. This is the law. It is one about to be rigorously pressed. . . .

The question before us is, *Whether we are to make resistance to the execution of this law?* Whether we are to recognize the principle that every man is innocent and free until he is proven to be otherwise, or to admit the Virginia doctrine that every black man is a slave—until proved otherwise? The South have President Fillmore, the Army and the Navy on its side—and they are determined to press this law to the "bitter end." This Convention must say what ought to be done. I am a peace man. I am opposed to the shedding of blood in all cases where it can be avoided. But this Convention ought to say to Slaveholders that they are in danger of bodily harm if they come here, and attempt to carry men off into bondage. I say to any Fugitive, that nothing short of the blood of the slaveholder who shall attempt to carry him off, ought to satisfy him. The Convention should say so. . . .

The efforts of Horace Greeley to send blacks back to Africa angered Douglass. He wrote a sharp criticism of Greeley's position and published it in Frederick Douglass's paper on May 29, 1852.

. . . What black man did not feel grateful to the *Tribune*, a few months ago, for the gallant manner in which it exposed the frauds and falsehoods practiced upon this nation in respect to the true character of Haiti? *Who* among us did not feel a thrill of gratitude when he read, in September last, the defense of the heroic colored men at Christiana? Why, every one of us. But while we do not forget all this, we must nevertheless, recognize Mr. Greeley as being among the most effective and dangerous of our foes. We say this more in sadness than in bitterness of spirit. We may misapprehend his motives: they are between himself and the Searcher of all hearts; yet we repeat, that by his present position he is, practically, among our deadliest enemies. He is the advocate of Colonization, which, to us, means *ultimate extermination*; . . .

Mr. Greeley is called a benevolent man; and, as such, we ask him, how he reconciles his course towards the Free Colored People with the spirit of benevolence? Does he not know that the certain effect of urging them to depart, and alarming them with the idea that it is impossible for them to remain here, is to damp their aspirations, to fill them with doubt, and to paralyze their energies for improvement and elevation? To us, this circumstance constitutes one of the strongest objections to the Colonization discussion.—Slaveholders will not emigrate with their slaves to New Mexico, while there are doubt and uncertainty of their ability to hold them when they get there; and colored people will not exert themselves to acquire property, and settle down as good citizens of the State, while they are alarmed and terrified by the prospect of being (ultimately) driven out of the country. This truth is *well* known by our oppressors; and it is, doubtless, one motive for the constant agitation of the Colonization scheme.

Douglass visited Harriet Beecher Stowe at her home, which he dubbed "Uncle Tom's Cabin," in March 1853. Her warm reception and her freedom "from the slightest tinge of affectation" won his respect.

It was our pleasure and privilege, during our recent visit to Massachusetts, to pass a day and a night in *"Uncle Tom's Cabin,"* at Andover. . . .

It is only when in conversation with the authoress of *"Uncle Tom's Cabin"* that she would be suspected of possessing that deep insight into human character, that melting pathos, keen and quiet wit, powers of argumentation, exalted sense of justice, and enlightened and comprehensive philosophy, so eminently exemplified in the *master book* of the nineteenth century.

The object of our visit was to consult with the authoress, as to some method which should contribute successfully, and permanently, to the improvement and elevation of the free people of color in the United States—a work in which the benevolent lady designs to take a practical part; and we hesitate not to say that we shall look with more confidence to her efforts in that department, than to those of any other single individual in the country. In addition to having a heart for the work, she, of all others, has the ability to command and combine the means for carrying it forward in a manner likely to be most efficient. She desires that some *practical* good shall result to the colored people of this country, by the publication of her book—that some useful institution shall rise up in the wake of *"Uncle Tom's Cabin."*—The good lady, after showing us, in the most child-like manner, any number of letters, in testimony of the value of her book, together with presents of various kinds, among the number the beautiful "Bronze Statue of a Female Slave," entered most fully into a discussion with us on the present condition and wants of *"the free colored people."* . . .

She who had walked, with lighted candle, through the darkest and most obscure corners of the slave's soul, and had unfolded the secrets of the slave's lacerated heart, could not be a stranger to us; nor could we make ourselves such to her.

She was our friend and benefactress. Aye, and the friend of all mankind—one like Burns or Shakespeare, those favored ones of earth, to whom the whole book of humanity unfolds its ample pages, and from whom nothing is hid. . . .

Mrs. Stowe's plan for improving the condition of the free colored people will be made known in due season. For the present, it is sufficient to know that her attention is now most earnestly turned to this subject; and we have no question that it will result in lasting benefit to our class.

Frederick Douglass' Paper, March 4, 1853

George Templeton Strong

During the years from 1851 to 1854, Strong made few references to the South or to slavery. Busy with his law practice and involved in affairs at home—in Columbia College, Trinity Church, and the Philharmonic—he showed little concern with politics.

An exception was the election of 1852, when he became interested in the party conventions.

June 7. After some forty-odd labor pains in the shape of balloting, the Democratic Convention has brought forth its candidate: Franklin Pierce of New Hampshire, with William Rufus King for Vice-President. Nobody knows much of Franklin Pierce, except that he is a decent sort of man in private life. Very possibly he may run all the better, as Polk did, for his insignificance. Democracies are not over-partial to heroes and great men. A statesman who is too much glorified becomes a bore to them. . . . Daniel Webster's chance for the presidency was gone forever when his friends dubbed him the Great Expounder of the Constitution. . . .

June 17, Thursday Afternoon. The great Whig palaver at Baltimore in full activity over its nominations, the three great sections of the party—Scott, Webster, and Fillmore—intriguing, caucusing, bragging, and betting in an excitement that must be very trying with the thermometer at 90°. Scott on the whole seems to stand the best chance, but the result of the incubation is mere matter of guess. . . .

June 22. Scott is the nominee at last: the fact was made known to the crowd that beset the *Courier's* office and half blocked the street, at twelve yesterday, and was received with a quartette or quintette of cheers, the mob being somewhat apathetic, and a few performers being left to do what enthusiasm was done.

His chance of election, I think, is small . . . he won't be helped by Horace Greeley's editorial of this morning, wherein he repudiates and spits upon the plank of the platform which affirms the Fugitive Slave Law. The General's old alliance with Native Americanism [the American Party, sometimes called the Know-Nothing Party, which opposed immigration] will tell against him with the immense foreign vote.

In the fall, Strong had little confidence in Winfield Scott's chances to win. Still he watched with interest until the election on November 2.

October 11 [1852]. Scott is brightening daily, I think. But this series of stump speeches is a lamentable anti-climax, a sad falling off from the Triumphal Entry into Mexico. . . .

October 15. Cold news for Scott from Ohio and Pennsylvania, though Greeley accounts for it all very much to his own satisfaction and proves that the state elections don't afford the least indication of the vote for President. Perhaps they don't. . . .

October 20. . . . I pronounce Scott to be in a bad way. No election ever drew near so quietly, no two candidates ever developed so little enthusiasm. Scott's stumping tour may have done good among the masses, but I'm sure it has lost him respect with sensible people everywhere. His speeches are awkward, strained, vapid, and egotistical. Pierce has a talent for silence that will serve far better than his antagonist's electioneering. . . .

October 22 . . . Daniel Webster is reported *in extremis*. A sad hole his death will leave, and one not easy to fill. From the old heroic race to which Webster and Clay and Calhoun belonged down to the rising race of Sewards and Douglases and Fishes [that is, Senator Hamilton Fish] is a dismal descent.

October 25. Webster died early yesterday morning, and seems from the brief notices that have come here by telegraph to have made a stately exit, to have died self-possessed, thoughtful, and resigned, in style fitting his great career and his lofty place in the eyes of Europe and America. It is the ending of one of the greatest men of this time; one of the greatest intellectually, not morally. His position in the North would have been far more commanding if there had been moral weight in his character. But love of office and improvidence in his private affairs sometimes made him do things unheroic to gain place or money. There was undue love of brandy and water, too. . . .

November 1, Monday. Prospects of the Whigs very bad for tomorrow, specially so in this city, if this foul weather lasts. . . .

I don't care much about the general result. I shall vote a hybrid ticket. . . .

November 3. Till the day when Babylon the Great shall be cast down into the sea as a millstone, there will not be such another smash and collapse and catastrophe as yesterday befell the Whig party. This morning's *Courier* began its revelations of calamity by avowing that it was certain that Pierce was yesterday elected by the largest vote ever given any candidate for the office, and the returns coming in during the day only certify the truth of this frank confession. It's a cataclysm of Democracy flooding the whole country and overwhelming the tallest Whig strongholds as the deluge of old covered the tops of the high mountains. The victory in this city, in the state, and in the Union is beyond all shadow of question. . . .

November 6, Saturday night. General opinion seems to be that the Whig party is dead and will soon be decomposed into its original elements. Shouldn't wonder. Where is its leader or leaders? No man commands the confidence or respect of the whole party. Even the Democracy is likely to be disintegrated by the election.

Abraham Lincoln

Lincoln delivered a eulogy for Henry Clay on July 6, 1852. Clay had been a model for Lincoln's career, and he felt intense loyalty to his ideas. After an extensive oration, he closed with remarks about Clay's opposition to slavery, and efforts to colonize Negroes to Africa, a position that Lincoln maintained until the middle of the Civil War.

Having been led to allude to domestic slavery so frequently already, I am unwilling to close without referring more particularly to Mr. Clay's views and conduct in regard to it. He ever was, on principle and in feeling, opposed to slavery. The very earliest, and one of the latest public efforts of his life, separated by a period of more than fifty years, were both made in favor of gradual emancipation of the slaves in Kentucky. He did not perceive, that on a question of human right, the negroes were to be excepted from the human race. And yet Mr. Clay was the owner of slaves. Cast into life where slavery was already widely spread and deeply seated, he did not perceive, as I think no wise man has perceived, how it could be at *once* eradicated, without producing a greater evil, even to the cause of human liberty itself. His feeling and his judgment, therefore, ever led him to oppose both extremes of opinion on the subject. Those who would shiver into fragments the Union of these States; tear to tatters its now venerated constitution; and even burn the last copy of the Bible, rather than slavery should continue a single hour, together with all their more halting sympathisers, have received, and are receiving their just execration; and the name, and opinions, and influence of Mr. Clay, are fully, and, as I trust, effectually and enduringly, arrayed against them. But I would also, if I could, array his name, opinions, and influence against the opposite extreme— against a few, but an increasing number of men, who, for the sake of perpetuating slavery, are beginning to assail and to ridicule the whiteman's charter of freedom—the declaration that "all men are created free and equal." . . .

The American Colonization Society was organized in 1816. Mr. Clay, though not its projector, was one of its earliest members; and he died, as for the many preceding years he had been, its President. It was one of the most cherished objects of his direct care and consideration; and the association of his name with it has probably been its very greatest collateral support. . . . If as the friends of colonization hope, the present and coming generations of our countrymen shall by any means, succeed in freeing our land from the dangerous presence of slavery; and, at the same time, in restoring a captive people to their long-lost fatherland, with bright prospects for the future; and this too, so gradually, that neither races nor individuals shall have suffered by the change, it will indeed be a glorious consummation. And if, to such a consummation, the efforts of Mr. Clay shall have contributed, it will be what he most ardently wished, and none of his labors will have been more valuable to his country and his kind.

Horace Mann

Mann continued to speak out against the Compromise of 1850, especially the Fugitive Slave Law. He prepared a long speech to be delivered on February 21, 1851, but was limited to five minutes by the Whig Speaker of the House. Mann erupted in anger: "Sir, I hold treason against this government to be an enormous crime, but great as it is, I hold treason against free speech and free thought to be a crime incomparably greater." In his shortened speech he made remarks as moving as those by Patrick Henry or John Quincy Adams: "In the name of my constituents, and by the memory of that 'old man eloquent,' in whose place it is my fortune to stand, I demand its repeal. I demand it because it is a law which wars against the fundamental principles of human liberty" and "because it is a law which conflicts with the constitution of the country, and with all the judicial interpretations of that constitution, wherever they have been applied to the white race." Brief as his remarks were, they showed Mann at his best, deeply committed to the cause of ending the return of fugitive slaves. He released his full text to the House and the press.

In the next year, Mann declined to run for reelection to the House of Representatives. However, he was nominated by acclamation for governor of Massachusetts by the Free Soil Party. Running a strong campaign, he received thirty thousand votes but failed to split the Whig vote. It was his last political campaign.

On September 15, 1852, Mann was appointed president of Antioch College in Yellow Springs, Ohio. Tired of political battles, he accepted his new position with enthusiasm. He began to build the school, its curriculum, and its students and faculty. It was to be coeducational, achieve excellence in academics, and stress sound ethical and moral principles.

In February 1853 he paid his last visit to the White House. Avoiding President Fillmore's reception line, he was unwilling to "touch the hand that signed the Fugitive Slave Law." Then he left Washington for the last time as a member of Congress. In a letter to his wife he wrote: "I am a free man again. What a Congressional life I have had, but I have fought a good fight, and I come out with a clear conscience." The last six years of his life were spent in higher education. He continued to reform and look for ways to make Antioch College thrive . He died on August 2, 1859, at Yellow Springs.

Sojourner Truth

In the summer of 1851, Truth began a lecture tour in western New York. The meetings were often disturbed or broken up by mobs. Truth learned to maintain her decorum and continue to speak in a dignified manner. Leaving New York, she traveled westward into Ohio where she attended a women's rights convention at Akron. Frances Gage presided over the meeting and kept an account of the proceedings.

The cause was unpopular then. The leaders of the movement trembled on seeing a tall, gaunt black woman, in a gray dress and white turban, surmounted by an uncouth sun-bonnet, march deliberately into the church, walk with the air of a queen up the aisle, and take her seat upon the pulpit steps. A buzz of disapprobation was heard all over the house, and such words as these fell upon listening ears:—

"An abolition affair!" "Woman's rights and niggers!" "We told you so!" "Go it, old darkey!"

On the second day the meeting heated up—some delegates talked about men having superior rights, others about the sin of Eve. The atmosphere at the convention was becoming stormy.

Slowly from her seat in the corner rose Sojourner Truth, who, till now, had scarcely lifted her head. 'Don't let her speak!' gasped half a dozen in my ear. She moved slowly and solemnly to the front, laid her old bonnet at her feet, and turned her great, speaking eyes to me. There was a hissing sound of disapprobation above and below. I rose and announced 'Sojourner Truth,' and begged the audience to keep silence for a few moments. The tumult subsided at once, and every eye was fixed on this almost Amazon form, which stood nearly six feet high, head erect, and eye piercing the upper air, like one in a dream. At her first word, there was a profound hush. She spoke in deep tones, which, though not loud, reached every ear in the house, and away through the throng at the doors and windows:—

'Well, chilern, whar dar is so much racket dar must be something, out o' kilter. I tink dat 'twixt de niggers of de Souf and de women at de Norf all a talkin' 'bout rights, de white men will be in a fix pretty soon. But what's all dis here talkin' 'bout? Dat man ober dar say dat women needs to be helped into carriages, and lifted ober ditches, and to have de best place every whar. Nobody eber help me into carriages, or ober mud puddles, or gives me any best place (and raising herself to her full height and her voice to a pitch like rolling thunder, she asked), and ar'n't I a woman? Look at me! Look at my arm! (And she bared her right arm to the shoulder, showing her tremendous muscular power.) I have plowed, and planted, and gathered into barns, and no man could head me—and ar'n't I a woman? I could work as much and eat as much as a man (when I could get it), and bear de lash as well—and ar'n't I a woman? I have borne thirteen chilern and seen 'em mos' all sold off into slavery, and when I cried out with a mother's grief, none but Jesus heard—and ar'n't I a woman? Den dey talks 'bout dis ting in de head—what dis dey call it? ' 'Intellect,' whispered some one near. 'Dat's it honey. What's dat got to do with women's rights or niggers' rights? If my cup won't hold but a pint and yourn holds a quart, wouldn't ye be mean not to let me have my little half-measure full?' And she pointed her significant finger and sent a keen glance at the minister who had made the argument. The cheering was long and loud.

'Den dat little man in black dar, he say women can't have as much rights as man, cause Christ want [wasn't] a woman. Whar did your Christ come from?' Rolling thunder could not have stilled that crowd as did those deep, wonderful tones, as she stood there with outstretched arms and eye of fire. Raising her voice still louder, she repeated, 'Whar did your Christ come from? From God and a woman. Man had nothing to do with him.' Oh! what a rebuke she gave the little man.

Turning again to another objector, she took up the defense of mother Eve. I cannot follow her through it all. It was pointed, and witty, and solemn, eliciting at almost every sentence deafening applause; and she ended by asserting that 'if de fust woman God ever made was strong enough to turn the world upside down, all 'lone, dese togedder [and she glanced her eye over us], ought to be able to turn it back and get it right side up again, and now dey is asking to do it, de men better let em.' Long-continued cheering. ' 'Bleeged [Obliged] to ye for hearin' on me, and now ole Sojourner ha'n't got nothing more to say.'

It was a powerful speech that turned the tide of the meeting. Hundreds rushed up to shake her hand and to wish her godspeed in her work.

Truth soon became a regular speaker for the abolition cause, but she needed to sell more of her "narrative" since it provided most of her income. This meant endorsements by notable people. She went to see Harriet Beecher Stowe and asked for her help. Stowe consented and wrote an endorsement of her work, Narrative of Sojourner Truth, A Bondswoman of Olden Time.

The following narrative may be relied upon as in all respects true & faithful, & it is in some points more remarkable & interesting than many narratives of the kind which have abounded in late years.

It is the history of a mind of no common energy & power whose struggles with the darkness & ignorance of slavery have a peculiar interest. The truths of Christianity seem to have come to her almost by a separate revelation & seem to verify the beautiful words of scripture: "I will bring the blind by a way that they knew not, I will make darkness light before them and crooked things straight."

This endorsement resulted in increased sales of Truth's autobiography and a friendship with Stowe in the years to come.

SOUTHERNERS

The issues of fugitive slaves being returned, the election of 1852, and growing signs of sectionalism were of considerable interest to men such as William Gilmore Simms and Jefferson Davis. But to Augustus Benners and others, they were of less importance, if noticed at all. Benners worried about cotton prices and the death of friends. Only the politicians seemed anxious about the future.

William Gilmore Simms

Simms was concerned about the days ahead. What hope could there be for South Carolina within the Union? "Unfortunately, the State is at sea without a pilot." Calhoun was dead. Where could one turn now for leadership?

To Nathaniel Beverley Tucker
Woodlands March 12. 1851.

. . . My own notion is that the Union, even if we remain quiescent, cannot last five years. Abolition, which is not a placable madness—not to be soothed—if let alone will so kick your state & others, that resistance becomes inevitable. I am willing to wait awhile in this hope,— making, in the meanwhile all possible preparations. My fear is that premature action of S. C. will retard the event & discourage the proper action when the moment really arrives. It is difficult to say what will be done by our Convention. The Legislature by calling it, has reduced us to a fearful dilemma. To escape discredit our only alternative is secession. I have been counselling as many as possible to make the Convention a Long Parliament. To gain time is the great duty of Politicians —and not to lose it. Unfortunately, the State is at sea without a pilot. It was the unfortunate effect of Mr. Calhoun's great popularity here, to dwarf all the men about him. As the great tree of the forest makes shrubs of all within its shadow, so has his ascendancy deprived of their proper growth & stature those who might have succeeded him on his departure. The people know not where to turn for guidance & protection. . . . Meanwhile, there are no attempts made to secure cooperation in the South. Each man paddles his own canoe, up & down stream, at his own pleasure, and without any effort at combination. . . .

Ever & Ever faithfully Yours.

W. Gilmore Simms

Despite the uncertainty about the future, Simms continued to edit the Southern Review. *It remained on shaky financial ground because he had little money to pay writers. He regularly lamented the lack of manuscripts submitted for publication by native Southern writers: "I know not to whom I shall turn for a proper article." Nevertheless he advised a generation of the South's writers in an effort to lift the quality of the region's literary output. To one young man he wrote: "Strike out an independent path and publish anonymously. . . . Make your book unique—seek for simplicity & wholeness . . . Be manly, direct, simple, natural."*

On April 5, 1852, he discussed several of the positions taken by the Southern Review *in recent years with a fellow writer.*

We believe also that Negro Slavery is one of the greatest of moral goods and blessings, and that slavery in all ages has been found the greatest and most admirable agent of Civilization. . . . In fact our system is *not* slavery, but a relation between white & black not dissimilar to that of Guardian & Minor. . . . We are conservative—we have an aristocracy which gives tone even to our mechanics,—and we consequently retain, measurably, our veneration. We believe that the South has all the Imagination of the U. S. which is the true source of all originality in production; that the South, however, has not the necessary training for authorship, and hence its want of symmetry and polish; its disregard of models; its eccentricities, irregularities, and want of performance; we believe that, except in oratory, we have done so little simply because our able men have got into an absurd habit of thinking that the only road to eminence is over the course of party.

Jefferson Davis

In the spring of 1851, Senator Davis conducted a speaking tour on behalf of the "Southern Rights Democratic Party." He traveled across central and northern Mississippi during May and June. Then in July he canvassed southwestern Mississippi in support of Albert G. Brown, who was seeking a third term in Congress. On July 11, Davis gave a speech reviewing the Compromise of 1850 that drew a large crowd.

The present time was one in which Mississippi would have to declare what position she would occupy. She had, on a previous occasion declared for her equality in the Union—she had declared that Congress had no right to interfere with slavery either in the territories or in States—that it had no right to interfere with any domestic institution whatever. Did she now support the same principle? Did her citizens still declare for a maintenance of those rights with which they were born, and which they had resolved they would maintain to the last? When she asserted she would have equality in the Union, what did she mean? Was it not because the Wilmot Proviso was proposed? And had they changed their opinions because the Wilmot Proviso was altered and adopted under a disguised form? They were deprived of their territory, and it was dedicated to free-soil. New Mexico was alleged to be free-soil; Mr. Clay asserted that the Mexican law excluded slavery, and when Congress was asked to remove the obstacle, it refused to do so, and so the South was to be excluded from her rights by a foreign law. . . . When Congress was asked to give a protection to slavery in New Mexico, the answer was "if a right could be possessed to protect slavery, by the same law a power would exist to take away or abolish slavery." This was the veriest sophistry—the meanest twaddle. What was government for but to protect life and property? Taxes were levied to support the strong arm of the government in giving protection to the interests of a community. Legislators and senators were elected to serve and protect the privileges [*sic*] and property of their constituents, but not to abolish their privileges or sacrifice their interests. The navy protected commerce on foreign seas; in fact, the primary object of government was protection. Why, therefore, could not the authority of government be extended to the territory of New Mexico, and give to the South justice by protecting the institution of slavery. Such a measure would be perfectly constitutional, but it would give no precedent for the destruction of any established rule.

For several months, Davis had been urged to resign his position as senator and run for governor. He was the only man who had a chance of defeating Henry Foote, the Whig candidate. On September 17 he resigned as senator and six days later was nominated for governor by the Democratic Party. He began his last canvass of Mississippi on October 21. The essence of his campaign can be seen in his speech at Athens on October 27.

Col. Davis very briefly reviewed the history of that abominable humbug, ycleped [called] the Compromise, and also of its monstrous progeny, the *Union party*. But he said as Mississippi had concluded to *bear* with it, in her voice, he was bound by every principle of his cherished democracy, to acquiesce. "The only question now before the people," Col. D continued, "was the *approval or disapproval of the Compromise measures*. If the good people thought fit to elect him, he would ever be thankful to them, as he was already for the honors they had conferred on him in the past, but it was not *himself* he was solicitous about; it was to the success of those great *democratic principles* for which he was battling, and for the advancement of which, he, contrary to his physician's advice, had come among them. But if, however, they disapproved his course, and sanctioned that of his opponent, and late colleague in the Senate, he would submit to the will of the people. He was not dead, he said, as had been said about him, and that he did not intend to die (politically) before the November election, and when he did die, he should die hard, clutching to the last the flag staff of the good old banner of [Andrew] Jackson and Jefferson and Madison Democracy.

The returns of the gubernatorial election on November 23 and 24 showed Davis losing by 999 votes out of 57,717 cast. Unfair campaign tactics by his opponent— a notice of Davis's death and exaggerated rumors of his ill health—led to his defeat. It was a bitter blow from which he slowly recovered. Deeply discouraged he withdrew from politics until the summer of 1852 when Franklin Pierce and William King became the Democratic nominees for president and vice president.

Davis was asked to speak in support of the ticket, which he did on June 9, 1852, at Jackson, Mississippi. He strongly backed Pierce and King but expressed concern about recent developments in the North.

Col. Davis expressed gratification at again meeting his old friends under auspices which promised a future far brighter than the recent past. . . .

He believed that at no former time had a Presidential election more deeply involved the great interests of the Union. Never before had we wandered so far from the political chart which had been left us by the founders of the republic, and never before so nearly been wrecked in the voyage. . . . The people had always come to the rescue, and by restoring it to democratic hands, the benign influence of democratic principles had speedily brought peace at home, and respectability abroad. He did not doubt but that the same event would soon be re-enacted, but so great a good was hardly to be achieved without sacrifice, and energetic effort. They had before them an organized foe, an army of Treasury dependents, and a host whose purpose was the consolidation of the States, and the destruction of that domestic institution of the South, the overthrow of which no intelligent man could contemplate as an evil to be measured. He called upon all Democrats, all the friends of State Rights, all the true friends of the Constitution, to rally shoulder to shoulder for the dispersion of the hosts of federalism, as the gales of November would scatter the yellow leaves of the forest.

During the following month, Davis actively supported the Democratic Party. His friendship with Pierce, which dated back to the 1830s, gave him a special reason to reenter politics and campaign on Pierce's behalf.

Franklin Pierce won the presidency and in early December wrote a letter to Davis asking for a meeting. He wanted his advice and was interested in sounding out Davis for a possible cabinet position.

Concord. N H. Decr. 7. 1852.
My dear General.
As the news of your illness filled with anxiety your friends in this northern region, so the intelligence of your convalescence has brought relief and joy. We earnestly hope that before now you have regained

your elasticity and vigor. You will not be surprised, that, under all the circumstances of our early acquaintance and present positions respectively, I much desire to see you, and to avail myself in connection with the duties and responsibilities before me of your advice. Can you gratify such desire without too great inconvenience. I wish to converse with you of the South and particularly of the formation of my Cabinet. I am not permitted to know, that you would accept a place in it if desired and I do not ask an interview on the ground, that I have arrived at any fixed conclusion upon the subject, but, because I wish to talk with you, as a friend, in relation to matters of high concernment not only to myself, but to you and every man, who has at heart the best interest of our party and the country, and because I feel an assurance, that whether our views concide or not, from you I shall receive a friends free and useful suggestions. . . .

Your friend.

Frank Pierce.

Initially unwilling to serve in the position of secretary of war in the Pierce administration, Davis reconsidered after the tragic death of Franklin Pierce's youngest son in a railway accident and accepted the offer on March 5, 1853. For the next four years, Davis enjoyed the challenge and the prestige of his cabinet post. He was to prove an effective administrator in dealing with the newly acquired lands of Texas, Oregon, and the Mexican cession. Next to John C. Calhoun (1817–1825), Davis is generally considered to be the best secretary of war of the nineteenth century.

The first year was a demanding one for Davis. He was busy reorganizing the War Department and its duties but kept in touch with political friends in Mississippi. Still bruised from the struggles of recent years, especially the loss of the gubernatorial race, he was unwilling to consider any political office except senator.

On April 17 he answered an old friend candidly.

To Eli Abbott
CONFIDENTIAL
Washington D.C. April 17th 1853
My dear friend,
. . . To the question you ask in relation to my personal wishes I answer, that to advance the doctrine of state rights is my first wish and

whatever will most promote this end will be most acceptable to me. If the use of my name would serve to unite (& strengthen) the Democracy, it is, as it has been at their service; but if it would tend to divide and weaken them, I ask of my friends to consider all personal feeling for me as but dust in the ballance, thus I will be assured they justly appreciate me. . . .

Jeffn, Davis

Later in the year, Davis referred to his satisfaction with his position as secretary of war and desired only that "a states rights Democrat" be chosen as the next senator to represent Mississippi.

Augustus Benners

During 1851 and 1852, Benners voted, worried about his cotton crop, and helped bury a friend. By the fall of 1852 his crop was indeed a "full one."

Monday, August 4th. [1851] Election day—very quiet voted in the morning & remained at home the balance of the day—We had a very hard rain on the 3rd evening & night—also on the evening—I am dreading the rains very much—worms will follow wet — . . .

Aug 27th. Rec'd note from Mrs Sawyer to come & see Mr Marbury on business and to bring Mr Bannister which I did found him very low, tho free from pain. he is evidently sinking. Staid to dinner & came home in the evening—How comforting to the dying man is the hope & trust he has of his acceptance with God. Mr M is calm & composed as he ever was. The christians hope looks beyond the grave.

Sept 2nd 51. Returned from plantation today having gone down on yesterday. found gins running at both places. the screw is nearly completed at the Walker—& Wilson is to come in a day or two & finish it. The cotton crop at the Cheney place has failed very much—the worms having destroyed all the middle crops—& such of the top crop as appeared. Mr Pitts has altered his figures since 1st Aug from 125 bales to 80—which he now thinks he will make—

Reached home before dinner and learned of the death of Rev J. S. Marbury on the 1st Sept. and attended his funeral in the evening at the Church. He was a man of unaffected piety and of great purity & excellence of character and died a christians death—his example should be long cherished by those who knew him and tears of affection will often bedew the grave of the young pastor who spent his life in the service of his Master & in doing good to the souls of his flock. . . .

Sept 9th. More rain this day—sun hot tho pleasant in the shade—rec'd from Mrs Sawyer Mr Marburys will in which I am named one of the executors—an office from which I would be glad to be excused—what will come of it? . . .

Septr 7th. [1852] I visited the plantation on friday 3rd Septr. The new screw had been raised on tuesday previous without accident. the cotton ginning was progressing at both places & Pitts reported that the hands the previous day at the Walker place had averaged 200—a great deal of cotton was open and picking was very fine. I rode over the new road for the first time—saw John Walthal who informed me he had changed his opinion as to his liability to keep up the partition fence between us—and would do his part—Pitts thought he would make 200 bales. Packed on Saturday at each place. The present impression seems to be that the crop will be a full one—my own conjecture is that it will be 2,600,000.

In 1853, Benners accepted a nomination by the Whig Party and then was elected to the lower house in Alabama. It was an active year, requiring him to campaign and then begin to serve his term in Montgomery.

April 21st 1853. . . . The weather still dry and rain much needed—upon my reaching home from my plantation I rec'd a letter informing me I had received the nomination for the legislature with Dr Anderson—have rec'd as yet no official information and have given no reply—. . .

July 20th 1853. Having accepted the nomination of the Whig party for the lower house in the legislature—we commenced our canvass at Newbern on Monday the 27th day of June—there was quite a large company assembled, a good deal of interest having been exerted on the Liquor selling question—Messrs Webb & Hunt were the Candidates for the Senate—and Mr Inge & myself the Whig candidates for the House & Judge Coleman the Democratic candidate for the house. We were all called out on the Ala Liquor Law to know if we would support it & we each refused to do so or to advocate its claims and were told by the Henden faction that if we did not agree to advocate it re its principles—they would have candidates of their own after us with a sharp stick. accordingly on tuesday the 28th of July Mr Huckabee appeared at Greensboro and announced himself a candidate for the senate and Mr Francis H. Hawks a candidate for the lower house— The latter commenced the speaking in the morning in Kennedy's yard and stated in substance that as there were now no issues between the two parties he was a candidate not as a Whig or a democrat but as an advocate for what he called the majority principle i.e. that the Legislature should pass an act to give to the people in each county & beat [election precinct] the right by a majority vote to regulate the liquor traffic in their beats. which I opposed on the grounds that in the first place it was unconstitutional and could not be legally enacted—and that if it could it would be productive of more harm than good to the cause of Temperance. It was unconstitutional because the Constitution has provided that the legislative or Law making power should be vested in the senate and house of Representatives and has not conferred upon them the authority to delegate said power—That if the Legislature should pass such an act they have not passed an act which regulates the liquor traffic but have attempted to confer upon a majority in the beats the right to do so and thus to make a Law which by the Constitution can be done only by the two houses of the Legislature. That even if it were constitutional it would be productive of immense evil to the cause of Temperance because individuals being by this prohibitory law prevented from getting liquor by the glass or quart as they saw proper would furnish themselves with whiskey by the barrel and being thus furnished in large quantities would drink more than they now do. And that the multiplication of private barrels of whiskey in this way would greatly aggravate the evils of our negroes being furnished with spirits—my argument was by many considered a successful refutation of his positions—on Wednesday we spoke to a small company at Oak Grove—and here Mr Huckabee dwelt prominently on the fact that he was a planter & made good corn the best proof of which he said was the fact that it staid in his crib all the year round— The crop being very short in this neighborhood one of the neighbors is said to have come to him after his speech & endeavored to get some corn which crop [he] agreed to sell to him at 40 cts a bushel, about 60 cts under the market price—he did not get one vote at this precinct.

Benners, confident of the result, ended his campaign.

The result of the Election was in the aggregate as follows

Hawks		228 in County Greene
Inge		895
Coleman		706
Benners		*941*
Webb	for senate	921
Hunt	"	503
Huckabee	"	139

I was very much pleased with the vote I rec'd & especially with the vote given me at Greensboro & Hollow Square & 5 Mile—

Unfortunately his pleasure at being elected was followed by the death of "my little boy Gus." It was a crushing blow.

Oct 27th. We had a white frost on the morning of the 24—at 1/2 past 2 on that day my little boy Gus died. He had been seized with croup the night before, about 8 o.clock. My wife came down stairs and informed me that he had symptoms of it and I went immediately up-stairs where he was sleeping to see him—he shewed some signs of it in his breathing but we were not alarmed at it—we applied a snuff plaster to his breast and greased and greased his little feet—it was a dreadful night—being unable to find Virgil I started off in a hard rain for the Doctor, not that I considered him bad off but fearing that something might come of it. upon Doctor Webbs arrival he manifested great alarm and administered an emetic of alum which operated promptly but did not relieve him. I was still of the opinion he was not very sick—again & again was he vomited but no relief his symptoms shewed little or no abatement. Spirits of turpentine was applied to his breast till it was raw—but no relief—I still did not permit myself to consider him dangerous—about 12 o'clock the Dr told me if he did not get relief in six hours he could not recover—oh my God how my heart sank at the announcement and how I watched the time—day came the six hours had passed and my sweet little Gus was still gasping with the horrid croup. Dr Osborne was called in to consult—but could give no assistance & told me he would certainly die—oh how my heart chilled as I was told again & again there was *no change* in him—my poor little boy gasped on till after two o clock when I was told he was most gone. I hurried to his little crib and sure enough he was breathing his last the Dr was closing his eyes. my poor wife was weeping near him my little

darling breathed a few small breaths and ceased to breathe forever—
May God have mercy on us. he took our little cherub to himself I
know it was for his good and ours but oh how bitter to loose [*sic*] my
little darling His smart little prattle will no more gladden my heart on
earth never again will his fat little feet paddle out to meet his pa and
give him a hug and a kiss—but God be praised he is still our child in
Heaven—He was buried in the town graveyard on tuesday at Two
oclock Mr Hatch performed the service—

*On December 11, Benners left for Montgomery and the convening of the Ala-
bama legislature. The day after Christmas was his thirty-fifth birthday.*

Dec 23rd. I left home on friday Nov {Dec.] 11th for Montgomery
to attend as a member of the House of Representatives from the County
of Greene. We found Selma looking very dreary and desolate by reason of the late epidemic and we concluded to stay all night at Stones
when we reached there instead of going in to Montgomery. We (Inge
Webb & myself) rode in to Montgomery on Sunday evening. I took
quarters at the Madison house—The Gov [John A.] Winston was inaugurated on the 20th and the two houses adjourned over to the 9th
Jany. I came off from Montgomery that night and reached home on
the night of the 21st—found all well—and was informed that 30 hogs
had been killed on the previous Monday, Dec 19th. it was a fine season
for killing but we have had warm drizzly weather since then. Mary
Hatch and Betsey Vail were at my house to day I reached home and
Mr Hatch came up yesterday with the carriage & mules staid last night
and started to day for Arcola.

Part II

Southern Successes, Northern Anxieties, 1854–1857

The relative peace that followed the Compromise of 1850 came to an abrupt end in the early months of 1854. The chairman of the Committee on Territories, Stephen Douglas, reopened the slavery question when he presented a bill to organize Kansas and Nebraska at the 40th parallel. All questions pertaining to slavery were "to be left to the people residing therein, through their appropriate representatives." Also he included a section repealing the Missouri Compromise, which prohibited slavery north of the 36°30' line of latitude. People were to decide the slavery question by popular sovereignty—a vote to accept or forbid slavery in the new territories.

Douglas's action destroyed any hope for sectional peace. Many Northern Whigs did not want slavery to expand into the territories and strongly opposed the measure. In order to pass it Southern support was needed. Douglas secured this support by including the provision repealing the Missouri Compromise, a concession that gave him the support of Southern Whigs and Democrats. The measure easily passed the Senate by a vote of 37 to 14 with the support of Southern Whigs and Southern Democrats. The real struggle was in the House of Representatives, where a vote in favor was, for many men, political suicide. Sixty-six Democrats revolted and defeated the bill, 110 to 95. After great pressure was brought upon them, the measure passed, 113 to 100, with 39 Democrats refusing to vote. The margin was 13 Southern Whig votes.

The Northern response was immediate and hostile. The Whig and Democratic Parties were badly split, resulting in the creation of a new party, first called the Anti-Nebraska Party and then, by the summer of 1854, the Republican Party. Antislavery sentiment in the North escalated, united by one common element—opposition to the extension of slavery in the territories.

Sentiment in the South strongly supported the new act. Southerners believed that slavery should be extended into the territories; it was essential to the prosperity of their region. After all, the Bible accepted slavery, confirming it as a social institution. In addition the majority of Southerners believed that blacks were inferior to whites, and this notion justified their bondage. Southern ideology was on a collision course with that of the North.

The clash came when settlers from the North and South moved into Kansas with the hope of influencing the decision on slavery. Many Northerners were financed by the New England Immigrant Aid Society, which provided them with breech-loading rifles called Beecher's Bibles, after Henry Ward Beecher, the Northern minister who said that rifles were more important than Bibles in the struggle against slavery. Southerners also moved in, supported by thousands of Missourians who crossed into Kansas and voted illegally in the elections. The result was more violence, and soon there were two governments—a Northern and Southern one—operating in Kansas.

In the election of 1856, for the first time, the Republican Party chose its presidential candidate: John C. Frémont, the western explorer. The Democrats selected James Buchanan, an experienced diplomat and politician from Pennsylvania. Millard Fillmore, the former president, ran on the ticket of the South's Know-Nothing Party. It was an election over the expansion of slavery, which Buchanan won with a plurality of the popular vote. This election made it apparent that sectionalism was now the dominant factor in American politics.

During the same year the Know-Nothing Party competed vigorously with the new Republican Party. Each had a different message. The Know-Nothings continued to focus on the rising number of immigrants and the consequent threat of Catholicism plus frustration with the political process, while the Republicans warned against religious bigotry and emphasized the danger of slavery to human rights. Two developments helped the Republican Party—the turmoil in Kansas, which showed that slavery, not Catholicism, was the greater danger; and a significant drop in nativism (hatred of foreigners) in the mid-1850s. Thus, the issue of Catholic versus Protestant no longer seemed as important as the conflict between North and South over the extension of slavery.

The reader will note that the two major themes mentioned earlier continue to appear in the following readings. The first, the growing rivalry between the sections, reaches new levels of violence in the Kansas territory. Both sides were deadly serious about expanding their way of life. John Brown and his sons were there to take part in the fights, and one of the sons died. There was less concern about the value of the Union, the second theme, because there was still hope that the compromises and court decisions would find a satisfactory answer. Still, Southerners such as William Gilmore Simms had little faith in the Union, and Northerners such as Charles Sumner were not interested in any compromise over slavery.

4

The Kansas-Nebraska Act, Bleeding Kansas, and the Republican Party

NORTHERNERS

Charles Sumner

The Kansas-Nebraska bill passed the Senate on March 3, 1854. Two days later, Theodore Parker sent Charles Sumner a letter thanking him for his speech opposing the measure. Parker wrote: "I hope you will always keep the integrity of your own consciousness. We shall be beaten—beaten—beaten—I take it. But must fight still." Sumner responded on March 9.

Senate Chamber
9th March 1854
My dear Parker,
Thanks for your words of cheer. Freedom is for a while defeated: but I turn to the country and to God, and do not despair.

[Missouri's Thomas Hart] Benton says that the North will never be on its legs. He speaks with infinite derision of the Senate, and says that it will be a bye-word of shame, to be repudiated by the country.

This wickedness has tried me much. It has taken from me sleep and appetite. Upon Chase and myself has fallen the [full?] brunt.

At midnight on the last day, I took the floor to speak for an hour or more again: but Douglass [Stephen A. Douglas] held it against me, and afterwards I was dissuaded by friends not to speak again. . . .

Ever yrs
Charles Sumner

P.S. In my course, you will observe, that I have been governed by my own individuality—not following others but myself. . . .

Several months later, Sumner wrote to Henry Wadsworth Longfellow about the continuing struggle in the House of Representatives. Thirteen days later the bill passed, 113 to 100.

Senate Chamber
9th May '54
Dearly-beloved Longfellow, . . .

The Nebraska-ites are pressing their purpose, & will, probably, triumph; it will be an evil day for them, unless the North is again lulled. Can this be so? Oh! for union among good men, forgetting whether they are Whigs or Democrats! This must be done or the Republic will become a great pirate. It now watches its chance,—when England & France have their backs turned—to make a quarrel with Spain. Great, magnanimous people!— . . .

Ever & ever yrs.

CS

Two abolitionists, Wendell Phillips and Theodore Parker, had been indicted by a grand jury over their effort to free Anthony Burns, a fugitive slave in Boston. Sumner wrote to Parker offering legal advice and support.

Senate Chamber
12th June 1854
My dear Parker,

Let the *dementia* work, even to the indictment of yourself and Phillips. Good will come of it.

The great petition for repeal of the Fugitive Slave Bill ought to be presented in the Senate, where its character and history can be recorded, and a debate upon it provoked. In the house it must be presented under the rule, without opportunity for even a word.

Bear these things in mind: but *without mentioning my name.* To present it would be a grateful service for me: but I would not seek the opportunity. I should follow it *at once* by notice of a Bill to repeal the Fugitive Slave Bill. My first impression was to give this notice to day: but I have concluded to wait the movement of the Boston petitioners; and to put myself in the position of carrying out their desires.

I am glad you liked those few words of mine. I had intended to make an elaborate speech of a different kind, but the determination to close the debate that night induced me to change my purpose. . . .

Ever yours

Charles Sumner

P.S. The threats to put a bullet through my head and hang me—and mob me—have been frequent. I have always said: "let them come: they will find me at my post."

In September, Sumner was reluctant to switch parties, but within a month his position changed. In a letter to William Henry Seward he revealed that he would become a Republican.

Boston 15th Oct. '55

My dear Seward,

I have devoured yr speech with admiration & delight. The latter half I read aloud to the Longfellows who enjoyed it with me. It is very finely thought & composed.

I am so happy that you & I are at last on the same platform & in the same political pew. I feel stronger for it.

I am to say something soon; but I know not what argument to build.

Remember me most kindly to Mrs Seward, who, I trust, is well at last.

Ever sincerely Yours,

Charles Sumner

At a Republican rally in Faneuil Hall on November 2, Sumner dismissed the Democrats as the slave party, the Whigs as dead, and the Know-Nothings as too isolated. The job of the Republican Party was to destroy the "Slave Oligarchy." A week later he wrote to Seward in glowing terms. He was now a Republican.

Boston 11th Nov. '55

My dear Seward,

At this moment we have in Mass. the best party, composed of the best men, with the best characters & best talents, that has ever been in

Massachusetts—& devoted to the best cause. It is humiliating that this American faction should have thus triumphed; but here in Mass it was done only through professions of Freedom. Large numbers of true men were thus carried off into this false coup. . . .

Ever Yours,

Charles Sumner

For the next six months, Sumner continued to be active in challenging slavery, in watching foreign affairs, especially with England, and in supporting Nathaniel Banks in his successful bid to be Speaker of the House of Representatives. Much of his attention, however, was on the situation in Kansas. Letters to Edward Everett Hale and John Jay show his deep concern about the possibility that Kansas would be a slave state.

On March 1 he wrote a private letter to Hale.

Washington 1st March '56

My dear Hale,

I wish I could have the advantage of direct conversation with you for a brief hour on Kansas.

It is clear that *this Congress* will do nothing for the benefit of Kansas. In the House we are weak; in the Senate powerless. This Know Nothing madness has demoralized Northern representatives. In the Senate, the small squad of Republicans constitute the only reliable friends. Nothing can be expected from [Lewis] Cass or [Stephen] Douglas. The latter in Executive session on [Kansas governor Wilson] Shannon's case, expressed great indignation with him for condescending to make a Treaty with rebels at Lawrence.

To what point, then, should we address ourselves? The first question will be on [Andrew H.] Reeder's case [removed as governor of Kansas]. This belongs exclusively to the House; but the facts evolved there will throw light on the whole subject.

Then comes the application for admission into the Union. Here is a difficulty arising (1) from the small population at the time the Constitution was adopted, & (2) from the slender support it recd. at the polls, owing doubtless to the invasion then proceeding.

How shall these matters be dealt with? Pray let me have yr counsels.

Of course the pretended Legislature & its acts must be exposed as invalid. But what next? . . .

Ever sincerely Yours,

Charles Sumner

In a letter to Salmon P. Chase, he wrote that he had the floor to make a speech on Kansas. It would be the most important one of his life.

Senate Chamber 15th May '56
My dear Chase, . . .
I have the floor for next Monday on Kansas, when I shall make the most thorough & complete speech of my life. My soul is wrung by this outrage, & I shall pour it forth. How small was all that our fathers endured compared with the wrongs of Kansas! . . .

Ever Yrs,

Charles Sumner

On May 19 and 20, Charles Sumner delivered "The Crime against Kansas" speech. He criticized the South for introducing slavery into Kansas and trying to have the territory admitted to the Union as a slave state. He bitterly attacked Stephen A. Douglas of Illinois and Andrew Pickens Butler of South Carolina, chastising the latter and asserting that Kansas had contributed more than South Carolina to human progress.

Congressman Preston Brooks, Butler's nephew, entered the Senate chamber late in the afternoon of May 22, walked over to Sumner, faced him and explained his reasons for coming, and then beat Sumner senseless with his cane. Caught unaware, Sumner was unable to rise out of his chair. It took him several years to fully recover, during which time he was easily reelected. His seat remained vacant for the next three years as a tribute to him.

Harriet Beecher Stowe

The introduction in January 1854 of the Kansas-Nebraska Act with its repeal of the Missouri Compromise alarmed Harriet. It meant the opening up of the western territories to slavery, a possibility too horrible for her to contemplate. Immediately she asked ministers to draw up a petition opposing the measure. Quickly a petition two hundred feet long with 3,050 names of ministers was gathered and sent to Washington. She believed that this gesture would make the difference in defeating the measure.

At the same time, Harriet wrote an "Appeal to Women of the Free States," *which appeared in the* Independent *on February 23. She hoped to persuade thousands of women to act to stop the expansion of slavery.*

Women of the free States! the question is not, shall we remonstrate with slavery on its own soil? but are we willing to receive slavery into the free States and territories of the Union?

Shall the whole power of these United States go into the hands of slavery?

Shall every State in it be thrown open as a slave State? This will be the final result and issue of the question which is now pending. This is the fearful crisis at which we stand. And now, is there anything which the women of a country can do? Oh women of the free States! what did your grave mothers do in the time of our revolutionary struggle? Did not *liberty* in these days feel the strong impulse of woman's heart? . . .

What, then, is the duty of American women at this time? The first duty is for each woman, *for herself* thoroughly to understand the subject, and to feel that as mother, wife, sister, or member of society, she is bound to give her influence on the right side.

In the second place, women can make exertions to get up petitions, in their particular districts, to our national legislature. They can take measures to communicate information in their vicinity. They can employ lecturers to spread the subject before the people of their town or village. They can circulate the speeches of our members in Congress, and in many other ways secure a full understanding of the present position of our country.

Above all, it seems to be necessary and desirable that we should make this subject a matter of earnest prayer. . . .

While, then, we seek to sustain the cause of free principle unwaveringly, let us hold it also to be our true office, as women, to moderate the acrimony of political contest, remembering that the slaveholder and the slave are alike our brethren, whom the law of God commands us to love as ourselves.

For the sake of both, for the sake of our dear children, for the sake of our common country, for the sake of outraged and struggling liberty throughout the world, let every woman of America now do her duty.

The next year, Harriet was busy writing a second antislavery novel entitled Dred: A Tale of the Great Dismal Swamp. *The name "Dred" was suggested by Nat Turner's insurrection in 1831; one of the participants was called Dred. By this time, Harriet had lost much of her hope for a peaceful resolution of the slavery question. It was now less likely that the South could be induced to abolish slavery by moral persuasion. Still, in her preface to the novel, she tried to convince the reader of the importance of resolving the issue peacefully.*

The issues presented by the great conflict between liberty and slavery do not grow less important from year to year. On the contrary, their interest increases with every step in the development of the national career. Never has there been a crisis in the history of this nation so momentous as the present. If ever a nation was raised up by Divine Providence, and led forth upon a conspicuous stage, as if for the express purpose of solving a great moral problem in the sight of all mankind, it is this nation. God in his providence is now asking the American people, Is the system of slavery, as set forth in the American slave code, *right*? Is it so desirable, that you will directly establish it over broad regions, where, till now, you have solemnly forbidden it to enter? And this question the American people are about to answer. Under such circumstances the writer felt that no apology was needed for once more endeavoring to do something towards revealing to the people the true character of that system. If the people are to establish such a system, let them do it with their eyes open, with all the dreadful realities before them.

By May 1856, Harriet was halfway through the book. A careful study of the effect of slavery on people in both the North and the South, it contained some of her best writing. It was proceeding on schedule when two major incidents happened in the country. One was the brutal murder of five proslavery settlers on Pottawatomie Creek in Kansas by John Brown; it was in retaliation for the sacking of Lawrence, an antislavery town. The second was the violent response of Congressman Preston Brooks to the "Crime against Kansas" speech given by Senator Charles Sumner.

These incidents caused Harriet to interrupt her work and write a letter, which was published in the Independent, *appealing to antislavery women. When she resumed writing her novel, it took a more extreme form. The heroine, Nina, was killed in the middle of the book. Other characters might have been more like Little Eva in* Uncle Tom's Cabin, *but now the spirit of revenge that possessed Dred turned him into an Old Testament prophet who thundered at the South in the language of the Bible.*

"Hear ye the word of the Lord against this people! The harvest groweth ripe! The press is full! The vats overflow! Behold, saith the Lord—behold, saith the Lord, I will gather all nations, and bring them down to the valley of Jehoshaphat, and will plead with them for my people, whom they have scattered among the nations! Woe unto them, for they have cast lots for my people, and given a boy for a harlot, and sold a girl for wine, that they may drink! For three transgressions of Israel, and for four, I will not turn away the punishment thereof, saith the Lord! Because they sold the righteous for silver, and the needy for a pair of shoes! And a man and his father will go in unto the same maid, to profane my holy name! Behold, saith the Lord, I am pressed under you, as a cart is pressed full of sheaves!"

Toward the end of the book the hero, Edward Clayton, was attacked by a South Carolinian, Tom Gordon—clearly an allusion to Brooks's caning of Sumner in the Senate.

This time the blow felled Clayton to the earth, and Tom Gordon, precipitating himself from his saddle, proved his eligibility for Congress by beating his defenseless acquaintance on the head, after the fashion of the chivalry of South Carolina.

Unfortunately the book lost its balance. Dred was no longer a credible figure, unlike his counterpart, Uncle Tom. It became a novel of despair, not of hope. Just as Harriet had written Uncle Tom's Cabin *with inspiration and dismay resulting from the Fugitive Slave Law, the impulse of passion and anger made* Dred *too shrill a work to be effective. Still, 150,000 copies were sold in the United States and 165,000 in Great Britain in the first year. Disappointed with the reviews of* Dred *in the newspapers and magazines, but happy with the sales of the* book and its serializing after publication, she remarked to her husband, *"Who cares what the critics say?"*

Abraham Lincoln

With the passage of the Kansas-Nebraska Act, Lincoln became deeply disturbed. The repeal of the Missouri Compromise especially bothered him, and he began to reconsider the issue of slavery and what could be done to stop its expansion. Now reenergized he began to speak out—first at Winchester, Illinois, and then at Springfield.

August 26, 1854

After the transaction of the regular business of the convention— adoption of resolutions, &c.,—the Hon. A. Lincoln of your city, who was present, was loudly called for to address the meeting. He responded to the call ably and eloquently, doing complete justice to his reputation as a clear, forcible and convincing public speaker. His subject was the one which is uppermost in the minds of the people—the Nebraska- Kansas bill; and the ingenious, logical, and at the same time fair and candid manner, in which he exhibited the great wrong and injustice of the repeal of the Missouri Compromise, and the extension of slavery into free territory, deserves and has received the warmest commendation of every friend of freedom who listened to him. His was masterly effort—said to be equal to any upon the same subject in Congress,— was replete with unanswerable arguments, which must and will effectually *tell* at the coming election.

On September 11, 1854, the Illinois Journal *published an unsigned article on the Kansas-Nebraska Act by Lincoln. He stated that "the Kansas and Nebraska territories are now as open to slavery as Mississippi or Arkansas were when they were territories." Then he provided his readers with an illustration.*

To illustrate the case—Abraham Lincoln has a fine meadow, containing beautiful springs of water, and well fenced, which John Calhoun had agreed with Abraham (originally owning the land in common) should be his, and the agreement had been consummated in the most solemn manner, regarded by both as sacred. John Calhoun, however, in the course of time, had become owner of an extensive herd of cattle—

the prairie grass had become dried up and there was no convenient water to be had. John Calhoun then looks with a longing eye on Lincoln's meadow, and goes to it and throws down the fences, and exposes it to the ravages of his starving and famishing cattle. "You rascal," says Lincoln, "what have you done? what do you do this for?" "Oh," replies Calhoun, "everything is right. I have taken down your fence; but nothing more. It is my true intent and meaning not to drive my cattle into your meadow, nor to exclude them therefrom, but to leave them perfectly free to form their own notions of the feed, and to direct their movements in their own way!"

Now would not the man who committed this outrage be deemed both a knave and a fool,—a knave in removing the restrictive fence, which he had solemnly pledged himself to sustain;—and a fool in supposing that there could be one man found in the country to believe that he had not pulled down the fence for the purpose of opening the meadow for his cattle?

In Springfield on October 4, Lincoln gave another speech on the need to limit the growth of slavery in the territories. Stephen A. Douglas remained afterward to deliver a two-hour rebuttal.

What *natural* right requires Kansas and Nebraska to be open to Slavery? Is not slavery universally granted to be, in the abstract, a gross outrage on the law of nature? Have not all civilized nations, our own among them, made the Slave trade capital, and classed it with piracy and murder? Is it not held to be the great wrong of the world? Do not the Southern people, the Slaveholders themselves, spurn the domestic slave dealer, refuse to associate with him, or let their families associate with his family, as long as the taint of his infamous calling is known?

Shall that institution, which carries a rot and a murrain [that is, pestilence] in it, claim any right, by the law of nature, to stand by the side of Freedom, on a Soil that is free?

What *social or political* right, had slavery to demand the repeal of the Missouri Compromise, and claim entrance into States where it has never before existed? The theory of our government is Universal Freedom. "All men are created free and equal," says the Declaration of Independence. The word "slavery" is not found in the Constitution. The clause that covers the institution is one that sends it *back* where it exists, not *abroad* where it does not. All legislation that has recognized or tolerated its extension, has been associated with a compensation—a Compromise—showing that it was something that moved forward, not by its own right, but by its own wrong.

It is said that the slaveholder has the same [political] right to take his negroes to Kansas that a freeman has to take his hogs or his horses. This would be true if negroes were property in the same sense that hogs and horses are. But is this the case? It is notoriously not so. Southern men do not treat their negroes as they do their horses. There are 400,000 free negroes in the United States. All the race came to this country as slaves. How came these negroes [to be] free? At $500 each, their value is $2,000,000. Can you find *two million dollars worth* of any other kind of property running about without an owner? These negroes are free, because their owners, in some way and at some time, felt satisfied that the creatures had mind, feeling, souls, family affections, hopes, joys, sorrows—something that made them more than *hogs or horses.* Shall the Slaveholders require us to be more heartless and mean than they, and treat those beings as *property* which they themselves have never been able to treat so?

For the next year, Lincoln remained a Whig and tried to find a way to "fuse" with those who opposed the extension of slavery. His greatest anxiety was the growth of the Know-Nothing Party. In a letter to Owen Lovejoy he discussed his plight.

Springfield,
August 11–1855
Hon: Owen Lovejoy:
My dear Sir:
Yours of the 7th. was received the day before yesterday. Not even *you* are more anxious to prevent the extension of slavery than I; and yet the political atmosphere is such, just now, that I fear to do any thing, lest I do wrong. Know-nothingism has not yet entirely tumbled to pieces—nay, it is even a little encouraged by the late elections in Tennessee, Kentucky & Alabama. Until we can get the elements of this organization, there is not sufficient materials to successfully combat the Nebraska democracy with. We can not get them so long as they cling to a hope of success under their own organization; and I fear an open push by us now, may offend them, and tend to prevent our ever getting them. About us here, they are mostly my old political and

personal friends; and I have hoped their organization would die out without the painful necessity of my taking an open stand against them. Of their principles I think little better than I do of those of the slavery extensionists. Indeed I do not perceive how any one professing to be sensitive to the wrongs of the negroes, can join in a league to degrade a class of white men.

I have no objection to "fuse" with any body provided I can fuse on ground which I think is right; and I believe the opponents of slavery extension could now do this, if it were not for this K.N.ism. In many speeches last summer I advised those who did me the honor of a hearing to "stand with any body who stands right"—and I am still quite willing to follow my own advice. . . .

Yours truly

A. Lincoln—

Two weeks later, on August 24, he responded to his old friend Joshua Speed about his political position regarding slavery.

You enquire where I now stand. That is a disputed point. I think I am a whig; but others say there are no whigs, and that I am an abolitionist. When I was at Washington I voted for the Wilmot Proviso as good as forty times, and I never heard of any one attempting to unwhig me for that. I now do no more than oppose the *extension* of slavery.

I am not a Know-Nothing. That is certain. How could I be? How can any one who abhors the oppression of negroes, be in favor of degrading classes of white people? Our progress in degeneracy appears to me to be pretty rapid. As a nation, we began by declaring that "*all men are created equal.*" We now practically read it "all men are created equal, *except negroes.*" When the Know-Nothings get control, it will read "all men are created equal, except negroes, *and foreigners, and catholics.*" When it comes to this I should prefer emigrating to some country where they make no pretence of loving liberty—to Russia, for instance, where despotism can be taken pure, and without the base alloy of hypocracy [*sic*]. . . .

And yet let [me] say I am Your friend forever

By early 1856 he was ready to choose a new political course. The Whig Party was but a shadow of itself. At the meeting of newspaper editors at Bloomington, Illinois, on February 22, Lincoln was the only nonjournalist attending. He helped the group draw up a conservative statement advocating the restoration of the Missouri Compromise, upholding the Fugitive Slave Act, pledging noninterference with slavery where it already existed, and affirming the Free Soil doctrine. The name "Republican" was not used because the editors called for an Illinois state fusion convention to meet in Bloomington on May 29. Lincoln agreed to participate in the upcoming battle with the Democrats.

The call went out on May 10 for a meeting of Sangamon County citizens to elect delegates to the Bloomington convention. The names of Lincoln and his law partner, William Herndon, headed the list of signers.

Call for Republican Convention
May 10, 1856
To the Citizens of Sangamon County.
The undersigned, citizens of Sangamon county, who are opposed to the Repeal of the Missouri Compromise, and who are opposed to the present Administration, and who are in favor of restoring the administration of the General Government to the Policy of Washington and Jefferson, would suggest the propriety of a County Convention, to be held in the City of Springfield, on SATURDAY, the TWENTY-FOURTH day of MAY, 1856, to appoint Delegates to the Bloomington Convention. . . .

Two hundred delegates attended the meeting to organize the Illinois Republican Party, which covered all shades of political opinion. The new party was based on the position that Congress had the duty to exclude slavery from the national territories. Recognizing the importance of his role in creating the party, Lincoln was asked to make the last major speech before adjournment, on May 29. It was the best speech of his life, full of passion and conviction. Unfortunately, there is no reliable record of it. The Alton Weekly Courier *published a brief report of its highlights.*

Speech at Bloomington, Illinois
May 29, 1856
Abraham Lincoln, of Sangamon, came upon the platform amid deafening applause. He enumerated the pressing reasons of the present movement. He was here ready to fuse with anyone who would unite with him to oppose slave power; spoke of the bugbear disunion which was so vaguely threatened. It was to be remembered that the *Union must be preserved in the purity of its principles as well as in the integrity of its*

territorial parts. It must be "Liberty and Union, now and forever, one and inseparable." Douglas once claimed against him that Democracy favored more than his principles, the individual rights of man. Was it not strange that he must stand there now to defend those rights against their former eulogist? The Black Democracy were endeavoring to cite Henry Clay to reconcile old Whigs to their doctrine, and repaid them with the very cheap compliment of National Whigs.

George Templeton Strong

In 1854, Strong once again became concerned with politics. His interest was also sparked by the Kansas-Nebraska Act with its repeal of the Missouri Compromise.

March 24, Friday. The Nebraska bill, which went so swimmingly through the Senate, has come to grief in the House, and is so referred as to be shelved indefinitely. This was on motion of [New York's] F. B. Cutting, who professes himself a friend of the bill, but has certainly stabbed it under the fifth rib. Probably he feels, like many other northern politicians, that it is one of those edged tools that it's dangerous to handle and better to shelve.

Several months later he briefly noted the passage of this bill by the House of Representatives.

May 23, Tuesday. Nebraska bill passed the House at two A.M. by a small majority. Senate will concur in the amendments. . . .

In June, Strong began to notice the presence of the Know-Nothing Party and the "vigorous reaction" of the North against the Kansas-Nebraska Act.

June 10, Saturday. The order of *Know-Nothings* seems to have become a material fact. Late elections at Washington and Philadelphia shew it to be a potent agency. "Street-preaching" rows here and in Brooklyn prove it aggressive and bellicose and capable of using not only the ballot box but the carnal [physical] weapon. Every recent indication of Northern sentiment points to vigorous reaction against the Nebraska bill and the formation of a strong anti-slavery party at the North.

By the fall elections the Know-Nothing Party had emerged as a powerful political force. Strong was concerned about its impact and longevity in New York.

November 8, Wednesday. . . . I'm surprised by the strength the Natives have shewn. The *Herald* and *Tribune* speak of Know-Nothingism as a mere temporary perturbation of our party system. Probably this secret organization will be short-lived, but taking its late triumphs in connection with those of the Natives ten years ago, it seems to me that its principle is likely to be an important element in political calculations for some time to come. If I were now entering on a political career and aimed at the Presidency, I should be very careful to keep on good terms with the O.U.A. [Order of United Americans], the Native Americans, the Know-Nothings, and all their friends. I should be wary about saying a word that could be remembered against me by those who distrust the Roman Catholic and foreign voters. But for the Nebraska and temperance questions, they would have controlled this election entirely, and reduced the Whig and Democratic parties to insignificance.

Strong kept an eye on the Know-Nothing Party, which continued to interest him. On December 29 he wrote: "There are some signs, however, of Know-Nothingism assaying itself against all wealthy ecclesiastical corporations."

Almost a year later, in the fall of 1855, Strong commented on the slavery situation, the showing of the Know-Nothing Party, and the possibility of "change in the Naturalization laws."

November 10. . . . I am glad this state declines uniting in a sectional Northern party. Washington Hunt thinks Ruggles's letters and influence did much to keep the Old Whigs of the West from coalescing with Fusionism. The nigger question is vast and momentous; it is of infinite importance that this our republic sanction and abet no wrong or injustice against Cuff and Dinah. But our system includes other elements beside Cuff and Dinah, and we cannot sacrifice everything to them without wrong to others; and there is the great fundamental question beside whether Cuff and Dinah, who were born into certain social institutions, possess natural inherent rights in virtue whereof they are entitled to have those institutions revolutionized.

November 11. Know-Nothing majority in the state not much under 6,000. So "Sam" rules here as in Maryland and Massachusetts. It's a resurrection from the dead. People thought "Sam" defunct or disorganized. Our antipathy to the Pope and to Paddy [that is, the Irish] is a pretty deep-seated feeling. Were I about to enter political life, and selecting an available set of principles, I should be very apt to cast in my lot with the Natives. I could very honestly pronounce in favor of material change in the Naturalization laws.

It was not until the spring of 1856 that Strong began to be seriously concerned about national political matters. The attack of Preston Brooks on Charles Sumner horrified him.

May 22 . . . News tonight that Charles Sumner of the Senate has been licked with a loaded cane by a certain honorable Carolinian Brooks for his recent rather sophomorical anti-slavery speech. I hold the anti-slavery agitators wrong in principle and mischievous in policy. But the reckless, insolent brutality of our Southern aristocrats may drive me into abolitionism yet.

May 23. Much angry feeling about the assault on Sumner at Washington. It will strengthen the Free-soilers and Abolitionists, and it's reasonable and right it should strengthen them, for it's an act of brutality and blackguardism that ought to tell against its authors and endorsers.

Six days later, Strong criticized the South in even harsher terms: "they are . . . a race of lazy, ignorant, . . . beggarly barbarians . . . breeding little niggers for sale."

May 29, Thursday. No new vagaries from the wild men of the South since yesterday. . . .

A few fine specimens have given them a prestige the class don't deserve. We at the North are a busy money-making democracy, comparatively law-abiding and peace-loving, with the faults (among others) appropriate to traders and workers. A rich Southern aristocrat who happens to be of fine nature, with the self-reliance and high tone that life among an aristocracy favors, and culture and polish from books and travel, strikes us (not as Brooks struck Sumner but) as something different from ourselves, more ornamental and in some respects better. He has the polish of a highly civilized society, with the qualities that belong to a ruler of serfs. Thus a notion has got footing here that "Southern gentlemen" are a high-bred chivalric aristocracy, something like Louis XIV's noblesse, with grave faults, to be sure, but on the whole, very gallant and generous, regulating themselves by "codes of honor" (that are *wrong*, of course, but very grand); not rich, but surrounded by all the elements of real refinement. Whereas I believe they are, in fact, a race of lazy, ignorant, coarse, sensual, swaggering, sordid, beggarly barbarians, bullying white men and breeding little niggers for sale.

Frederick Douglass

The year 1854 was a difficult one for Douglass. The efforts of Stephen A. Douglas and the Democratic Party to repeal the Missouri Compromise and to allow slavery to expand anywhere in the new territories alarmed him. Unfortunately, there were only a few congressmen who recognized the danger and tried to stop the legislation.

Douglass was especially pleased with a speech by Charles Sumner opposing the Kansas-Nebraska bill.

To Hon. Charles Sumner
Rochester, February 27th, 1854
My Dear Sir:
All the friends of freedom, in every State, and of every color, may claim you, just now, as their representative. As one of your sable constituents, my dear Sir, I desire to thank you for your noble speech for freedom, and for your country, which I have now read twice over.

When Messrs. Chase, [Benjamin F.] Wade, and Seward had spoken, I could not see what remained for you to say. The result shows that the world is larger than it looks to be from the little valley where I live. If I thought you were, or could be, dissatisfied with your speech, I should have to consider you a hard master, and a very unreasonable man.

It is sad to think that after all the efforts of your Spartan band, this wicked measure will pass. A victory now for freedom would be the turning point in freedom's favor. But "God dwells in eternity," and it may be time enough yet. Heaven preserve you and strengthen you.

Yours most truly and gratefully,

Frederick Douglass

Later in the spring, Douglass published an editorial entitled "The End of All Compromises with Slavery—Now and Forever." He was angry with the "audacious villainy of the slave power."

But what is to be done? Why, let this be done: let the whole North awake, arise; let the people assemble in every free State of the Union; and let a great party of freedom be organized, on whose broad banner let it be inscribed, All compromises with slavery ended—The abolition of slavery essential to the preservation of liberty. Let the old parties go to destruction, whither they have nearly sunk the nation. Let their names be blotted out, and their memory rot; and henceforth let there be only a free party, and a slave party. The banner of God and liberty, and the bloody flag of slavery and chains shall then swing out from our respective battlements, and rally under them our respective armies, and let the inquiry go forth now, as of old, Who is on the Lord's side? Let the ministers of religion, all over the country, whose remonstrances have been treated with contempt—whose calling has been despised—whose names have been made a byword—whose rights as citizens have been insolently denied—and whose God has been blasphemed by the plotters of this great wickedness, now buckle on the armor of their master, and heartily strive with their immense power, to arrest the nation in its downward progress, and save it from the deep damnation to which it is sinking.

> If ye have whispered truth, whisper no longer,
> Speak as the tempest does, sterner and stronger.

The time for action has come. While a grand political party is forming, let companies of emigrants from the free States be collected together—funds provided—and with every solemnity which the name and power of God can inspire. Let them be sent out to possess the goodly land, to which, by a law of Heaven and a law of man, they are justly entitled.

Frederick Douglass' Paper, May 26, 1854

In the summer of 1855, Douglass predicted the doom of the Slave Power. He hoped for the continued growth of the abolition movement.

The days of the Black Power are numbered. Its course, indeed, is onward, but with the swiftness of an arrow, it rushes to the tomb. While crushing its millions, it is also crushing itself. —The sword of Retribution, suspended by a single hair, hangs over it. That sword must fall. Liberty must triumph. It possesses an inherent vitality, a recuperative energy, to which its opposite is a stranger. It may to human appearances be dead, the enemy may rejoice at its grave, and sing its funeral requiem, but in the midst of the triumphal shout, it leaps from its well guarded sepulchre, asserts the divinity of its origin, flashes its indignant eye upon the affrighted enemy, and bids him prepare for *the last battle, and the grave.* . . .

Frederick Douglass' Paper, July 27, 1855

In November, Douglass proclaimed again that he did not fear the great effort to end slavery. It would be "the final struggle," and he was confident that slavery would soon be abolished.

. . . in the final struggle, in order to be successful, there must exist a thorough organization of freemen, with the single issue presented, Liberty everywhere, Slavery nowhere; there must be unity of effort; every man who loves freedom, must array himself in her defence, whatever may have been his past political predilections. The magnet of Human Freedom, must be held high above the din of party tumult, and every man who is willing to peril his life, his fortune, and his sacred honor, in its defence, will ultimately be attracted to the magnet, whether Whig, or Democrat, or Freesoiler, or Abolitionist. This will form the great Abolition Party of the land. In fact, there must be, and there will be, but two Parties in the country; these will be known not as Whigs, nor as Democrats, nor as Republicans, so far as party names are concerned, but simply as the Anti-Slavery and Pro-Slavery parties of the country. All who are desirous of maintaining a sort of assumed neutrality on the question, as well as the most inveterate haters of the Abolition movement, will constitute the Pro-Slavery Party. Neither of these parties, in the last conflict, will be *wheedled* from the arena, by the presentation of incidental issues. Each party, forming a unit, and rallying under its own banner, will fight for the triumph of its respective Principles.

We do not fear the result of such a struggle. The sooner the last battle shall be fought, the sooner victory will perch upon the standard of the free. . . . The throne of the despot is trembling to its deep foundations. There is a good time coming. We yet shall make the welkin [that is, Heaven] ring with the mighty hallelujahs of the free.

Frederick Douglass' Paper, November 16, 1855

Charlotte Forten Grimké

At the same time, in nearby Salem, Massachusetts, Charlotte Forten, a young black woman of sixteen, began to keep a diary. She hoped that it would "enable me to judge correctly of the growth and improvement of my mind from year to year." The first day's entry on May 24, 1854, was full of hope and happiness. Her entry on the second day was quite the opposite, however.

Thursday, May 25—Did not intend to write this evening, but have just heard of something that is worth recording;—something which must ever rouse in the mind of every true friend of liberty and humanity, feelings of the deepest indignation and sorrow. Another fugitive [Anthony Burns] from bondage has been arrested; a poor man, who for two short months has trod the soil and breathed the air of the "Old Bay State," was arrested like a criminal in the streets of her capital, and is now kept strictly guarded,—a double police force is required, the military are in readiness; and all this is done to prevent a man, whom God has created in his own image, from regaining that freedom with which, he, in common with every other human being, is endowed. I can only hope and pray most earnestly that Boston will not again disgrace herself by sending him back to a bondage worse than death; or rather that she will redeem herself from the disgrace which his arrest alone has brought upon her.

Two days later, Charlotte went to Boston to observe the trial of Anthony Burns.

Wednesday, May 31. . . . Everything was much quieter—outwardly than we expected, but still much real indignation and excitement prevail. We walked past the Court-House, which is now lawlessly converted into a prison, and filled with soldiers, some of whom were looking from the windows, with an air of insolent authority, which made my blood boil, while I felt the strongest contempt for their cowardice and servility. We went to the meeting, but the best speakers were absent, engaged in the most arduous and untiring efforts in behalf of the poor fugitive; but though we missed the glowing eloquence of [Wendell] Phillips, [William Lloyd] Garrison, and [Theodore] Parker, still there were excellent speeches made, and our hearts responded to the exalted sentiments of Truth and Liberty which were uttered. The exciting intelligence which occasionally came in relation to the trial, added fresh zeal to the speakers, of whom Stephen Foster and his wife [Abigail Kelley] were the principal. The latter addressed, in the most eloquent language, the women present, entreating them to urge their husbands and brothers to action, and also to give their aid on all occasions in our just and holy cause. —I did not see father the whole day; he, of course, was deeply interested in the trial.—Dined at Mr. Garrison's; his wife is one of the loveliest persons I have ever seen, worthy of such a husband. At the table, I watched earnestly the expression of that noble face, as he spoke beautifully in support of the non-resistant principles to which he has kept firm; his is indeed the very highest Christian spirit, to which I cannot hope to reach, however, for I believe in resistance to tyrants, and would fight for liberty until death. We came home in the evening, and felt sick at heart as we passed through the streets of Boston on our way to the depot, seeing the military as they rode along, ready at any time to prove themselves the minions of the South.

On Friday, June 2, her fears that Burns would be sacrificed to propitiate the South were realized.

Friday, June 2. Our worst fears are realized; the decision was against poor Burns, and he has been sent back to a bondage worse, a thousand times worse than death. Even an attempt at rescue was utterly impossible; the prisoner was completely surrounded by soldiers with bayonets fixed, a canon [*sic*] loaded, ready to be fired at the slightest sign. To-day Massachusetts has again been disgraced; again has she showed her submissions to the Slave Power; and Oh! with what deep sorrow do we think of what will doubtless be the fate of that poor man, when he is again consigned to the horrors of slavery. . . . In looking over my diary, I perceive that I did not mention that there was on the Friday night after the man's arrest, an attempt made to rescue him, but although it failed, on account of there not being men enough engaged in it, all honor should be given to those who bravely made the attempt. I can write no more. A cloud seems hanging over me, over all our persecuted race, which nothing can dispel.

Still, in the summer, antislavery meetings kept her from losing all hope. They lifted her spirits.

Tuesday, August 1. To-day is the twentieth anniversary of British emancipation. The joy that we feel at an event so just and so glorious is greatly saddened by thoughts of the bitter and cruel oppression which still exists in our own land so proudly claiming to be "the land of the free." And how very distant seems the day when she will follow the example of "the mother country," and liberate her millions of suffering slaves! This morning I went with Mr. and Mrs. R[emond] to the celebration at Abington. The weather was delightful, and a very large number of persons was assembled in the beautiful grove. Mr. Garrison, Wendell Phillips and many other distinguished friends of freedom were present and spoke eloquently. Mr. Garrison gave an interesting account of the rise and progress of the anti-slavery movement in Great Britain. I had not seen Mr. [Thomas Wentworth] Higginson before. He is very fine looking, and has one of the deepest, richest voices that I have ever heard. I was much pleased with Mr. [John] M'Cluer, a genial, warm-hearted Scotchman who was arrested in Boston during the trial of Burns. He has a broad, Scotch accent which I was particularly delighted to hear as I have been reading very much about Scotland lately. The sadness that I had felt was almost entirely dissipated by the hopeful feelings expressed by the principal speakers.

In the fall of 1855, Charlotte entered the Normal School. She looked forward to the year despite her continued fears of discrimination.

Wednesday, September 12. To-day school commenced. Most happy am I to return to the companionship of my studies, ever my most valued friends. It is pleasant to meet the scholars again; most of them greeted me cordially, and were it not for the thought that *will* intrude, of the want or *entire sympathy* even of those I know and like best, I should greatly enjoy their society. There is one young girl and only one—Miss Sarah Brown, who I believe thoroughly and heartily appreciates anti-slavery, *radical* anti-slavery and has no prejudice against color. I wonder that every colored person is not a misanthrope. Surely we have everything to make us hate mankind. I have met girls in the school-room—they have been thoroughly kind and cordial to me—perhaps the next day met them in the street—they feared to recognize me; these I can but regard now with scorn and contempt, once I liked them, believing them incapable of such measures. Others give the most distant recognition possible. I, of course, acknowledge no such recognition, and they soon cease entirely. These are but trifles, certainly to the great, public wrongs which we as a people are obliged to endure. But to those who experience them, these apparent trifles are most wearing and discouraging; even to the child's mind they reveal volumes of deceit and heartlessness, and early teach a lesson of suspicion and distrust. Oh! it is hard to go through life meeting contempt with contempt, hatred with hatred, fearing, with too good reason to love and trust hardly any one whose skin is white, however lovable, attractive and congenial in seeming.

On the weekend of February 2–4, 1856, Garrison and his wife stayed with Charlotte and her host family. It was a special time for her.

Saturday, February 2. This evening our beloved Mr. [William Lloyd] Garrison and his wife arrived.—Most gladly did we welcome them. The Remonds and Putnams spent the evening with us, and we had a delightful time. Mr. Garrison was very genial as he always is, and sang delightfully.

Sunday, February 3. This has been one of the happiest days of my life. More and more do I love and admire that great and good man. His wife is a lovely woman; it is indeed delightful to see so happy and noble a couple. This evening Mr. Garrison gave us one of the best lectures I ever heard him deliver. Always interesting to me, to-night he was unusually entertaining. Just before the lecture Mr. Innis announced the fact of Mr. [Nathaniel] Banks' election, which was received with tumultous [sic] applause. Mr. G. spoke beautifully of the "*Banks* of Massachusetts impeding the onward progress of the waves of the southern despotism."

Monday, February 4. This morning Mr. and Mrs. G left. This was the first time they have staid with us since I have been here. And the pleasure, the great pleasure which I experienced from this visit, will prevent me from soon forgetting it.

SOUTHERNERS

Most citizens living in the South were pleased with the Kansas-Nebraska Act; it meant that slavery could extend into the new territories. Jefferson Davis was active behind the scenes as the secretary of war in the Pierce cabinet. William Gilmore Simms still wanted the South to secede, but only when other states were ready. Recurring violence in Kansas caught their attention as a mini-civil war began in the territory.

John J. Crittenden

During 1854 the issue of the Kansas-Nebraska Act troubled Crittenden. The agitation surrounding the passage of the bill deeply divided his Whig Party. Replying to a question about his position on the repeal of the Missouri Compromise, his answer was simple—to do nothing that increased the agitation in the North.

J. J. Crittenden to Archibald Dixon.
Frankfort, March 7, 1854.
My dear Sir,— . . .
Considering the question as an open one, it seems to me clear that Congress ought to leave it to the people of the Territories, preparing to enter the Union as States, to form their constitutions in respect to slavery as they may please, and ought to admit them into the Union whether they have admitted or excluded slavery; but that question, it seems to me, can scarcely be considered as an open one.

The country has long rested in the belief that it is settled by the Missouri Compromise, so far as it respects all the territory embraced by it, and of which Nebraska and Kansas are parts. I hope, however, that the North may consent to yield that compromise, and concur in substituting the principle of the Nebraska bill for the rule fixed by the Missouri Compromise. But without such a concurrence of Northern representatives as would fairly manifest the assent of the North to such substitution, I do not think the South ought to disregard or urge the repeal of that compromise to which she was a party.

The Missouri Compromise has long been considered as a sort of landmark in our political progress. It does not appear to me that it has ever been superseded or abrogated; and I think it is to be apprehended that its repeal, without sincere concurrence of the North, will be productive of serious agitations and disturbances.

That concurrence will relieve the subject from difficulty, as the parties to compromise have an undoubted right to set it aside at their pleasure. By such a course it seems to me the North would lose nothing, and would but afford another evidence of her wisdom and her patriotism. This, however, is a subject for her own consideration. . . .

I am your friend,

J. J. Crittenden.

A day earlier he had replied with the same answer to another friend.

To Hon. Presley Ewing, Washington City.

Frankfort, March 6, 1854.

. . . In reply to telegraph, I am clear that Congress ought to leave it to the States preparing for admission into the Union to form their constitutions in respect to slavery *as they please*.

Hope the North may concur in substituting this principle for the rule *fixed* by the *Missouri Compromise*. But without such numerical concurrence of Northern representatives as would fairly indicate the assent of the North to such substitution, I don't think the South ought to disregard that compromise, to which it was a party.

J. J. Crittenden.

Crittenden was elected to the U.S. Senate in 1855. The following spring he discouraged a friend, A. T. Burnley, from working for his nomination to the presidency.

That the Presidency is an office neither to be sought nor declined, is a sentiment that accords so well not only with my judgment, but with my *natural* temper and constitution, that I adopt and follow it rather from instinct than from any nobler or more patriotic consideration. It costs us no exertion to follow where our nature leads. I have never, therefore, *put forward* any *pretensions* to the Presidency, much less pressed them; nor have I ever endeavored, from any selfish feeling, to put back the claims or pretensions of any man. But, notwithstanding all this, I have a pride of character which does not permit me to humble myself so far as to shrink from or to decline even the Presidency itself, if such an honor and station should unexpectedly be offered me. But I am no candidate, —no seeker for the office. I have said *no word*, taken no step in that direction. Nor will the nomination of another be any disappointment to me. I can willingly witness the nomination of another, and support that nomination, too. And of all the persons who have been named for that high office, I prefer our friend Davis. I would throw no obstacle in his way to a nomination, and would support that nomination with all the little power or influence I may have. I verily believe that Davis would do the same by me. And is not this all that could be required of either of us? I can say further, that if I could, by my word, close up all uncertainties of the future by accepting or making Davis the successor of Pierce, I would do it with an unalloyed feeling of gratification.

Crittenden was disappointed when Millard Fillmore lost his bid for the presidency. He made many speeches on his behalf, but Crittenden's efforts were in vain. James Buchanan was elected president.

The Jones Family

The most explosive issue in Boston in the spring of 1854 was not the Kansas-Nebraska bill with its repeal of the Missouri Compromise; rather, it was the Burns fugitive slave case. Anthony Burns had been arrested, and the South was demanding that he be returned to his slave home. Public sentiment in Boston was strongly opposed to the return of Burns.

Charles Jones, a student at Harvard Law School, was deeply troubled by the response of Bostonians. As a Southerner and owner of slaves, he supported the Fugitive Slave Law. Jones's law professor, Judge Edward Greely Loring, had been appointed special commissioner with authority to send Burns back to the South. He was under heavy pressure to release him. Charles's letter to his father showed his unhappiness with the situation.

Mr. Charles C. Jones, Jr., to Rev. C. C. Jones
Harvard University,
Cambridge, Massachusetts
Tuesday, May 30th, 1854
My dear Father,
Your very welcome letter, presenting me in such charming colors with all the pleasures which you are all now enjoying at home, and especially with the engagements and recreations of dear Mother, was yesterday morning received. To me the picture, always so attractive, is

rendered even more dear in consideration of the endless confusion, turmoil, and bloody scenes which are now hourly transpiring in our very midst.

Mob law, *perjury*, free-soilism, and *abolitionism* are *running riot*. Never before in all my life have my feelings been so severely tried as they have been during these past and present occurrences. For two days I have been present in the courthouse attending this trial. The room is filled with armed men; even the counsel at bar have their revolvers and bowie knives. The passages are strictly guarded night and day by the military, of whom over one hundred marines from the navy yard are garrisoned in the courthouse proper, besides two other companies, while the city hall contains four volunteer companies ordered out by the mayor. All the military of Boston are under arms, ready at a moment's notice to appear at any given point. Hourly are the streets opened around the courthouse and cleared of the mob by companies marching in solid columns for that purpose. The drum and fife, the challenge of the guards, the commands of the officers, the shouts of the mob, all mingling in such confusion, often prevent you, although even within a few feet of counsel arguing at the bar, from hearing them. The halls of justice are literally thronged with armed men. Singular and I may say awful sight! . . .

Excuse this meager letter. I am tired, downhearted, and vexed at the scenes and opinions which are running rife in our midst. Hope that the matter will be settled in a day or two. With warmest love to you, dear Father, dear Mother, Sister, Brother, and all relatives I remain, in haste,

Your ever affectionate son,
Charles C. Jones, Jr.

The response of his father was more measured and suggested that the young man might "gather experience from all these things."

Rev. C. C. Jones to Mr. Charles C. Jones, Jr.
Arcadia Plantation,
Liberty County, Georgia
June 12th 1854
My dear Son, . . .

Your last letter was one of great interest to us, and I am glad that you were with Colonel Suttle and gave him sympathy and support.

Although he appears to be a gentleman capable of any emergency, yet as a gentleman he would and no doubt did appreciate your attentions and those of other young gentlemen from the law school. . . . I agree with you that the conduct of the abolitionists was infamous. They demonstrate themselves in this case to be fanatics of the worst sort, setting at defiance all laws human and divine, the constitution of their country, all truth, all decency, without one redeeming quality—not even the common courage of men! However, I think the Bostonians *deserve credit for the execution of the law. They did execute it,* and the whole matter will do good in our country, even in New England itself. And your worthy professor came out with flying colors. The creatures of the law school hissed him as he came into his lecture room! They should have been *expelled* by the college authorities. The Southern and right-minded students did well to *cheer him.*

I do not at all regret that you have been an eye- and ear-witness to all this matter. . . . Gather experience from all these things; make your observations; and learn self-control, calm self-possession under circumstances of excitement and danger. This gives a man vast advantages, and enables him to act wisely and successfully. . . .

Your ever affectionate father,

C. C. Jones

His mother, Mary, worried about him. She feared that he might be carrying a pistol.

Mrs. Mary Jones to Mr. Charles C. Jones, Jr.
Maybank,
Monday, June 12, 1854
My dear Son, . . .

Today I asked Joe if he knew where your *pistol* was; he said you had carried it. I hope, my dear child, you will never carry arms about you. This *awful and cowardly practice,* from the evidence in the Ward trial, seems to be very common in Kentucky. I think the man who carries concealed weapons places himself beyond the divine protection, and is in the broad road to the commission of some rash if not murderous act. Your grandfather always regarded it as a never-failing sign of a *coward*—and a "*dastardly one,*" as I have frequently heard him express it. . . .

Ever your affectionate mother,

Mary Jones

On the following day, June 13, Charles wrote to his parents praising the city, state, and federal officers' conduct in the Burns case. There had been serious potential for violence.

Mr. Charles C. Jones Jr., to Rev. and Mrs. C. C. Jones
Cambridge
Tuesday, June 13th, 1854
My dear Mother and Father, . . .

The excitement in reference to the rendition of Burns, Colonel Suttle's slave, which for so many days kept Yankeedom in perfect commotion, is ceasing. The war of words is heard in more subdued tones, the mobs have dispersed, and we are flooded with pamphlets purporting to be "sermons of the times" and "lessons for the day"—incendiary in their character, bitter against the South, Southern men, Southern institutions, and particularly vehement upon topics of "Chains and Slavery," Nebraska Bill, Fugitive Slave Law. And what will appear most remarkable to the sober, pious mind is that they all come as emanations from the respective *pulpits* of this vicinity—promulgated, moreover, upon a day which the Lord has consecrated for His especial service. Strange and enormous must be the stupefying fanaticism of that man who, professing to be called of God for the revelation of holy things unto men, can so far forget his sacred office, and the solemnities of the season, as to indulge openly in vituperations against his country and fellow man, not only unbecoming a minister but unworthy a sensible person upon a secular occasion. It is really surprising to what an extent a person becomes an actual *fool* who, possessed of one prejudice, one misconceived idea, surrenders himself a total slave to its miserable influence. I have recently from observation formed an estimate of the elements of fanaticism more vivid and real than ever before, and willingly subscribe to the old rule: "Never dispute or argue with fools or bigots either in religion or politics."

Our professor, Judge Loring, deserves the approbation of the entire country for the manly, open, and determined manner in which he conducted himself during the entire trial and finally disposed of the case. You have no idea what he endured and what indignities he is still forced to suffer at the hands of the thousand miserable monomaniacs by whom he is surrounded. He has, as Professor [Theophilus] Parsons remarked to me, acted as well as mortal man could, regarding only the laws of his country, upheld by a stern sense of justice and an approving conscience. . . .

You have, I hope, received the papers which I forwarded containing a minute account of all the incidents of trial, the excitement in Boston, and final rendition of the fugitive. Therefore I will not indulge in any account of the scenes which then and there transpired, but will merely remark that due praise must be given to the officers both of the state and city as well as of the United States for the promptitude with which they conducted themselves in all arrangements requiring decision, accuracy, firmness. The powerful military force on the ground and the efficient disposition of the soldiers is all that prevented Boston from becoming one miserable arena of riot, blood, and lawlessness. . . .

Your ever affectionate son,
Charles C. Jones, Jr.

Charles Jones had been thinking about where to practice law after his graduation from Harvard. A letter from his father (November 8, 1854) advised him to be careful in making that choice. Moreover, to be successful in his profession he should not own slaves. Managing a plantation would take up too much of his time.

In relation to your settlement in life, my dear son, I wish you to exercise your preference and discretion. Do not confine yourself to the South if any other part of the Union is more agreeable to you. And I wish to make the impression upon you with the point of a diamond *that you never can succeed and attain to any eminence in your profession if you have anything at all to do with the management of Negro property. No man in any profession* within my knowledge ever has—and for the obvious reason that no man can succeed in either profession who follows *two.* I am certain my necessary and unavoidable connection with the management of Negroes and the conduct of planting has been a most serious drawback to me in a professional point of view; and nothing but the most industrious habits and indomitable perseverance ever kept me up at all; and I have rid myself of the drawback several times in accepting calls out of this county. Planting requires such a consumption of time, and the property you manage makes such a draft upon your attention, etc., etc., that no student and professional man can prosper under it all. I wish you to profit by my experience, if nobody's else, and make up your mind to *live by your profession and to be totus in illis.* We shall endeavor to render you every assistance in our power.

Charles decided to practice law in the South. When an offer came from a prominent lawyer in Savannah, John Elliott Ward, he readily accepted it since he had always liked the city. In a letter of June 11, 1855, his father congratulated him but shared some concerns about the political situation.

The "Know-Nothing" skies have become overcast with the shadows of abolitionism; and while I could not enter their body because it is a *secret political organization*, which the times do not exactly justify, I certainly can wish them no success whatever while stained with a connection with those who are not only enemies of our own section of the Union but even of the Union itself. Let us have the flag at the masthead, declared principles, an open sea, and a fair fight. That is the best way in everything.

Augustus Benners

Benners was an active politician in the Alabama legislature in late January and early February 1854. He made a number of speeches, opposed a bond issue for railroads, and helped hammer out a compromise on a bill establishing a system of public schools, which finally passed after considerable debate.

March 1st 1854. I left Greensboro on the 6th January to return to the Legislature at Montgomery which assembled on the 9th . . . The session commenced on Monday—and continued till the 18th. The prominent and leading question during the session was State aid to Rail Roads The first known as the omnibus way for the Governor to issue State bonds to each of [the] roads at the rate of $8000 a mile which complied with the terms of the bill. This proposal gave great concern to the members who were opposed to the state incurring additional liabilities—and its success was for a long time regarded as probable—& many speeches were made for it. I opposed it and made a speech against it in reply to Mr Curry of Talladega Chairman of the Com. of internal improvements. after considerable parliamentary tactics we came to a vote and the bill was defeated by a vote of 54 nays to 40 ayes. The main reasons of my opposition to the bill were that the State already involved with a large debt should not whilst it was so considerably incur additional liabilities—and because from the geographical structure of the Country if The principle of indorsing bonds were initiated there was great reason to apprehend that in future all legislative freedom would be destroyed by the coalition of the roads interested in getting more aid. The more especially as it would not be very difficult to persuade the people that future burthens which were now so useful to them would be no great incubus as their payment was to be so distant not less than 10 nor more than 20 years—After the defeat of the main bill, the attempt was made to divide out by an omnibus bill the money in the treasury at the rate of $8000 a mile to Railroads this passed the Senate and was defeated in the House. The Mobile & Ohio road received a loan of $400,000 for two years on mortgage & personal security. This I voted for considering it in a business view as proper—the security not only being ample but readily convertible into the money without embarrassing the operations of the Company—they having a great quantity of property which could be sold for the money before the loan would be needed. The other roads applying for aid having nothing with which to secure the State for advances but anticipated profits—. I voted against loans to them.

The bill to establish a system of free public schools appropriating about $200,000 per Annum including 16th Section monies was also of great general importance. The feature of the bill diverting the 16th Section moneys from the townships to which it belonged I considered wrong. as also the immense discretion vested in the superintendent & for these & other reasons voted against the bill. The Bill introduced by me as a substitute for the Committee bill on the Statute of Limitations, to repeal Section 2502 of the code. After a hard battle over it was finally passed in both houses and is become the law—

The following year he was offered the chance to be renominated but declined. Benners was uncertain about the future and was not willing to sacrifice the necessary time and money.

April 27 [1855] . . . I wrote to the Whig this week and declined the Legislature—There is so much indifference on the subject that I did not care to be a candidate P.S. I was subsequently very warmly pressed to run by both sides but having declined I concluded to stick to it. I was also much pressed to be a candidate for senate which I also declined—

By 1860 he owned eighty-four slaves to work his two plantations. Still he needed to rent a number each year, a process that took time and often frustrated him. Furthermore, Benners was finding his overseer, Mr. Boyd, "incompetent."

January 1st 1856. The new years day has been on the whole a pleasant one tho quite cool part of the day cloudy and wet under foot. Not a great many people have been in town and I have hired only one negro to day. Mr Webbs Joe at $150 and he is to be allowed once in a while to come to town. Orris from Jno B Williams at $150 and Margaret & Phillis at $190 are all hired up to this time. . . .

January 18 1856 after a long spell of very cold gloomy weather a great deal of rain & wretched roads we have to day a fine day. I went [to] Eutaw on the 14 Jany and bought Mary for $920—cash. . . . Went in the stage & returned same day bringing Mary with me. . . .

Jany 25 Hired Rachel and Laura from Dr. Wordsworth for $150.00— . . .

Feby 21st 1856 Thursday, . . . Boyd incompetent to keep up the discipline of plantation—as his wife is of her own family. Fuss about Webbs fence cant get the rails out of the timber pointed out—verily planting is a troublesome business—an everlasting want to supply—an everlasting fuss to settle—ever settling— ever giving. Never settled— never satisfied—I could wish I had never seen a negro—and dont in the least doubt I would have been more of a man if not a better one if I had never owned one—

The next month there was a report of the murder of a fellow plantation owner, Thomas Borden. It surprised him and caused "immense excitement" in nearby Newbern.

March 29th, 1856— . . . Before I reached Newbern I met a white boy riding—who informed me that Thomas R. Borden had been shot the night previous—in his bed asleep—thro the window with balls. I found immense excitement in Newbern on account of it and went to the house where the murder had been committed and examined the place from which he was shot—he was lying on the bed, the head of which was between the front windows in the right hand room on the first floor—and the gun was fired thru the lower panes of glass of the side window—about 3 1/4 yards from where he lay—the balls entered his head making as I was told a large hole and scattering the brains. A number of men under Frank Hawks as magistrate were sitting as Coroners inquest in the office in the yard when I was there about Eleven oclock in the morning. Some one the night before he was shot had thrown a brick at the window as was said and shortly there after another brick was thrown upon which a gun was fired by Jim Borden. It was said that the dogs which were very ferocious made no noise—a strong suspicion existed that Jim Borden was the man who had done the deed—Mr Borden was buried on Saturday at 10 clock about which time Jim left.

April 2nd I hired Mansfield to take charge of the Walker Place at the rate of $300 a year from the time he takes charge with a distinct understanding if he dont suit we are to separate—he is to go down with his wife and children on friday next—Jim Borden was arrested at Lauderdale Springs in Miss—and brought here yesterday evening—was before the magistrate today and trial put off till tomorrow—

On May 24, Benners noted the sale of a slave mother and her five children. No special mention was made of the transaction except that it netted him $2,500.

May 24th Sold Silvey and her five children on 21st May—Bonaparte[,] Frank, Wm. Henry, Jacob & Melisa to J. O. K. Mayfield for $2500—of which 1600 was paid in a northern check and $900 in a draft accepted by the Palmers. And gave bill of sale signed by self & Wm. P. Webb as trustees—Payt for them was made by C. S. Bray as agent for Mayfield and I went up to the house opposite Southern University grounds where B. D. Palmer lives and where sd negroes were and there delivered them to said Bray as agent for Mayfield—He told Beckham to keep them for Mayfield till he called for them. Sent the bill of sale at Brays request to W. P. Webb to have registered and returned to him delivery of negroes was made on 24th May 1856.

William Gilmore Simms

During December 1854, Simms's article, "Our Parties and Our Politics, A Southerner's View of the Subject," was published by Putnam's Magazine. *In sixteen pages, Simms expressed his fears about the future of the Union. Disturbed by the growing opposition to the introduction of slavery into the western territo-*

ries, he warned that "the time for separation" may have arrived: "we had better part, while we may part in peace."

But there can be no peace until the North agrees to let the slavery question alone. If slavery be the sin and evil they conceive it, it is all ours; to borrow the words of a fanatical preacher in the West— "ours by solemn compact; our small-pox, our cholera, our plague, our leprosy." The writer to whom we have previously referred, admits that some years since "every intelligent and judicious Northerner was glad to concede that slavery was a system exclusively within the control of the States." We beg to know what new light has dawned upon them, to modify their construction of constitutional right. If no assault upon slavery in the States be designed, why this warfare against the entrance of the South into the territories? Has there been any other single question presented to our people, upon which sectional lines have been drawn? Combinations of men from the North and the South have sustained, and similar combinations have opposed, the establishment of national banks, and protective tariffs, and every contested measure of federal policy. Upon this single question is the South a unit. The worm, when trodden under foot, will turn upon the oppressor, and the unanimity of the South here is explicable upon the instincts of self-defence. The interdiction of slavery in the territories is avowedly designed as an indirect blow at the same institution in the States, from direct attacks upon which, all, save the most radical fanatics, admit that the Constitution protects us. The policy of Abolition is to encircle us with a cordon of free States, and thus to confine us in the limits of the present slave territory, until the increase of that class of our population shall coerce emancipation, if not amalgamation. We do not desire to dwell upon the dark future which the success of such a policy foreshadows. By Southhampton and Hayti the South is forewarned, and forewarned, she is forearmed.

We had designed to notice the impudent claim which is asserted for "the outcast republicans of Europe," to exclude us from the enjoyment of our own property, because "our form of society can never advance beyond a semi-barbarism." We envy not the heart that could conceive, or the tongue that could utter such a sentiment, libelling as it does, without discrimination, the whole body of a Christian community. However, the statement of the proposition carries with it to every fair-minded man its own reply, and time and space admonish us to hurry to a close.

. . . 'Tis idle to close the eye to the peril of the day. Sectionalism is arming for a struggle of life or death. No sane man imagines that success, in any of her designs, is consistent with the stability of the Union. When the North shall repudiate her constitutional obligations, by repealing an act to carry into effect one of the fundamental provisions of the Constitution—when the defunct restrictive policy of excluding us and ours from the common territory of the Union shall be revived—when the covenant with Texas shall be ignored—and the hand of fellowship be refused to an incipient State, unless she rejects our social polity—when thus a circle of fire is forming around us, and the preponderance of the hireling States to an extent sufficient to amend the Constitution, and invest the Federal Government with control over our institutions—ensured at no distant day—when all, or either of these events shall occur, the time for separation will have more than arrived. If upon them or either of them our Northern brethren are madly bent, we had better part, while we may part in peace. "Let there be no strife between our people and your people, for we be brethren. Is not the whole land before us? Separate yourselves from us. Go you to the North, and we will go to the South."

But we are not despondent. Our confidence in the ultimate decision of the Northern masses is still unshaken. There is too much of sound and practical sense in this Union to permit a sentimental abstraction to shiver it into fragments. In the sober second thought of the yeomanry of the land, is its hope, and will be its salvation. The Old Guard is up and doing. Strong in the inherent justice of their cause, they gather themselves once more to throttle the demon of discord. With unwavering step, in the confident expectation of certain triumph, they press boldly onward, bearing in the advance the time-honored banner of the Republic, radiant with the gathered glories of the past, and suggestive of still more unfading glory in the future, emblazoned with the simple, but august device—THE CONSTITUTION AND THE UNION!

Jefferson Davis

During 1854 and 1855, Secretary of War Davis remained active behind the scenes. He approved of the Kansas-Nebraska bill and helped arrange a meeting of Stephen A. Douglas, David Atchison, and other congressmen with the president in which Pierce reluctantly approved the repeal of the Missouri Compromise. Davis continued to bring pressure on his fellow Democrats to ensure passage of the measure.

On May 15, 1854, Davis wrote to Kentucky congressman John C. Breckinridge favoring the dropping of an amendment by Delaware's John Middleton Clayton prohibiting unnaturalized foreign immigrants from voting in the territories. He believed that it would be favored by Northern Democrats.

To John C. Breckinridge
May 15th 1854
Dear Sir, . . .
Mr. Stephens of Michigan remarked to me this morning that all the northern Democrats would vote for Douglass' [Stephen Douglas] original substitute.

I remarked that it was preferable to me and he repeated that every Democrat of the north would support it. As the principal difficulty with the Southern men has arisen from the modifications the bill underwent in the Senate after the substitute was offered, I thought it might be important and write that you may see the Hon Mr. S. or take such other course as you may deem best.

Very truly yrs.
Jeffn Davis

The bill passed on May 22, and three days later the Senate agreed. It went to the president for his signature on May 30, 1854. Davis played a vital role in persuading a reluctant Pierce to accept the repeal of the Missouri Compromise.

In the fall of 1855, Davis responded to a request for him to serve in the U.S. Senate. In an expansive letter, Davis answered affirmatively and then spoke gloomily about the future.

To Thomas J. Hudson
Washington, Nov. 25, [1855]
Dear Sir: I have the pleasure to acknowledge your favor of the 13th instant, and thank you for the kind estimation you place upon my capacity to serve Mississippi as her representative in the United States Senate. You ask me to say whether if elected by our Legislature, [I] would accept the station, and assure me that I am for that office your

first choice, and, you believe, that of your constituency. I answer without circumlocution. I would accept, and were the office one of less distinction or less agreeable to me, I should have given the same reply under a rule of conduct I have long entertained, and which requires me to hold myself subject to the call of Mississippi for service in any station to which it may be her pleasure to assign me. In the same spirit of frankness with which you have addressed me, I will say that were I disposed to select the station which would be most agreeable to myself without waiting for an indication from my fellow-citizens, it would be that named by you—Senator from Mississippi.

Events seem to be hurrying us on to a crisis, alike dangerous to the peace of the South and the preservation of the Constitutional Union. My hope for safety is in resolute adherence to our time honored doctrine of State rights, and a strict construction of the compact made between the States, when the Union was ordained and established. It is equally a violation of good faith to the States to refuse to exercise powers delegated, and thus to defeat the purpose for which they were given, as it is to usurp those powers which were reserved. When the States surrendered to their agent the general government, the conduct of all foreign intercourse, the obligation was clearly imposed to use the power for the general interest, and the common defense. . . .

As a member of the present administration I am gratified by your expressed wish to see the President renominated, and though I cannot claim to be an impartial judge, it has seemed to me both just and polite that the South should give such recognition of her regard for the faithful manner in which she has asserted and maintained her constitutional rights. Sensibly impressed with the high compliment you offer me in selecting [me as] your preferred candidate for the Vice-Presidency, I must in all sincerity assure you that is an office for which I do not consider myself suited and in no degree to possess. Moreover, I have conclusively made up my mind never again to hold office unless it be in the service of Mississippi.

I would be glad to hear from you whenever your convenience will permit.

Very respectfully, your friend, etc,

Jefferson Davis.

Two weeks later, Davis was even more candid. The South must expand to California and Oregon if it is to regain its equality with the North.

To William Cannon
December 7, 1855

. . . We of the South have been too much disposed to rely on the intrinsic merits of our cause, and to neglect all the necessary defences whilst an active enemy was seizing the outposts preparatory to an attack upon the citadel. Abolitionism would gain but little in excluding slavery from the territories if it was never to disturb that institution in the states, and Northern supremacy in both houses of Congress would not have been pursued through so many years of labor if it had been a thing which was not to be employed against the equal rights of the other section. A direct attack they have too much sagacity to make for that would be met by open resistance, but through the forms of legislation, and ostensibly for the public service, a section having the control of both houses of Congress can gradually work an inequality which will reduce the other section to a tributary condition. We have lost our equality in the Senate, and it is of vital importance that we should endeavor to regain it. We should not allow the Abolitionists to Colonise Kansas by emigrant societies without making an effort to counteract it by throwing in a Southern population, and so of New Mexico. The country on the Pacific is in many respects adapted to slave labor, and many of the citizens desire its introduction. As I have been in the habit of looking to the great interest of the communities to find the cause of their public policy, this case has led me to ask why the advocates of domestic slavery should not have acquired the control of California and Oregon. The answer has seemed to me to be this: The only convenient route for emigrants is now by sea and across the Isthmus, and the vessels for this line of communication start from Northern ports, thus shutting out those who must take with them their servants, their flocks and herds and [thus] securing a Northern Immigration to that country which would first unite our population. If we had a good railroad and other roads making it convenient to go through Texas into New Mexico, and through New Mexico into Southern California, our people with their servants, their horses and their cows would gradually pass westward over fertile lands into mining districts, and in the latter, especially, the advantage of their associated labor would impress itself upon others about them and the prejudice which now shuts us out of that country would yield to the persuasion of personal interest. This border once established from East to West, future acquisitions to the South would insure . . . to our benefit, thus the equality might be regained and preserved which is incumbent to a fair construction of the Constitution and the fulfillment of the great purpose for which our Union was established.

The panacea of 1850 has already lost its efficacy, and the disease it was promised to check for all future time seems to have been rendered chronic by the treatment.

5

The Election of 1856 and Its Aftermath

In the election of 1856 the Republican Party chose a presidential candidate for the first time, James C. Frémont, the military hero and explorer. The party opposed the extension of slavery and urged its containment to the current boundaries. The Democrats chose James Buchanan, an experienced diplomat and politician who did not have strong positions on slavery or its extension into the territories. The third candidate was former president Millard Fillmore, chosen by the American Party, which was composed of Southern Whigs and took no position on slavery.

The election became a contest between Buchanan and Frémont, with Fillmore having little impact. Buchanan received votes from those who feared that Frémont's election would anger the South and lead to the secession of Southern states. Those voters who were concerned about the expansion of slavery cast their ballots for Frémont. Buchanan won 45 percent of the popular vote, while Frémont won 33 percent and Fillmore 22 percent. Thus, Buchanan carried the South, except for Maryland and five free states, with 174 electoral votes; Frémont carried eleven free states, with 114 electoral votes; and Fillmore, one state. For the second time in American history a president received less than a majority of the popular vote (the first was John Quincy Adams in 1824). The divided outcome revealed a country in which sectionalism was now the most important factor. The Republicans were elated and redoubled their efforts for the future.

NORTHERNERS

Abraham Lincoln

During the summer and fall of 1856, Lincoln made more than fifty speeches in his effort to elect John C. Frémont as president and stop the expansion of slavery. In Galena, Illinois, he spoke in July against "Disunion." As reported by the Weekly Gazette, Lincoln stated: "We WON'T dissolve the Union, and you SHAN'T."

127

Speech at Galena, Illinois
July 23, 1856
Lincoln on Disunion

Hon. Abraham Lincoln hits the nail on the head every time, and in this instance it will be seen, he has driven it entirely out of sight,—if we succeed as well as we anticipate in re-producing from memory his argument in relation to "Disunion."

Mr. LINCOLN was addressing himself to the opponents of FREMONT and the Republican party, and had referred to the charge of "sectionalism," and then spoke something as follows in relation to another charge, and said:

"You further charge us with being Disunionists. If you mean that it is our aim to dissolve the Union, for myself I answer, that is untrue; for those who act with me I answer, that it is untrue. Have you heard us assert that as our aim? Do you really believe that such is our aim? Do you find it in our platform, our speeches, our conversation, or anywhere? If not, withdraw the charge. . . . We the majority, being able constitutionally to do all that we purpose, would have no desire to dissolve the Union. Do you say that such restriction of slavery would be unconstitutional and that some of the States would not submit to its enforcement? I grant you that an unconstitutional act is not a law; but I do not ask, and will not take your construction of the Constitution. The Supreme Court of the United States is the tribunal to decide such questions, and we will submit to its decisions; and if you do also, there will be an end of the matter. Will you? If not, who are the disunionists, you or we? We, the majority, would not strive to dissolve the Union; and if any attempt is made it must be by you, who so loudly stigmatize us as disunionists. But the Union, in any event, won't be dissolved. We don't want to dissolve it, and if you attempt it, *we won't let you*. With the purse and sword, the army and navy and treasury in our hands and at our command, you *couldn't do it*. This Government would be very weak, indeed, if a majority, with a disciplined army and navy, and a well-filled treasury, could not preserve itself, when attacked by an unarmed, undisciplined, unorganized minority.

"All this talk about the dissolution of the Union is humbug—nothing but folly. *We* WON'T dissolve the Union, and *you* SHAN'T."

He continued to make speeches for the next few months. At Belleville, Lincoln argued that there were just two parties to consider, the Democrats and Republicans, not Fillmore's third party.

Speech at Belleville, Illinois
October 18, 1856

. . . He [Lincoln] showed that there are only two parties and only two questions now before the voters. A Kentuckian, as he is, familiar with Slavery and its evils, he vindicated the cause of free labor, "that national capital," in the language of Col. Fremont, "which constitutes the real wealth of this great country, and creates that intelligent power in the masses alone to be relied on as the bulwark of free institutions." He showed the tendency and aim of the Sham Democracy to degrade labor to subvert the true ends of Government and build up Aristocracy, Despotism and Slavery. The platforms of Buchanan and Fremont were contrasted, and the opposite tendency of each to the other was shown with the clearness of light. The rights of man were eloquently vindicated. The only object of government, the good of the governed, not the interests of Slaveholders—the securing of life, liberty and the pursuit of happiness; this true end of all Government was well enforced. The Kentuckian, Lincoln, defended the Declaration of American Independence against the attacks of the degenerate Vermonter, Douglas, and against Breckenridge and the whole ruling class of the South. Here was a Southerner, with eloquence that would bear a comparison with Henry Clay's, defending Liberty and the North against the leaders of the Border Ruffians and Doughfaces of Illinois. Stephen A. Douglas, the traitor to Freedom, was exposed, and his arguments refuted by Lincoln.

Lincoln was discouraged by the defeat of Frémont but believed that there would be opportunities for success in the future. At the end of the year he attended a Republican banquet in Chicago. The initial toast was given: "lst THE UNION—The North will maintain it—the South will not depart therefrom." Then, Lincoln responded.

He said he could most heartily indorse the sentiment expressed in the toast. During the whole canvass we had been assailed as the enemies of the Union, and he often had occasion to repudiate the sentiments attributed to us. He said that the Republican party was the friend of the Union. (Cheers.) It was the friend of the Union now; and if it had been entirely successful, it would have been the friend of the Union more than ever, [Loud and long continued cheers]. He maintained that the Liberty for which we contended could best be obtained by a firm, a steady adherence to the Union. As Webster said, "Not Union without liberty, nor liberty without Union; but Union and liberty, now and forever, one and inseparable."(Loud cheers.) . . .

Can we not come together, for the future. Let every one who really believes, and is resolved, that free society is not, *and shall not be*, a failure, and who can conscientiously declare that in the past contest he has done only what he thought best—let every such one have charity to believe that every other one can say as much. Thus let bygones be bygones. Let past differences, as nothing be; and with steady eye on the real issue, let us reinaugurate the good old "central ideas" of the Republic. We *can* do it. The human heart *is* with us—God is with us. We shall again be able not to declare, that "all States as States, are equal," nor yet that "all citizens as citizens are equal," but to renew the broader, better declaration, including both these and much more, that "all *men* are created equal."

George Templeton Strong

Strong was excited by the nominations of John C. Frémont and William L. Dayton for president and vice president by the Republican Party. For the first time, Republicans ran candidates for the highest two positions in the land.

June 17 [1856] . . . . *Hurrah for both*. I shall vote the Republican ticket, if alive and capable of locomotion to the polls next fall. Northern discords and splits will defeat that ticket beyond question, but I want it to have a respectable minority in its favor. I belong to the insurgent plebeians of the North arming against a two-penny South Carolina aristocracy. . . .

On July 15 the House of Representatives resolved the case against Preston Brooks, who had attacked Charles Sumner in the Senate chamber. Most members wanted to expel him, but there was not a two-thirds majority. It was enough to make Strong consider abolitionism.

July 15. House of Representatives has disposed of the Brooks and Sumner case. The motion to expel Bully Brooks failed for want of a two-thirds vote, but the majority in favor of expulsion was considerable, so the *Cheval*, or *Hoss* (his nearest approach to a chivalric title) made an allocution to his Southern admirers and refractory Northern liegemen and indignantly resigned his seat. It's said that Butler is to leave the Senate and that this caitiff [that is, despicable person] will be instantly promoted to Butler's seat. Even South Carolina can hardly be so blind and drunken with insolence and folly. Reasonable men and gentlemen, North and South, must be unanimous as to Brooks's harangue, which has rarely been equaled for bad taste, self-importance, and brutality. . . .

Vivat Frémont—I fear I shall come out a "damned Abolitionist" after all.

Two months later, Strong worried about the South seceding if Frémont were elected. It seemed likely that South Carolina would lead the exodus.

September 21, Sunday. . . . The pestilent little state of South Carolina, mad with metaphysics and self-conceit, gasconading [that is, boasting] itself day by day into greater wrath and keener sense of imaginary wrong, means to secede if the North elect Frémont. It may by its legislature declare itself an independent nation, November 15th, or it may back out a little later, if it can secure Georgia or Virginia as allies, by refusing to go into ballot for President and Vice-President, and forming a Southern Confederacy. If it stand alone, it is easily dealt with; a couple of frigates can blockade its ports, and it will be starved into submission in about two weeks, being as poor and weak as it is insolent and irrational. But should it find aid and comfort from the sympathy of other slave states, *which is not an improbable thing*, if it put itself forward as champion of "Southern rights," the situation becomes a grave one and admits of but two probable solutions: a long and fierce civil war, or what's worse, dissolution of the Union.

Election results began to trickle in—the Republicans won Maine in September and Connecticut and Ohio in October. However, on October 19, Strong was filled with despair.

October 19. Alas for Frémont! Woe is me on account of the prospects of the Republican ticket! Everything is out of joint. Seward and Thurlow Weed have got hold of the cosmos by the wrong handle, as the Great [Bronson] Alcott would express it. We are all exchanging despondencies and condolences and confident predictions of being *nowhere* next November. Perhaps we were unduly elated a fortnight ago, when everything looked so bright and Frémont was so sure of every

Northern state, and are immeasurably disgusted by discovering that he has more to do than to walk over the course at his leisure. . . .

It strikes me that this institution—slavery as it *exists* at the South with all its "safe-guards" and "necessary legislation"—is the greatest crime on the largest scale known in modern history; taking into account the time it has occupied, the territory it covers, the number of its subjects, and the civilization of the criminals. It is deliberate legislation intended to extinguish and annihilate the moral being of men for profit; systematic murder, not of the physical, but of the moral and intellectual being; blasphemy, not in word, but in systematic action against the Spirit of God which dwells in the souls of men to elevate, purify, and ennoble them. So I feel now; perhaps it's partly the dominant election furor that colors my notions. Of course, slaveholders are infinitely better than their system. And we have nothing to say about this system where it is established, and we have no right to interfere with it, no responsibility for it. The question for the North is whether we shall help establish it elsewhere, in the "territories" our nation owns.

Strong still believed as late as October 24 that the Republicans could win. Frémont could be elected or the election might go to the House of Representatives. Even on November 2 he hoped that many people who usually did not vote might cast their ballots for Frémont.

On Election Day, November 4, he voted early and waited for the results. His initial optimism gave way to anxiety, and by late evening he believed that "Republicanism was in a bad way." The next day the results were in—Buchanan won, though with only 45 percent of the popular vote.

November 4, Tuesday. Four P.M. Voted after breakfast. Spent an hour or two at the polls of my election district at the corner of Twenty-second Street and Third Avenue. Went downtown to a Trust Company meeting, and then spent two or three hours more in political service. In spite of the foul weather, there is an immense vote; never larger in this city, I think. People form in queues, and so far as I've seen, everything is orderly and good natured; no crowding or confusion. . . .

Indications are not discouraging. The strength of the Frémont vote went in early in the day. This afternoon Fillmore is gaining and Buchanan still more. So it seems, but ordinary inferences from the appearance of voters are not *perfectly* reliable this time. For example, a party of Irishmen came along this morning asking for Republican electoral tickets. They were going to vote the Democratic ticket in the Fifth Ward where they belonged, except for President, and they didn't like to ask for a Republican ticket there. Frémont, I think, will run largely ahead of his ticket, and I don't expect over 10,000 against him in this city. The signs from Pennsylvania are good as far as they go, and the feeling this morning is that Frémont may well be elected. It's a momentous business; thank God, the responsibility of its decision doesn't rest wholly on me. Either way, fearful disaster may come of this election. . . .

November 5. Pennsylvania goes in for slavery extension and Buchanan by 20,000 majority. New Jersey the same way. New York Republican by an immense vote. Maryland probably gives her little all (eight votes) to Fillmore. So Buchanan is elected, unless Fillmore shall have got some Southern state besides Maryland. That would carry the election into the House, a thing rather undesirable.

Strong's last reference to the election was on November 8. He recorded in his diary that the Republicans did well and the Democrats barely won.

November 8. Everybody, except a few Fillmoreans, is delighted with the election. The Democrats, because Buchanan is in—that's nearly beyond dispute now—and the Republicans because New York is with them actually by near 70,000, because the New England states stand unanimous on the same side, and because the Democracy has had such a bad scare that it will probably be cautious about affronting the North much farther.

Charles Sumner

During the remainder of 1856 and the early months of 1857, Sumner slowly regained his strength after Brooks's assault. In August he wrote to Ralph Waldo Emerson about riding his horse again and his hope to make a speech.

To Ralph Waldo Emerson
Cresson—Alleghany Mts—
Penn. 16th Aug. '56
My dear Emerson, . . .

At last I am physically convalescent. Three times, in this mountain air, have I ridden on horse-back, & I begin to feel returning strength.

How long I shall be obliged to forego mental exertion & especially the excitement of public speaking; I know not. Never did I renounce any thing with deeper regret than I renounced the opportunity of speaking again this session from that seat where I was struck down. This has been hard to bear. . . .

> Ever sincerely Yours,
> *Charles Sumner*

Salmon Chase suggested that he consider becoming governor of Massachusetts. Sumner was not interested.

To Salmon P. Chase
Cresson—Alleghany Mts—
Penn. 26th Aug. '56
My dear Chase, . . .

There are many things on which I should be glad to commune with you—both public & personal. As to the governorship, I have no question on its comparative honor by the side of the post I now hold. I remember that J. Q. Adams kept himself aloof from local politics, & thought that a person, who wished to be useful on the national field, should do this. It is said that no man can be governor of Mass. without entanglements. These I wish to avoid. My aim is to serve *our cause*, & I am unwilling to enmesh myself in the questions, & controversies, both personal & public, which are peculiar to our State. . . .

> Ever sincerely Yours,
> *Charles Sumner*

In January 1857 he wrote about his problems to William Herndon, the law partner of Abraham Lincoln.

To William Henry Herndon
Boston 12th. Jan. '57
My dear Sir,

With a pang I have seen time pass, & found myself constrained to silence; especially during the Presidential canvass. My prostration has been great; but at last I see my recovery sure. Sometimes I think it has almost come; but I am still obliged to take to my bed at the beginning of the evening.

My hope is to reach Washington before the session closes.

I rejoice in all the good news from Illinois. With [William H.] Bissell for Governor surely this mighty prairie State can be put actively on the side of Freedom. I had expected to take part in the late canvass there; but this is among the satisfactions which I lost.

But the Future is safe. I am sure of it. The ruffians & their allies will be defeated, in serious, solemn battle. Meanwhile all of us must work; & I am glad the cause has a friend so faithful as yourself. . . .

Faithfully Yours,

Charles Sumner

It would be three years before Sumner became an active senator again.

Frederick Douglass

In the spring of 1856, Douglass wrote against the misguided efforts of some advocates to resolve the slavery problem by colonization in Africa. Years ago he had lost faith in such a proposal. Thus, he penned letters in an attempt to "expose the Colonization movement."

To Benjamin Coates, Esqr.
Rochester, April 17th, 1856
My dear Sir:

. . . I am not about to write you an argument against Colonization. You are already acquainted with the argument. It has been repeatedly pressed upon your attention far more ably than I am able to press it, and I know that when the truth strongly presented fails to convince, convincement is not likely to follow when the same truth is but feebly and imperfectly stated. Still I am almost compelled by your eloquent plea for Colonization, briefly to state my conviction touching the Colonization movement. I believe then, that the agitation of Colonization, has a direct tendency to divert attention from the great and paramount duty of abolition, and stands directly in the way of the latter, that it serves to deaden the national conscience when it needs quickening to the great and dreadful sin of slavery, that it furnishes an apology for delaying emancipation until the whole four millions can be sent to Africa, thus interposing a physical impossibility between the slave and his deliverance from chains, that it aims to extinguish the hope of ultimate elevation for the free Negro in this country, and to unsettle all his plans of progress here, that it robs his future in this country of all that can gladden his heart and nerve him to manly endeavor, that it serves to confirm existing prejudice as a thing natural and unsurmountable. Believing all this and more—however I may feel towards Liberia as an existing fact, I cannot do other than expose the Colonization movement. . . .

Your true and grateful friend,

Frederick Douglass

At the end of the summer he published an editorial supporting the candidacies of Frémont and Dayton for president and vice president of the United States. For him the Republican Party offered the only hope for stopping the expansion of slavery.

. . . let us not be unreasonable or impatient with the Republican Party. In considering this defect in the Anti-Slavery character and creed of the Republican Candidates, it should be borne in mind that they stand now in respect to this doctrine precisely where the Liberty Party stood ten years ago. The Right and duty of the Federal Government to abolish Slavery everywhere in the United States, is entirely true and deeply important; and yet, it must be confessed that this doctrine has been made appreciable but to a few minds, the dwellers in the mountain peaks of the moral world, who catch the first beams of morning, long before the slumberers in the valleys awake from their dreams. This new doctrine, we think, may very properly be left to take its turn in the arena of discussion. Time and argument will do more for its progress, and its final adoption by the people, than can be done for it in the present crisis, by the few votes of the isolated Radical Abolitionists. . . . A great crime against Freedom and Civilization is about to be perpetrated. The Slave Power is resolved to plant the deadly Upas [that is, an Asian tree whose sap is poisonous], Slavery, in the virgin soil of Kansas. This great evil may be averted, and all the likelihoods of the case, the election of John C. Frémont and William L. Dayton, will be instrumental in averting it. Their election will prevent the establishment of Slavery in Kansas, overthrow Slave Rule in the Republic, protect Liberty of Speech and of the Press, give ascendency to Northern civilization over the bludgeon and blood-hound civilization of the South, and the mark of national condemnation on Slavery, scourge doughfaces from place and from power, and inaugurate a higher and purer standard of Politics and Government. Therefore, we go for Fremont and Dayton.

Frederick Douglass' Paper, August 15, 1856

Charlotte Forten Grimké

In the fall of 1856 there was much discussion about "bleeding Kansas" and the presidential elections. Charlotte Forten began to learn about the violence in Kansas and then the election of James Buchanan, a pro-Southern politician from Pennsylvania. These were disquieting times.

Sunday, October 26. Mr. [Charles Lenox] R[emond] lectured for us this evening. His lecture was very good. I particularly liked what he said about Kansas. Everybody has so much sympathy for the sufferers there, and so little for the poor slave, who for centuries has suffered tenfold worse miseries.—Still I am glad that *something* has roused the people of the North at last.

October. Went with Mr. [Joseph] Putnam to hear Mr. [Richard] Dana, who taught me more about Kansas than I ever knew before. A very great political excitement prevails.

Saturday, November 8. Alas! for the hope of the people! Again has Might triumphed over Right; Falsehood over Truth; Slavery over Freedom. But these things cannot last much longer. Surely a just God will not permit them.

In the winter, Charlotte was thrilled by letters from John Greenleaf Whittier and Wendell Phillips. They were unexpected but very welcome.

Friday, December 19. Came home from school, weary and cold, but found something which refreshed and inspirited me,—filled me with joy and astonishment,—a letter from Whittier,—the 'Great Poet of Humanity'! It was an answer to one which I wrote to him—because— I *could not help it*; the Spirit moved me. *His* letter, most unexpected by me, is *very* kind and beautiful, most worthy of his noble self. I thank him for it with all my heart. A letter in *his own* handwriting. He can never know the happiness—the delight it gives me. But oh, it grieves me deeply to know that he is ill,—that his health has failed fearfully of late. How *could* we bear to lose him? *I will not* think that it is possible. . . .

Thursday, January 22. [1875] Came from school cold and weary, found to my joyful surprise a letter from Mr. [Wendell] Phillips.— How *very* kind he was to *write.* I feel *very* grateful to him. He is indeed a noble-hearted man. I can never, never express all the reverence and admiration which I feel for him. How delightful it would be to be admitted to his society. Alas, I can never hope to be fitted for that great privilege. But I *can* love and admire him, and shall ever do so, with all my heart.—Looked over many old letters, which gave me rather a sad and lonesome feeling.

During the same months, Charlotte's spirits were lifted by antislavery lecturers. "They excited me to such a degree of enthusiasm."

Sunday, December 21. Have just returned from Parker Pillsbury's lecture. One of the best Anti-Slavery lectures I ever heard. While listening to him I could not help thinking of [Martin] Luther of old. Indeed as it has been said of Luther, I believe, "his words were half battles." Glorious indeed they were—those battles for suffering humanity. They excited me to such a degree of enthusiasm, that I could have risen and thanked and blessed him for them, then and there. As [Sir Philip] Sidney says of the Ballad of Chevy Chase, "they stir the soul like the sound of the trumpet," but to a higher, nobler impulse than that of *physical* resistance; to a stern *moral* resolve of sternest *moral* warfare against the terrible curse of our country and of the age.—Such a lecture renews one's strength; makes one feel equal to any labor, for the ennobling of mankind.

Charlotte continued to read about slavery and its cruelty. The recently published Autobiography of a Female Slave *was deeply distressing to her.*

Saturday, February 7. . . . "The Autobiography" is very thrilling. Some parts of it almost too horrible to be believed, did we not know that they cannot exceed the terrible reality. It is *dreadful, dreadful* that *such* scenes can be daily and hourly enacted in this enlightened age, and *most* enlightened republic. How long, Oh Lord, how long, wilt thou delay thy vengeance? . . .

Sunday, February 8. Finished "The Autobiography of a Female Slave." To me it is deeply interesting. The writer's style has not, perhaps, that perfect elegance and simplicity which distinguishes the *best* writers, but she evidently *feels* deeply on the subject, and her book is calculated to awaken our deepest sympathies. I thank her for writing it. Hers must be a brave, true soul thus to surmount all obstacles, to soar above all the prejudices, which, from childhood, must have been instilled into her mind, and take upon herself the defense of a downtrodden and degraded race!

SOUTHERNERS

The Kansas issue and the election of 1856 looked very different to Southerners. They saw the necessity of Kansas becoming a slave state so that the "peculiar institution" would continue to expand westward. Moreover the election of a Republican president was a threat to the Southern way of life. It was becoming more difficult to see a peaceful solution.

The Jones Family

In his letters to his parents, Charles Jones, now living in Savannah, discussed the presidential election of 1856 and disunion.

Mr. Charles C. Jones, Jr. to Rev. and Mrs. C. C. Jones
Savannah, Wednesday, October 8, 1856
My dear Father and Mother,
. . . Buchanan's prospects seem by no means as encouraging as they were at first. The union of the Fillmore and Frémont men in Pennsylvania will, it is seriously feared, cause the old Keystone State to deviate from her hitherto unshaken adherence to Democratic principles. What a shame it will be if she repudiates her noble, trueborn son for such a miserable offspring of fanaticism as Frémont "the Pathfinder"! Fillmore is not in the race. The whole aim of the combination is to defeat Buchanan; and regarding Frémont as the most available of the two to accomplish that purpose, regardless of all principles and sound national considerations, the masses are declaring allegiance to him.

The Union, in the event of Frémont's election, will, at least in this section of the state, be decidedly below par. Disunion sentiments are already entertained to a very general extent. Our country was probably never before to such a degree disturbed by factions at home, and those of a purely sectional character. To what this will all lead, time only will reveal. It is to be sincerely hoped that every true lover of his country, of the liberties guaranteed under the Constitution, will come to the rescue. . . .

> Your affectionate son,
> *Charles C. Jones, Jr.*

After the election, Charles rejoiced over the results but worried about the future of the country. What would happen after the "expiration of the term of office of the President- and Vice-President-elect"?

Mr. Charles C. Jones, Jr., to Rev. and Mrs. C. C. Jones
Savannah
Saturday, November 8th, 1856
My dear Father and Mother,

Since last writing you the people of this country have met and decided an important issue, boldly and broadly presented; and happy am I that we are able to congratulate ourselves upon the result. For at least four years, under the administration-elect, may we hope for peace and prosperity. Beyond that period we scarce dare expect a continuance of our present relations. Unless there be a material reaction in the sentiments of at least a portion of our common country at the expiration of the term of office of the President- and Vice-President-elect, it is to be feared that the cohorts of fanaticism will claim one of their own persuasion as the officer-elect to preside over the destinies of this great republic. Whence that reaction will arise, and whether there is the least probability of its occurring, is more than problematical. Buchanan and Breckenridge are elected, and owe their election to the South mainly; while the vote of the North with but few exceptions has been cast for Frémont. The next issue will doubtless be purely sectional in its character. The prospect is fearful, but everything indicates such a future condition of affairs. And when it does come, we of the South must and will be prepared to meet it bravely and without concession. . . .

Peace will now, I hope, again spread her white wings over our land; the angry and excited passions of men be calmed; and everyone, dismissing the excitement of this late political struggle from the mind, attend once more to the more quiet yet not less important duties of life. . . .

> Your affectionate son,
> *Charles C. Jones, Jr.*

For a time it appeared that one of the Joneses' slave families would be sold to a General Harrison, but his offer was not the highest one. Still the entire family was sold to one person who lived near Macon, Georgia.

Rev. C. C. Jones to Mrs. Mary Jones
Savannah, Wednesday,
December 10th, 1856
My dear Wife, . . .

Charles has effected a sale: $4500 cash, Joe's little man *included*, making $642.85 each, expenses to be deducted. The best sale that could be effected at present. Some four hundred now in the market; money scarce and hard to be obtained. They have all been sold to one person—not to be separated, but remain on his own farm in the vicinity of *Macon*. General Harrison did not purchase; his offer in the end not as advantageous. They have been sold as we desired, and of this we should be glad, although more might have been obtained had they been sold separately. Conscience is better than money. Have not seen Charles yet, and the letter must go at once to the office. . . .

Your ever affectionate husband,
C. C. Jones.

However, in March 1857, Charles's father found out that the slave family subsequently had been broken up and its members sold individually. It was a bitter disappointment.

Rev. C. C. Jones to Mr. Charles C. Jones, Jr.
Montevideo,
Thursday, March 26th, 1857
My dear Son,

We were happy to hear today of your own and your brother's good health. . . . Enclosed you will find a letter received today which will be as great a surprise to you and Joe as it has been to us. The man Lilly who writes the letter is evidently a Negro trader, and not the permanent owner of the Negroes! The internal evidence of the letter proves it. In addition, I have learned that *Lyons* at the Boro received a *friendly* letter from Old Cassius this evening in which he speaks of not yet being *at home*—dated in New Orleans. My opinion is that they are there on sale! *Lilly* says *he bought them in Savannah*. This was not the *name* of the man who appeared in the purchase, nor was *New Orleans* his home. Was it not a *planter* near Macon who bought for his *own use* and not to sell again? Here seems to be deception—a wheel within a wheel!

So soon as you hear from the ostensible purchaser you will know more about it—should he answer your letter. Do not let him know of Lilly's letter. He may request you to send him the money for the people. Do not do so. It will be a roundabout way, and they may never get it. All we wish to learn of him is to know how the game has been played. If we have been deceived by Wright and the purchaser, we have been deceived. We were endeavoring to do the best we could.

Rev. Dr. Palmer is now in New Orleans, and we might enclose the money to him; and at our request, stating our fears that the people have fallen into the hands of a trader, he would pay it over to Cassius and Phoebe himself and then inform us of the fact. This, I think, my son, will be the safer course. You can write him at my request as the only friend I have in New Orleans upon whom I could confidently call in the matter. If you can get no draft for the amount on New Orleans, a draft on New York sent to New Orleans in favor of Dr. B. M. Palmer will answer the purpose. It will be best to write in this way to Dr. Palmer without delay. The list sent in Lilly's letter you see is different from the one given me by Cassius himself. Send a copy of the account I sent you to Dr. Palmer. . . .

Your affectionate father,

C. C. Jones.

Charles's response to the news was equally sad. All his efforts had been in vain.

Mr. Charles C. Jones, Jr., to Rev. and Mrs. C. C. Jones
Savannah,
Saturday, March 28th, 1857
My dear Father and Mother,
Your kind favor, Father, has been duly received. The news contained in the enclosed communication was as unexpected as it was unpleasant. The death of Jane is sad. I hope she may have made some preparation for the great change, but the probabilities under the circumstances are unfavorable. The revelation confirms me in the hitherto unshaken conviction that no confidence whatever can be placed in the word of a Negro trader. It is the lowest occupation in which mortal man can engage, and the effect is a complete perversion of all

that is just, kind, honorable, and of good report among men. The plan you propose with regard to the transmission of the money realized from the sale of Cassius' property is without doubt the best, and I will see that a check is duly purchased and forwarded on Monday. . . .

Your affectionate son,

Charles C. Jones, Jr.

Augustus Benners

In the fall of 1856 he mentioned for the first time that year's presidential race. Benners no longer considered himself a Whig, but he distrusted the other parties. The first election news came in late October and the final results in early November.

October 21st 1856 . . . News of election in Pennsylvania is still very conflicting the Buchanan party claiming a triumph by a small majority & the Filmore & Frémont fusionites also claiming that they have carried it. Intense interest is felt in the result . . .

Nov 3rd 1856 . . . Tomorrow is the day for election of president & vice president of U States—intense interest is felt in the result. the South dreading the possible success of J. C. Frémont who is the candidate of the Black republicans. Filmore who is supported by the American party stands we think no chance and the best opinion is that Buchanan & Brackenridge will be elected. I shall vote for them, the destruction of the Whig Party by the formation of American party a know nothing party—having left me as it were without a party—and besides other objections to it believing that the American party has been measurably free soilized. I have felt it my duty to support the Democratic candidates believing that their platform of principles contains the true doctrine on the Slavery issue non interference by Congress with the subject—May God in his mercy overrule the election to the good of our people.

Jefferson Davis

In the fall of 1856, Davis received an invitation to attend a public dinner honoring Preston Brooks, the protagonist of Charles Sumner. He declined but expressed sympathy for a Southern brother who, in his opinion, had been unfairly vilified.

To South Carolina Citizens
Washington, Sept. 22, 1856.

Gentlemen: I have the honor to acknowledge your polite and very gratifying invitation to a public dinner to be given by the people of the 4th Congressional District, to their Representative, Hon. P. S. Brooks.

It would give me much pleasure, on any occasion, to meet you, fellow citizens of the 4th District of South Carolina; and the gratification would be materially heightened by the opportunity to witness their approbation of a Representative whom I hold in such high regard and esteem. Circumstances will not permit me, however, to be with you, as invited, and I have only to express to you my sympathy with the feeling which prompts the sons of Carolina to welcome the return of a brother, who has been the subject of vilification, misrepresentation, and persecution, because he resented a libellous assault upon the reputation of their mother. . . .

Jefferson Davis.

In October 1856, just prior to the election, Henry Wise put the state of Virginia in a state of readiness and called for Southern governors to come to a conference on the 13th. Only the governors from North and South Carolina attended.

To Herschel V. Johnson
[October 1856]

Should another controversy arise, I think the conduct of the South at that period will embolden the North to expect her to shrink from the redemption of her pledges, and that the chances of a resort to force are thereby greatly increased. The recent demonstration of Gov Wise in relation to the militia of Virginia would indicate that he looks to an appeal to the last argument of sovereigns, but he has Judiciously left all men to draw what inferences the tendency of their own minds may suggest, and certainly no one has a right to object because the Governor of a State seeks to give to its militia the greatest possible efficiency. In a single sentence then my idea of our present condition is, that we should make all the preparation proper for sovereign States—should hasten slowly, and be temperate in all things—as ever

very truly your friend—

Jeffn., Davis

William Gilmore Simms

In the late summer of 1856, Simms once again expressed interest in politics. In a letter to James Orr, a Democratic congressman from South Carolina who would soon become speaker of the House of Representatives, Simms expressed his concerns about the value of the Democratic Party to Southerners. The two men had taken a trip earlier in the summer and talked about the future of the South.

To James Lawrence Orr
Charleston, Aug. 30. [1856]
My dear Orr.

I know not where you are, nor what you are doing, but take for granted that you are still at your post in Washington. I have little to say, being immensely busied at this moment, preparing for a course of Lectures at the North, whither I have been summoned by a flood of invitations; and where, unless the dissolution takes place before we look for it, I am in hopes to earn a much needed amount of money. But what I have to say is briefly this: It is time that you should begin seriously to calculate the value, at once to yourself and the South, of the Democratic Party. I fancy you begin to see for yourself what I long ago urged upon you, that, even if successful in electing their President, the D. P. was too feeble to maintain their pledges to the South, and would not retain their organization very long after. It is barely possible, I think, that Buchanan will be elected. He may carry a sufficient Northern vote to secure this result. The South, I take it, will sustain him entirely. As for Fillmore, I suppose him nowhere. But even if elected, the Democratic Party, like the Whig under Fillmore, will not possess the proper administrative power for good. If you agree with me, you will see the propriety of recognizing, with all your sympathies, the *Sectional* organization. The South, as a Section, has the power to rule this country through its products—to acquire the commerce & manufactures, to grow eminently great for all purposes. We are by nature independent & powerful. Were we but united, all would be right. Now, *self & country*, in your case, may be served equally, if you seize upon the proper moment, to show to your people that you are not simply a *national man*, which is the charge most frequently brought against you. Take an early opportunity to identify yourself with the South, especially, making it understood that you go with the D. P. only as that Party is able to promote the interests & safety of the South. Do not be tardy. Do not be a minute too late. There is no reason, so far as I see, why you should not represent your country, in a sectional organization, as successfully as under a national one. —I throw out these hints to you frankly, as—you will credit me —I really desire to see you in all cases successful, where the propriety and patriotism of your course may claim recognition. You are a man of energy, strength, resolution. You have youth & zeal. Bring these to bear upon the new necessities of the country—the new relations which we may be about to form —and I have no doubt you can achieve a far superior and less questioned position than that which you now occupy. Do not suffer the harness of party, to render you oblivious in any degree, of that new course, to which the necessities of the country are now driving your section of it. I am satisfied that the disintegration of all existing parties is inevitable— . . .

Truly yr friend

Simms

Part III

The Union Comes Apart, *1857–1861*

On March 6, 1857, two days after James Buchanan was sworn in as president, the Supreme Court issued the Dred Scott Decision. It ruled that the Missouri Compromise was unconstitutional since Congress did not have the power to deprive citizens of their property. Slaves could not be differentiated from other types of property and their owners were protected by the Fifth Amendment. Thus, slavery could not be kept from expanding into the territories and the North. Southerners were delighted with the decision and thought for the first time in ten years that slavery was now completely protected. They had been worried about the increasing attacks on slavery and the continuing efforts to pass the Wilmot Proviso. Now, with the Kansas-Nebraska Act and the Dred Scott Decision, Southerners believed that the issue of slavery had finally been settled.

Despite the Supreme Court decision, Kansans remained deeply divided over the slavery issue. A group of pro-slavery settlers met in Lecompton, Kansas, and drew up a constitution. It was submitted to the voters, and with the help of several thousand Missourians who were not eligible to vote, the pro-slavery constitution was approved. Several months later, there was another vote on the complete constitution. This time, with many antislavery settlers casting ballots, the constitution was decisively rejected. Most citizens in Kansas were opposed to slavery and favored freeing all of the slaves in the territory. Disregarding the second vote, President Buchanan tried to force Congress to admit Kansas as a slave state. In the Senate, Stephen Douglas refused to cooperate with the president and, with the help of Republicans, defeated the effort. Douglas continued to argue for popular sovereignty, which allowed the settlers, not Congress, to decide the issue. This controversy resulted in a split in the Democratic Party that delayed the admission of Kansas into the Union until 1861.

In the next year, Stephen Douglas ran for reelection to the Senate. Midway through his campaign, Abraham Lincoln, the Republican candidate, challenged him to a series of debates. He accepted, and there were seven open-air debates in the last two months of the campaign. The main topic was slavery. Douglas attacked Lincoln as a black abolitionist (that is, someone favoring the abolition of enslavement of blacks) who promoted sectionalism, while Lincoln denounced the Dred Scott Decision and insisted that slavery be placed in a position that would ensure its eventual extinction. Lincoln won the majority of popular votes, but because the state legislature elected the senator, its Democratic majority returned Douglas to his seat. Although Lincoln lost the election, he became a national figure thanks to his performance in the debates.

On October 16, 1859, John Brown, an unstable man of intense convictions, gathered sixteen whites and five blacks and marched to Harpers Ferry, Virginia. The town was easily taken as well as the federal armory and arsenal, Brown's target. By morning nearby towns were mobilized and their citizens rushed to defend Harpers Ferry. A detachment of U.S. Marines led by Col. Robert E. Lee arrived on October 18, and Brown and his followers were quickly captured.

In the next six weeks, Brown was tried, found guilty, and sentenced to death. For one month while held in jail, he proclaimed against the evils of slavery and the need to abolish the institution. Then, on December 2, Brown was executed. Almost immediately he became a martyr to the North and a symbol of violence to the South. The Southern reaction was extreme anger because many believed that Republicans wanted to make war on the South. They expected another attack unless measures were taken to stop it.

As the 1860 presidential election approached, the turmoil in American politics escalated. In Charleston, South Carolina, the Democratic Party split over the slavery issue. The convention failed to choose a candidate; six weeks later, Stephen Douglas became the nominee for the Northern Democrats and John C. Breckinridge, the candidate for the Southern wing of the party. The Republican Party met in Chicago with William Seward as the front-runner. However, after three ballots, Abraham Lincoln was nominated. A fourth party, the Constitutional Unionists, chose John Bell of Tennessee. Thus, there were four candidates for the presidency. Lincoln stayed at home, avoiding any discussion of slavery and writing letters urging no compromise on the extension of the issue. Breckinridge did little more than assert his love for the Union, while Bell talked of returning to the good old days. The most active candidate was Douglas, who campaigned in the North and South and argued for preservation of the Union. Only Douglas recognized the danger of secession and warned the South that such an effort would be met with force. The other candidates ignored the possibility, and thus the issue was not seriously discussed in the campaign.

The outcome was in serious doubt until Election Day, November 6. Then it was clear that Lincoln won a majority of the electoral vote and just under 40 percent of the popular vote. Every Northern state except New Jersey voted for Lincoln. Breckinridge carried the lower South while Douglas received 29 percent of the popular vote but only twelve electoral votes. Bell carried three states in the upper South. It was the most sectional election in American history with the winner, Abraham Lincoln, carrying the North but getting no votes in the South and with Breckinridge carrying the seven states of the lower South but receiving not a single electoral vote in the North.

The election of a Republican president who continued to oppose the expansion of slavery was considered a serious threat to Southerners, who began to hold conventions to decide whether or not to secede. South Carolina was the first to meet and on December 20, 1860, passed an ordinance declaring: "The Union now hitherto existing between South Carolina and states under the name of the United States of America, is hereby dissolved." Other states held similar conventions, and by February 1, 1861, Mississippi, Florida, Alabama, Georgia, Louisiana, and Texas voted to secede. The new nation was named "The Confederate States of America."

In the following month, on March 4, Abraham Lincoln was sworn in as the sixteenth president of the United States. He made a plea to the Southern states, and especially to the eight remaining slave states, to "think calmly and well upon this whole subject." There was no reason for hasty actions since the old Constitution remained unchanged and provided opportunities for redress. He hoped that his plea would forestall any impetuous moves.

Determined to hold the Union together, he faced an immediate problem—what to do about Fort Sumter, in Charleston Harbor? Federal troops there needed supplies or would soon be forced to surrender. Lincoln talked to Winfield Scott and the cabinet before taking the next step, which was to send a number of ships to provision the fort. He also decided to send advance notice to Francis W. Pickens, the Confederate governor of South Carolina.

How would President Jefferson Davis react? Should he allow Fort Sumter to be provisioned? If he did, it could be seen as an act of weakness on his part. Davis, considering the effort to provision Sumter as an act of aggression, ordered General Pierre G. T. Beauregard to take the fort before it could be resupplied. Efforts to convince Major Robert Anderson to surrender Sumter were unsuccessful. Thus, there was no other choice but to order firing on the fort. It began at at 4:30 A.M. on April 12 and continued until 1:30 P.M. the next day, when Anderson surrendered. The war had begun.

The reader will note a continuance of the two major themes of the book. The first, the conflict between the North and South, reached new heights with the unwillingness of the North to accept the Dred Scott Decision, the making a martyr of John Brown, and the election of Abraham Lincoln as president. Panic seized parts of the South as its citizens waited for more John Browns and for the actions of an "abolitionist president." The second theme, a reconsideration of the nature and value of the Union, was on the minds of many Southerners. Unless there could be federal protection for slavery and their way of life, why remain in the Union any longer? Conversely, many in the North were more certain than ever that the Union must be maintained at all costs. They agreed with Daniel Webster: "Liberty and Union, now and forever, one and inseparable." Others were less certain about the value of a Union that could only be held together by force. Why not let the erring Southern sisters go their own way?

6

Dred Scott, Kansas, and the Events of 1858

NORTHERNERS

Abraham Lincoln

When Lincoln read the Dred Scott Decision, he waited several months before making public remarks about it. He was not anxious to challenge the Supreme Court but thought that such a misinterpretation of the Declaration of Independence and the Constitution could not be ignored. He addressed the decision in a speech at Springfield on June 26, 1857.

That decision declares two propositions—first, that a negro cannot sue in the U.S. Courts; and secondly, that Congress cannot prohibit slavery in the Territories. It was made by a divided court—dividing differently on the different points. . . .

We think its decisions on Constitutional questions, when fully settled, should control, not only the particular cases decided, but the general policy of the country, subject to be disturbed only by amendments of the Constitution as provided in that instrument itself. More than this would be revolution. But we think the Dred Scott decision is erroneous. We know the court that made it, has often over-ruled its own decisions, and we shall do what we can to have it over-rule this. We offer no *resistance* to it. . . .

I have said, in substance, that the Dred Scott decision was, in part; based on assumed historical facts which were not really true; and I ought not to leave the subject without giving some reasons for saying this; I therefore give an instance or two, which I think fully sustain me. Chief Justice [Roger] Taney, in delivering the opinion of the majority of the Court, insists at great length that negroes were no part of the people who made, or for whom was made, the Declaration of Independence, or the Constitution of the United States.

On the contrary, Judge [Benjamin R.] Curtis, in his dissenting opinion, shows that in five of the then thirteen states, to wit, New Hampshire, Massachusetts, New York, New Jersey and North Carolina, free negroes were voters, and, in proportion to their numbers, had the same part in making the Constitution that the white people had. He shows this with so much particularity as to leave no doubt of its truth; and, as a sort of conclusion on that point, holds the following language:

"The Constitution was ordained and established by the people of the United States, through the action, in each State, of those persons who were qualified by its laws to act thereon in behalf of themselves and all other citizens of the State. In some of the States, as we have seen, colored persons were among those qualified by law to act on the subject. These colored persons were not only included in the body of 'the people of the United States,' by whom the Constitution was ordained and established; but in at least five of the States they had the power to act, and, doubtless, did act, by their suffrages, upon the question of its adoption."

During the same year, Lincoln maintained the party position of no further expansion of slavery. President Buchanan pushed for the admission of Kansas as a slave state while Stephen Douglas continued to support popular sovereignty—the people in Kansas deciding whether or not to accept slavery. In a letter to Lyman Trumbull, Lincoln tried to distance himself from the other two positions.

Chicago, Nov. 30, 1857.
Hon: Lyman Trumbull.
. . . What think you of the probable "*rumpus*" among the democracy over the Kansas constitution? I think the Republicans should stand clear of it. In their view both the President and Douglas are wrong; and they should not espouse the cause of either, because they may consider the other a little the farther wrong of the two. . . .

On June 16, 1858, Lincoln, named the Republican's choice for the U.S. Senate, responded by delivering the "House Divided" speech at the party's convention. No one who heard it was in doubt about Lincoln's position.

Mr. PRESIDENT and Gentlemen of the Convention.
If we could first know *where* we are, and *whither* we are tending, we could then better judge *what* to do, and *how* to do it.

We are now far into the *fifth year*, since a policy was initiated, with the *avowed* object, and *confident* promise, of putting an end to slavery agitation.

Under the operation of that policy, that agitation has not only, *not ceased*, but has *constantly augmented*.

In *my* opinion, it *will* not cease, until a *crisis* shall have been reached, and passed.

"A house divided against itself cannot stand."

I believe this government cannot endure, permanently half *slave* and half *free*.

I do not expect the Union to be *dissolved*—I do not expect the house to fall—but I *do* expect it will cease to be divided.

It will become *all* one thing, or *all* the other.

Either the *opponents* of slavery, will arrest the further spread of it, and place it where the public mind shall rest in the belief that it is in course of ultimate extinction; or its *advocates* will push it forward, till it shall become alike lawful in *all* the States, *old* as well as *new*—*North* as well as *South*. . . .

Our cause, then, must be intrusted to, and conducted by its own undoubted friends—those whose hands are free, whose hearts are in the work—who *do care* for the result.

Two years ago the Republicans of the nation mustered over thirteen hundred thousand strong.

We did this under the single impulse of resistance to a common danger, with every external circumstance against us.

Of *strange, discordant*, and even, *hostile* elements, we gathered from the four winds, and *formed* and fought the battle through, under the constant hot fire of a disciplined, proud, and pampered enemy.

Did we brave all *then*, to *falter* now? —*now*—when that same enemy is *wavering*, dissevered and belligerent?

The result is not doubtful. We shall not fail—if we stand firm, we shall not fail.

During the late summer and early fall, Lincoln and Stephen Douglas engaged in seven debates to decide who would be elected senator from Illinois. Those debates centered almost entirely on slavery. Douglas saw no reason for slavery not to continue indefinitely if the people so desired. It would be their choice if they wanted it extended to the territories. Lincoln, on the other hand, believed that slavery must be put in a position where it would eventually die out. He spelled out this position over a two-month period. His first speech was in Ottawa, Illinois, on August 21, 1858.

Now gentlemen, I don't want to read at any greater length, but this is the true complexion of all I have ever said in regard to the institution of slavery and the black race. This is the whole of it, and anything that argues me into his idea of perfect social and political equality with the negro, is but a specious and fantastic arrangement of words, by which a man can prove a horse chestnut to be a chestnut horse. (Laughter.) I will say here, while upon this subject, that I have no purpose directly or indirectly to interfere with the institution of slavery in the States where it exists. I believe I have no lawful right to do so, and I have no inclination to do so. I have no purpose to introduce political and social equality between the white and the black races. There is a physical difference between the two, which in my judgment will probably forever forbid their living together upon the footing of perfect equality, and inasmuch as it becomes a necessity that there must be a difference, I, as well as Judge Douglas, am in favor of the race to which I belong, having the superior position. I have never said anything to the contrary, but I hold that notwithstanding all this, there is no reason in the world why the negro is not entitled to all the natural rights enumerated in the Declaration of Independence, the right to life, liberty and the pursuit of happiness. (Loud cheers.) I hold that he is as much entitled to these as the white man. I agree with Judge Douglas he is not my equal in many respects—certainly not in color, perhaps not in moral or intellectual endowment. But in the right to eat the bread, without leave of anybody else, which his own hand earns, *he is my equal and the equal of Judge Douglas, and the equal of every living man.* (Great applause.)

Later, on October 15, in Alton, Illinois, he concluded his campaign with what he considered the essence of his debate with Douglas.

That is the real issue. That is the issue that will continue in this country when these poor tongues of Judge Douglas and myself shall be silent. It is the eternal struggle between these two principles—right and wrong—throughout the world. They are the two principles that have stood face to face from the beginning of time; and will ever continue to struggle. The one is the common right of humanity and the other the divine right of kings. It is the same principle in whatever shape it develops itself. It is the same spirit that says, "You work and toil and earn bread, and I'll eat it." (Loud applause.) No matter in what shape it comes, whether from the mouth of a king who seeks to bestride the people of his own nation and live by the fruit of their labor, or from one race of men as an apology for enslaving another race, it is the same tyrannical principle. I was glad to express my gratitude at Quincy, and I reexpress it here to Judge Douglas—*that he looks to no end of the institution of slavery.* That will help the people to see where the struggle really is. It will hereafter place with us all men who really do wish the wrong may have an end. And whenever we can get rid of the fog which obscures the real question—when we can get Judge Douglas and his friends to avow a policy looking to its perpetuation— we can get out from among them that class of men and bring them to the side of those who treat it as a wrong. Then there will soon be an end of it, and that end will be its "ultimate extinction." Whenever the issue can be distinctly made, and all extraneous matter thrown out so that men can fairly see the real difference between the parties, this controversy will soon be settled, and it will be done peaceably too. There will be no war, no violence. It will be placed again where the wisest and best men of the world, placed it.

Lincoln lost the election although he received a majority of the popular vote. Apportionment favored the Democrats in the legislature, and they elected Douglas by a vote of fifty-four to forty-six.

Lincoln's performance won him considerable publicity, which augured well for the future. In a letter to a friend he reflected on his loss.

Springfield,
Nov. 19, 1858.
Anson Miller, Esq.
My dear Sir
 . . . In the last canvass I strove to do my whole duty both to our cause, and to the kind friends who had assigned me the post of honor; and now if those friends find no cause to regret that they did not assign that post to other hands, I have none for having made the effort, even though it has ended in personal defeat. I hope and believe seed has

been sown that will yet produce fruit. The fight must go on. Douglas managed to be supported both as the best means to *break down*, and to *uphold* the slave power. No ingenuity can long keep those opposing elements in harmony. Another explosion will come before a great while.

Yours very truly

A. Lincoln.

Charles Sumner

During these years, Charles Sumner was suffering the effects of his severe beating by Preston Brooks. Traveling to England, France, and Germany, he sought medical advice and healing. His recovery finally came in the summer of 1859.

Sumner maintained an active interest in national affairs and kept in touch with important political figures. The Kansas situation was especially troublesome to him. On April 27, 1857, he wrote a letter from France to his friend Samuel Gridley Howe.

I tremble for Kansas, which seems to me a doomed territory. How disgusting seems the conduct of those miserable men who thus trifle with the welfare of this region. My blood boils at this outrage & I long to denounce it again from my place. *Le Jour viendra.* [The day will come.]

Several months later, on September 18, he shared his concerns with Governor Salmon P. Chase of Ohio.

Poor Kansas! I am pained by the trials & sorrows of this territory; & my indignation overflows when I see the President & Cabinet lending themselves to the cruel work. I envy you the opportunity & the ability of speaking for our cause thus imperilled.

In December, Sumner returned home and attempted to become active again as a senator. The Kansas issue was still unresolved; in February 1858, Sumner objected to President Buchanan's intention to station troops in Kansas in order to protect the new government. He explained his position to Senator William Pitt Fessenden.

New York—Brevoort House—
28th Feb. '58.
My dear Fessenden,
You first made the point, that the Presdt. had no authority under the laws of the U.S. to fill Kansas with Federal troops as a *posse comitatus* [power of the country]. It has never been answered. I do not think it can be.

The wolf must be held by the ears, & kept in that condition. In other words, the Administration must be held before the country, as violating the laws for a *tyrannical & sectional purpose*, & kept so completely in the wrong, that the troops will be innoxious. At all events, try; & it belongs to you to make the effort.

Let it be by resolution, calling upon the Presdt. for reasons why he undertakes to keep troops in K. as a *posse comitatus?* Or, introduce a bill, ordering the withdrawal of the troops. At all events make the point, & do it constantly. Challenge an answer.

I wish that I could help you. I should enjoy following you in the attack. But my time will come—pretty soon, I think.

Ever Yours,

Charles Sumner

Sumner returned to England in June 1858. His physical relapse required additional medical treatment. He remained abroad for fifteen more months in an effort to recover his health.

There had been rumors of his resignation. He refused to resign, explaining his position to his friends.

To Samuel Gridley Howe
Paris—24th Nov. '58
Dear Howe,
If I send any letters of resignation *you* will know it as soon as any body.

But I am to be a well man. This is the solemn judgt. of the drs after consultation— . . .

If my position were merely political I should resign at once; but I am unwilling to renounce the opportunity of again meeting the enemies of Freedom in the Senate. My resignation would delight the slave-drivers, & I have some reason to believe, it would pain, the true

A-Sl. [Anti-Slavery] men of the country. Unless something occurs which I do not anticipate that delight & that pain shall not come from me. . . .

George Templeton Strong

Strong had little interest in national politics in the years from 1857 to 1859. A busy lawyer, he also dabbled in spiritualism and remained active in many philanthropic efforts. The only political matter that he noted with any regularity was the situation in Kansas. There were efforts to have Kansas admitted as a slave state with the Lecompton Constitution, which recognized the right of slavery. He watched the Kansas issue for many months.

January 5. [1858] That firebrand Kansas threatens incendiarism again, and I fear we're on the eve of a critical period. General [John Adams] Dix tells me that the fractious cabal of fire-eaters, which has so much more power than it deserves, has made up its mind to disunion or the Lecompton Constitution. I doubt if the North can submit to the latter. Will it have the pluck to repress and punish any movement toward the former? Doubtful. Our very remarkable executive head is a mere man of expediencies, I fear, without principle (moral or political) and devoid of all decision and courage, a jellyfish, able to sting a refractory officeholder, but able to do no more.

Several months later he again referred to the Lecompton Constitution.

March 24. People talk in these days mostly of:
1. "Lecompton." It has just scratched through the Senate, after a tough struggle, in a dilapidated and disreputable state. Opinions differ as to its fate in the lower house, but I predict that the Administration will triumph and the Senate will pass without material amendment. Maybe the world will come to an end in consequence, but I shall be surprised if it does, at least for some little time.

The next month there was more news from Washington.

April 2. . . . News from Washington important. The knell of our liberties is understood not to have tolled yet. We are all supposed to be rejoicing over a great crisis happily past. Perhaps we are. Executive dictation, proslavery propagandism, and so forth, by an uncorrupted and so forth. Infamous invasions of popular right, nigger-driving oligarchy, fraud, violence, and the border ruffians of Missouri are put down, rebuked, driven home to the obscene dens from which they emerged, and so on, by and so on rising in its majesty. Hoo-ray! By 120 to 112 the House has so amended the Senate Lecompton bill as to provide for submission of the Lecompton Constitution to the people of bleeding Kansas. May that hemorrhagic territory rest in peace! But I fear it won't, and that old Buchanan & Co. won't give it up without further contest. And the chances are in favor of Buchanan's success after all. Three or four dirty little Representatives can surely be bought off by executive Patronage.

On May 3 he noted that "Lecompton has triumphed in Congress! But will probably be squashed and squelched in Kansas." In fact, it was defeated when it was sent to the people for a vote. The issue was not finally resolved until the war began, when Kansas was admitted to the Union as a free state.

In the next eighteen months, Strong showed little interest in political matters. The only exception was the election of 1858, when he noted that the Republicans carried New York and that Stephen Douglas won reelection to the Senate. There was no reference to the Lincoln-Douglas debates.

Frederick Douglass

Speaking before the American Anti-Slavery Society in New York City on May 11, 1857, Douglass condemned the Dred Scott Decision. He believed that it could not stand, nor could it blot out the hopes of an enslaved people.

This infamous decision of the Slaveholding wing of the Supreme Court maintains that slaves are within the contemplation of the Constitution of the United States, property; that slaves are property in the same sense that horses, sheep, and swine are property; that the old doctrine that slavery is a creature of local law is false; that the right of the slaveholder to his slave does not depend upon the local law, but is secured wherever the Constitution of the United States extends; that Congress has no right to prohibit slavery anywhere; that slavery may go in safety anywhere under the star-spangled banner; that colored persons of African descent have no rights that white men are bound to respect; that colored men of African descent are not and cannot be citizens of the United States. . . .

God will be true though every man be a liar. We can appeal from this hell-black judgment of the Supreme Court, to the court of common sense and common humanity. We can appeal from man to God. If there is no justice on earth, there is yet justice in heaven. You may close your Supreme Court against the black man's cry for justice, but you cannot, thank God, close against him the ear of a sympathising world, nor shut up the Court of Heaven. All that is merciful and just, on earth and in Heaven, will execrate and despise this edict of [Chief Justice Roger] Taney. . . .

Furthermore, Douglass thought that there was no reason to consider the "dissolution" of the Union in order to escape from slavery.

There is nothing in the present aspect of the anti-slavery question which should drive us into the extravagance and nonsense of advocating a dissolution of the American Union as a means of overthrowing slavery, or freeing the North from the malign influence of slavery upon the morals of the Northern people. While the press is at liberty, and speech is free, and the ballot-box is open to the people of the sixteen free States; while the slaveholders are but four hundred thousand in number, and we are fourteen millions; while the mental and moral power of the nation is with us; while we are really the strong and they are the weak, it would look worse than cowardly to retreat from the Union. . . .

At times, Douglass appeared to be uncertain about the success of peaceful means to end slavery. In an 1857 article entitled "Peaceful Annihilation of Slavery is Hopeless," he expressed grave doubts.

While we feel bound to use all our powers of persuasion and argument; to welcome every instrumentality that promises to peacefully destroy that perpetual contemner [that is, scorner] of God's laws, and disturber of a nation's peace—Slavery; we yet feel that its peaceful annihilation is almost hopeless, and hence stand by the doctrines enunciated in those resolutions, and contend that the slave's right to revolt is perfect, and only wants the occurrence of favourable circumstances to become a duty. . . . We cannot but shudder as we call to mind the horrors that have ever marked servile insurrections—we would avert them if we could; but shall the millions forever submit to robbery, to murder, to ignorance, and every unnamed evil which an irresponsible tyranny can devise, because the overthrow of that tyranny would be productive of horrors? We say not. The recoil, when it comes, will be in exact proportion to the wrongs inflicted; terrible as it will be, we accept and hope for it. The slaveholder has been tried and sentenced, his execution only waits the finish to the training of his executioners. He is training his own executioners.

Several months later, on August 4, 1857, on the twenty-third anniversary of emancipation in the British West Indies, Douglass spoke in celebration of that event.

The whole history of the progress of human liberty shows that all concessions yet made to her august claims, have been born of earnest struggle. The conflict has been exciting, agitating, all-absorbing, and for the time being, putting all other tumults to silence. It must do this or it does nothing. If there is no struggle there is no progress. Those who profess to favor freedom and yet deprecate agitation, are men who want crops without plowing up the ground, they want rain without thunder and lightning. They want the ocean without the awful roar of its many waters.

This struggle may be a moral one, or it may be a physical one, and it may be both moral and physical, but it must be a struggle. Power concedes nothing without a demand. It never did and it never will. Find out just what any people will quietly submit to and you have found out the exact measure of injustice and wrong which will be imposed upon them, and these will continue till they are resisted with either words or blows, or with both. The limits of tyrants are prescribed by the endurance of those whom they oppress. In the light of these ideas, Negroes will be hunted at the North, and held and flogged at the South so long as they submit to those devilish outrages, and make no resistance, either moral or physical. Men may not get all they pay for in this world, but they must certainly pay for all they get. If we ever get free from the oppressions and wrongs heaped upon us, we must pay for their removal. We must do this by labor, by suffering, by sacrifice, and if needs be, by our lives and the lives of others.

Sojourner Truth

In 1858, Truth traveled in Michigan and Indiana. Well known by this time, she drew large and enthusiastic crowds. Parker Pillsbury provided an account of one of her meetings where a rumor had circulated that she was an imposter—a man in a woman's clothes.

At her third appointed meeting in this vicinity, which was held in the meeting-house of the United Brethren, a large number of democrats and other pro-slavery persons were present. At the close of the meeting, Dr. T. W. Strain, the mouthpiece of the slave Democracy, requested the large congregation to "hold on," and stated that a doubt existed in the minds of many persons present respecting the sex of the speaker, and that it was his impression that a majority of them believed the speaker to be a man. The doctor also affirmed (which was not believed by the friends of the slave) that it was for the speaker's special benefit that he now demanded that Sojourner submit her breast to the inspection of some of the ladies present, that the doubt might be removed by their testimony. There were a large number of ladies present, who appeared to be ashamed and indignant at such a proposition. Sojourner's friends, some of whom had not heard the rumor, were surprised and indignant at such ruffianly surmises and treatment.

Confusion and uproar ensued, which was soon suppressed by Sojourner, who, immediately rising, asked them why they suspected her to be a man. The Democracy answered, "Your voice is not the voice of a woman, it is the voice of a man, and we believe you are a man." Dr. Strain called for a vote, and a boisterous "Aye," was the result. A negative vote was not called for. Sojourner told them that her breasts had suckled many a white babe, to the exclusion of her own offspring; that some of those white babies had grown to man's estate; that, although they had sucked her colored breasts, they were, in her estimation, far more manly than they (her persecutors) appeared to be; and she quietly asked them, as she disrobed her bosom, if they, too, wished to suck! In vindication of her truthfulness, she told them that she would show her breast to the whole congregation; that it was not to her shame that she uncovered her breast before them, but to their shame. Two young men (A. Badgely and J. Horner) stepped forward while Sojourner exposed her naked breast to the audience. I heard a democrat say, as we were returning home from meeting, that Dr. Strain had, previous to the examination, offered to bet forty dollars that Sojourner was a man! So much for the physiological acumen of a western physician.

Unfortunately little is known about her activities in the next few years.

Harriet Beecher Stowe

Anxious to secure an international copyright for her novel, Dred: A Tale of the Great Dismal Swamp, *Harriet took a trip to Europe that began in August 1856. In a letter to her husband from London, she expressed pleasure at the positive response of her friends to the new book.*

The duchess, last night, showed me her copy of "Dred", in which she has marked what most struck or pleased her. I begged it, and am going to send it to you. She said to me this morning at breakfast, "The Queen says that she began 'Dred' the very minute she got it, and is deeply interested in it."

Stowe was also pleased with the continuing interest in England in the events in the United States.

The news from America is eagerly watched by them, and the Duchess said: "I only wish Fremont could be elected while you are here. I would have the castle illuminated." You have no idea of the feelings of good people here about America. They say it is a ship freighted with the world's future; and they watch its struggle in the breakers with the deepest emotion.

Her close friend, Lady Byron, was so moved by Dred *that she asked for advice about sending £50 to those settlers in need in Kansas (the novel dealt in part with the conditions there).*

Feeling that the sufferers in Kansas have a claim not only to sympathy, but to the expression of it, I wish to send them a donation. It is, however, necessary to know what is the best application of money and what the safest channel. Presuming that you will approve the object, I ask you to tell me. Perhaps you would undertake the transmission of my £50.

Harriet's response was gratitude for such a large and unselfish gift.

Thank you, my dear friend, for your sympathy with our poor sufferers in Kansas. May God bless you for it! By doing this you will step to my side; perhaps you may share something of that abuse which they who "know not what they do" heap upon all who so feel for the right. I assure you, dear friend, I am *not* insensible to the fiery darts which thus fly around me.

The response in Paris was equally satisfying, especially that of three French gentlemen.

There were three French gentlemen who had just been reading 'Dred' in English, and who were as excited and full of it as could be, and I talked with them to a degree that astonished myself. There is a review of 'Dred' in the 'Revue des Deux Mondes' which has long extracts from the book, and is written in a very appreciative and favorable spirit. Generally speaking, French critics seem to have a finer appreciation of my subtle shades of meaning than English. . . . It is wonderful that the people here do not seem to have got over 'Uncle Tom' a bit. The impression seems fresh as if just published. How often have they said, That book has revived the Gospel among the poor of France. It has done more than all the books we have published put together. It has gone among les ouvriers [the workers], among the poor of Faubourg St. Antoine, and nobody knows how many have been led to Christ by it. Is not this blessed, my dear husband? Is it not worth all the suffering of writing it?

It was a successful trip lasting ten months, and Harriet returned home in June 1857 with renewed health and satisfaction. Then, on July 9, her eldest son, Henry, drowned while swimming in the Connecticut River. This death had a profound effect on her. Similar to that experienced with the loss of her first child in 1849, her intense suffering lasted for several years and resulted in the writing of a book. This time the book involved a reconsideration of her religious beliefs; Calvinism no longer offered her help in her times of crisis. The Minister's Wooing was about the callous treatment by male clergymen of women who were in mourning.

The heroine lost a son, and in her sorrow she was comforted by a black slave woman rather than by a minister of the church.

The story elevated the informal "priesthood" of women who comforted the afflicted and buried the dead as well as undermined the entire male Calvinistic religious structure. It would soon be serialized in the most prestigious literary magazine in the country, The Atlantic Monthly. Harriet continued to write novels in the following years that were financial, if not literary, successes. She was one of the first American women to make a living through writing.

SOUTHERNERS

Southerners were pleased with the Dred Scott Decision since it meant that slaves could be taken into the territories or to the North, but they were worried about the situation in Kansas. Unless Kansas became a slave state, the future of the institution seemed very bleak. The South could not grow without more slave states joining the Union.

John J. Crittenden

Crittenden was opposed to the Lecompton Constitution, which made slavery legal in the Kansas Territory, because it had not been legally drawn up. Only one-fifth of the registered voters chose the delegates who wrote the constitution, and Free Soil delegates had refused to participate in what they considered a rigged convention.

In a speech on March 17, 1857, Crittenden explained his position on the Lecompton Constitution.

I say, then, Mr. President, upon the record evidence, upon all the evidence, this is not the constitution of the people of Kansas. It is not the constitution under which they desire that you shall admit them into the Union. Now, will you, against their will, force them into the Union under a constitution which they disapprove? That is the question. You know the fact that ten thousand against six thousand are opposed to the constitution. You know that by the act of their Territorial Legislature that they entreat you not to admit them with this constitution. They tell you, moreover, as one of their reasons, not only that they disapprove of the whole constitution, but that it is particularly hateful to them because the votes given for it, or apparently given for it, were, to a great extent, fraudulent and fictitious. The Legislature tells you that nine-tenths of the people there are opposed to it. . . .

Speaking as a Southerner, Crittenden argued that Kansas could never be a slave state.

Mr. President, I am, according to the denominations now usually employed by parties in this country, a southern man. I have lived all my life in a southern State. I have been accustomed from my childhood to that frame of society of which slavery forms a part. I am, so far as regards the necessary defense of the rights of the South, as prompt and as ready to defend them as any man the wide South can hold; but in the same resolute and determined spirit in which I would defend any invasions of its rights, and for which I would put my foot as far as he who went furthest, I will concede to others their rights, and I will maintain and defend them. With the same feeling with which I know I would defend my own rights, I will respect theirs. I never expected Kansas to be a slave State. . . .

Now, Sir, what considerations are there, apart from these which I have stated, which could lead me to give, or could compensate me for giving, a vote against my sense of what was right and just? What is the advantage to our whole country, or to any portion of it, to result from taking Kansas into the Union now with this constitution? Is anything to be gained? Is the South or the North to gain anything by it? I see nothing to be gained by it. . . .

Crittenden concluded with a plea for a fair vote for the settlers of Kansas, and he promised to work for the admittance of the territory with whatever constitution they approved. He expected more slave states to be admitted to the Union but only if a majority of their citizens voted for slavery.

There had always been an interest by Southerners in acquiring Cuba. In 1859, President Buchanan tried to buy Cuba from Spain, but Crittenden, though a Southerner, opposed the effort.

It was once the policy of this government to preserve amity and kind relations with all the states of North and South America, and we succeeded. They came into the world as free nations under our auspices. We were an exemplar to them. What has become of that feeling? Where is it, you rulers of our people? How have we lost all this? The good will of a whole continent is a mighty fund of national strength, and we have lost it. We are gathering up little accounts with these nations and making quarrels with them. Do these little clouds of war promise additional prosperity or increase of revenue to meet our debts? Fighting is an expensive luxury—there is cost in it. This bill proposes to let the President make war at his discretion. The power to make war belongs to the Senate and House of Representatives. We cannot abdicate it,—the people have given it to us as trustees.

Tryphena Fox

Upon her marriage to David Fox, a physician in Plaquemines Parish, Louisiana, Tryphena became the mistress of a plantation and looked forward to a bright future. However, the move to Louisiana from Mississippi, where she had tutored a planter's daughter, was not what she expected. There were no schools near her new home (she had ten children in the next twenty-two years), the nearest church was thirty-five miles away, and there were few neighbors and little intellectual stimulation. On January 4, 1857, she wrote to her mother in Massachusetts about her new life.

Mrs Pickens left home last week to be absent about a month. I am very sorry as she is so good a neighbor & the only person I visit familiarly; there is no ceremony between us and she does many little favors for me. I probably told you before, that she was not an educated woman; but their wealth has enabled them to travel and mix in refined society, so that she has acquired good manners and taste from observation. It is said that they are about to "sellout." Then my nearest neighbor will be Mrs Stackhouse & Mrs Brooks her mother. I do not like them at all, for though the Mssrs Stackhouse are the wealthiest planters here, the whole family is exceedingly illiterate. All the visiting I do there is to call occasionally, just to keep on the right side, on account of the Doctor's practice there. Perhaps you would like to know who lives next door, just across the intervening acre; Mr Sarpy—a creole & overseer, on a very large plantation above has bought the house and ground, and is now repairing and arranging it for his—let me see—not negro *wife*, but his *negress*, and his four mulatto children. They have been living upon the plantation where he oversees, but are now to remove to the "new place". The occupant of the next house is known as "Old Bru"— a fugitive from justice in France who has been here for the last three or four years. He lives by the *very honorable* and profitable calling of receiving stolen goods from the negroes, for which he pays them a mere trifle and which he sells after getting a sufficient quantity of each kind, at a good profit in N. O. [New Orleans]. The family below are quite respectable—the man a native of France, an honest & industrious carpenter, who works on the plantations. Then comes a widow of some sort. Her husband disappeared one morning very *suddenly*, was last seen going back through the fields toward the swamp, and has never been heard of since. They are Creoles. Below these, is a family of the name of Geoffrey, also Creoles—a good for nothing lazy set. . . . Although these people live so near, yet I know no more of them personally, than as if I lived in Pittsfield; only seeing them as I ride by in the buggy with the Dr.

Tryphena found it difficult to stay healthy in Louisiana. She contracted a fever but recovered with the help of a slave woman who soon became ill herself.

I have been quite ill, with an attack of bilious fever. I am not able to sit up yet, but am recovering fast under the Dr's prompt treatment and kindness of nursing and Mary's (the new servant) attentive care. I was imprudent in doing too much about the house myself not being accustomed to housework for some time and unwilling to wait for Mary's arrival from N. O which I feared would be two or three weeks yet & the house wanted fixing so badly as far as dust and smoke & dirty windows was concerned. And I was having callers every few days and it annoyed me to see things look so, and I went to work myself & this is the result. . . .

I am quite well this morning, so that I am able to go about the house, and such confusions, as I find things in, you can hardly imagine, for my sickness has not been all. The negro girl Mary who came last Sunday waited upon me & did considerable housework until Thursday when she began to complain. Friday morning while the Doctor was gone she was taken with a violent cramp in her stomach, which lasted all day in spite of all his efforts on his return to lessen it. That night there was no sleep for any one and the next morning he thought she would die, and sent for her master; he came and said if she was well enough or better by night, he would take her away for there was no one here to wait upon her and she needed constant attention. During the evening, after cupping her & giving her powerful medicines, she became better and a waggon was brought & she was lifted into it upon her bed & taken home—four miles distant. she is so much prostrated that it will take her a long time to recover her former strength. That is the way with all diseases in this country, they must be cured quickly or they kill quickly, and if one recovers from a short attack, they find it has been so severe as to leave but little strength.

Especially troubling to her were the insects—mosquitoes and ants—and the rats.

Aside from the annoyance of these high winds the mosquitos are very troublesome to-day—more so than I have ever known them before. It is just the weather for them, cold nights, when they cannot move about much and warm, damp, or sultry days when they can bite the hardest. It is like having someone near you, touching you every now and then with a coal of fire. You jump and it is gone, to be applied in some other place. Even my shoes are no protection to my feet or kid gloves for my hands. They are not large, but black & fine. Ants, are another source of annoyance. They are everywhere, in the fields, forests, houses and barns. Anything eatable weather [*sic*] flesh or vegetables attracts them. I have learned by the dear experience of having a great quantity of clothing ruined by them, to put everything carefully away at night, if I do not care to see it full of little holes in the morning. All my provisions have to be carefully wrapped up or stowed away into the safe, the legs of which stand in little basins of water and into which they cannot penetrate. As I have commenced telling you of my *weighty grievances* I might as well finish at once and make a *clean breach* of it. Now dont think I am going to "fess" how many quarrels I have had with a certain Dr. because we have not had *one* yet, and I am only going to *tell you* about—*rats.* They infest the cornhouse and stable, destroying great quantities of corn; but I would not care so much for this if they would only let my *ducks* alone, for out of twenty-five of the last brood, only nine are left; they are getting big enough to defend themselves.

She gave birth to a nine-pound baby on September 20. The delivery was quick and painless.

Sunday P.M. Sept. 20th '57
Dear Mother,
I was taken sick last Sunday night about twelve o clock and safely delivered of a little girl in about *two hours.* My confinement so far, has been unusually free from the maladies attending that of most women.

I have had no milk fever or trouble with my breasts. As this is my seventh day I hope soon to get up & attend to my household duties & the claims of the little one. It is a fine, plump child & weighed about nine pounds! It is not decided yet who it resembles, but I think its father, as her little eyes are very dark & she has plenty of very dark hair. Dr R— is well. I will write more when I can sit up. Mails must have failed for I have heard nothing from you in a long time. Write soon— . . .

Affectionately Your Daughter

T. B. Fox

Tryphena's greatest problem concerned the running of the plantation and especially the work of the slaves. It taxed her patience to the limit. Born in the North, she had no experience with slavery and did not understand the hope of many slaves for freedom or the desire of black husbands and wives to remain together. To her, it was disloyalty. Her outlook was becoming decidedly Southern.

I could tell you a long lingo about the purchase of Reuben, his fidelity for about six months, then his taking a wife from the next plantation, her ruining him putting him up to steal, & lie & drink & finally persuading him to run away, *she going at the same time*, but it would be too long a story. It would show you though, that he has not run away because he has such hard task-masters, or such quantities of work to do, or because he is not properly clothed & fed & cared for when sick. But I know what those ranting abolitionists will think that *Triphen Holder*, has turned out to be a Southern monster, so you must keep my troubles to yourself. We don't know when we shall get him, but Dr Raymond will probably dispose of him as soon as possible after he returns. His wife, Phillis, was caught some time ago & it is very probable that she feeds him. He has been tracked in various places, with other negroes. There are three or four out, besides him from this neighborhood. His conduct for the last three months shows that he is a grand old scoundrel & was probably sold in Virginia for some rascality.

Mary came back about two weeks ago, & has done so well that she hardly seems like the same servant.

Dr Raymond is somewhat out of health & very much "out of spirits." He is so mortified & angry to think a negro would run away from him, when so many around here on the plantations, would be glad to have him for master & envy Reuben his place so much. He has so little to do & so many privileges.

Even a greater problem than Reuben was the new slave, Susan, and her two daughters. The price for the three slaves was only $1,400, but despite warnings, the Foxes bought her. Susan was to be "troublesome property."

My health is quite good now—but my *temper is quite bad*—these darkies "do plague me to death" sometimes. Susan goes by fits & starts—good three or four weeks & then so ugly & contrary that an angel could hardly keep mild & pleasant. To-day it has been push, hurry, push, to get the washing any where near done & though it is four o clock she is just hanging out the colored clothes. The white things have only been washed in *one* water & boiled—she has done nothing but wash since six o clock this morning, so you may know how slow she is—only three Dr R— baby & myself to wash for. . . .

[November 15, 1858] . . . Everything went smoothly, but Tuesday morning to my great disappointment & annoyance Susan was taken violently with headache & high fever so that we had to bring her into the house & watch her to save her life; she was very sick all the week; yesterday I had to send her back to her room, as we had put her into our only spare room & it was getting so soiled I feared it would never be passable for a stranger again. Negroes are *so* peculiar—so utterly void of white folks habits of cleanliness & energy! . . . Our expenses will be heavy this year, for the house has to be painted outside & we have had to build Susan a cabin with a *fireplace* on account of her having young children. She has been living in the ironing room next to the kitchen & using my kitchen fireplace, but I find it is not a good plan to allow her to do that; besides the ironing room was neither large or close enough for health. . . .

. . . Susan is worrying me again, beyond endurance & were it not for the tightness in our money affairs, Dr— would hire me another woman in her place, but as matters now stand we can neither hire or buy & I shall have to put up with many things which would otherwise be intolerable. She is *impudent & lazy & filthy* & the latter with even my ideas of neatness, I cannot overlook. Perhaps I do not treat her right—probably I do not for I do not like her & never did, & *never shall*; it is not pleasant to live on the same place & in as close proximity as one is obliged to do, with the cook & be all the time at enmity with her & feel angry, whether I say any thing or not.

William Gilmore Simms

Simms continued to write to his close friend, James Hammond, the newly elected senator from South Carolina, who had asked him for advice on January 20, 1858. Simms's lengthy reply was on January 28.

To James Henry Hammond
Woodlands, Jany. 28, 1858.
My dear Hammond.

The question is not so much whether you will be better able than your predecessors to do, or recover any thing for the South; —whether you will succeed in organizing her representatives for more efficient action; for a hope in short, whether you will aggrandize her by gains of territory, or strengthen her by increase of representation & states;— but, whether you shall maintain her *status*, that of your State, & your own. Not one of your friends, or fondest admirers, ever expected that, with all your powers, you could bring about any immediate results of advantage. These will depend pretty much on the chapter of accidents; which will continually afford opportunities; of which, a brave, quick, intelligent mind, will take due advantage. In the conflict between South & North, the great object with us, is the extrication of the former from the folds of the latter. If we could get our Southern representatives up to your standards & mine, the game would be an easy one; for we are stronger in the sinews of war, really; in fighting men & wealth, than our enemies. . . . The dissolution of the Union will, I say, be the result of casualties & events which are not within the pale of mere calcula-tion; and, as I have long been satisfied, no revolution can be effected, among any people, of the cautious, calculating nature of the Anglo-Norman, or Anglo-American race, until the usurpation shall invade the household, & be brought home to every man's door, in a sense of [per]sonal danger, or pecuniary loss & privation. . . . "You say the South (in Congress) is utterly disorganized, & you fear demoralized." I know that. I knew it long ago. And what could you expect? Weak men in power, can neither be brave, nor honest. But what of that? You call a council of war, and all your officers shrink back from the proposition of battle. What then? You *know*, in general issues, that battle is life. Shall *you* shrink? Shall you reduce yourself to the level of these under-lings whom you despise? No! You give battle. You may be defeated. But your sense of what is right sustains you; and the very instincts of the cowards sustain you! And your country will sustain you, even though they share the apprehensions of the cowardly. Take the responsibility as old [Andrew] Jackson did! I grant you that these people all regard you as a rival; but all ordinary men, in the moment of battle, submit to a rival, whom they fear, & whom they hate, perhaps, but whose courage & wisdom brings them safety; extricates them from meshes from which they cannot extricate themselves. But, if you go into battle with this spirit, you can not be defeated. Public opinion is growing with you. . . .

In the fall of 1858, tragedy struck Simms. Two of his sons died, felled by yellow fever, on the same day.

> To James Henry Hammond
> Charleston, Sep. 24. [1858]
> Oh! dear Hammond, weep for me! I am crushed to earth. I have buried in one grave, within twelve hours of each other, my two brave beautiful boys, Sydney, & your little namesake, Beverley Hammond, two as noble little fellows as ever lived. It was a dreadful struggle of 12 days with one, & nine with the other. It is a terrible stroke of fate, leaving us almost desolate. I feel heart broken, hope crushed, and altogether wretched. I can write no more. God's blessing upon you & yours. Weep for me & mine, dear friend, for I know that your sensibilities are keen enough to feel for the great agonies of mine.
> > Yours ever faithfully even now.
> > *W. Gilmore Simms*

For the next month, Simms worried about his other children. Finally, in November he commented on Hammond's speech at Barnwell Court House in which he advised South Carolina to remain in the Union unless pushed to the wall by abolitionists.

> To James Henry Hammond
> Woodlands, S. C. Nov. 22 [1858]
> My dear Hammond. . . .
> I have read and meditated [on] your speech a very great deal. It is a very noble & masterly performance, immeasurably superior to most of the things that you have done, and simply because it was done under a coercive strain, which, in spite of your ailments of body, brought all

your mind to bear upon it. It will, it ought & will, give you a national reputation. It is as profound, comprehensive & thoughtful, as any speech delivered for 20 years in Congress. It places you fairly within the ranks occupied by Clay, Calhoun & Webster. It is the speech of a statesman, such a speech, my dear Hammond—you will suffer me the egotism—as I alone, of all your friends, well knew that you were capable of making. I have long since been satisfied that your mind only wanted the adequate field, *and the adequate provocation*, to assert its perfect mastery, over all the contemporary politicians. I knew what you could do, when, a year ago, I counselled you to strike at *Douglas*. Perhaps, Seward, would have been your better mark, but Douglas was more certainly the popular idol. I do not say all this to please, but to provoke you. I believe, the field open, & your true position reached, *your health* will improve. But you are not to mind health. You have made an *entree*. This speech secures *that*. . . .

W. G. S.

Jefferson Davis

Davis became a U.S. Senator one day after ending his four-year term as secretary of war. He said little about his views until November 4, 1857, when he spoke to the Mississippi legislature at Jackson.

He spoke of the perils to which the South would be exposed by the admission of Kansas as a free State. Missouri would then be surrounded on three sides by States hostile to Slavery, and would inevitably be lost. New Mexico and the Indian Territory [now Oklahoma], and probably a portion of Texas, would be wrested from us; and with these additions to the power of the Northern majority, the way would be opened for new and more fatal aggressions upon our rights.

What then was to be the course of the South? Would she be content with mere resolutions, expressive of high determination, but not to be followed up with corresponding action? Was she to draw one circle after another, with a constantly diminishing radius, until she would be powerless to resist, and have but little left that would be worth contending for? He could not allow himself to think that the craven policy of acquiescence under admitted and flagrant wrongs would be carried so far. As a brave and high-spirited people, jealous of the rights which our revolutionary fathers had left us, we would prepare for the worst, while hoping for the best. He was gratified to believe that we were getting ready for the momentous struggle, which the signs of the times so strongly indicated was rapidly approaching. The completion of our internal improvement system would place us in a better position to meet the emergency. It would give us additional means and increased facilities for resistance; and, in the face of the conviction that we were able to defend ourselves, aggression on our rights and honor, if it did not cease, would at least hesitate and reflect and look to consequences. . . .

Later in the speech, Davis affirmed his loyalty to "maintain the Union and the Constitution" but stated an even higher loyalty to Mississippi.

As long as he occupied a seat in the Senate, he would stand as a sentinel on the watchtower, ready to sound the note of alarm whenever the rights of Mississippi should be invaded or her honor assailed, and prepared to go as far as the farthest in their defense and vindication. He would consecrate whatever ability God had given him to maintain the Union and the Constitution. He would do no act and speak no word to impair the harmony which it was so important to preserve between the States. His position would be equally distant from disunion on the one hand, and submission on the other. But while he was not for a dissolution of the Union, it was not to be understood that he had abandoned or modified his views in relation to the right of secession; on the contrary, he gloried in recognizing it as a fundamental part of his political creed; it was the doctrine of the old Republican party—the [ess]ential and vital principle of State rights, and [sho]uld not be surrendered without leaving the States abject and powerless at the [f]eet of a consolidated and omnipotent Federal Government.

In the next year his health began to deteriorate. His doctor urged him to go to Europe, but Davis went north to Maine instead. The weather was cooler and he quickly regained his physical well-being. During the two-month period he made a number of speeches and received an honorary doctorate at Bowdoin College. In a speech at Portland on September 11, 1858, Davis stressed the common bond of the Democratic Party and the need to understand the Southern view on recent problems.

Democrats, patriots, by whatever, political name any of you may be known, you have a sacred duty to perform to your ancestry and to posterity. The time is at hand when for good or for evil, the questions which have agitated the public mind are to be solved. Is it true as asserted by northern agitators that there is such contrariety between the North and the South that they cannot remain united? Or rather, is it not true as our fathers deemed it, that diversity in the character of the population, in the products and in the institutions of the several States formed a reason for their union and tended to secure to their posterity the liberty which was the common object of their love and cultivating untrammeled intercourse and free trade between the States to duplicate the comforts of all? . . .

Then he spoke of Southern interests.

We of the South, on a sectional division, are in the minority; and if legislation is to be directed by geographical tests—if the constitution is to be trampled in the dust, and the unbridled will of the majority in Congress is to be supreme over the States, we should have the problem which was presented to your Fathers when the Colonies declined to be content with a mere representation in parliament.

If the constitution is to be sacredly observed, why should there be a struggle for sectional ascendancy? The instrument is the same in all latitudes, and does not vary with the domestic institutions of the several States. Hence it is that the Democracy, the party of the constitution, have preserved their integrity, and are to-day the only national party and the only hope for the preservation and perpetuation of the Union of the States.

Returning from Maine to Mississippi, Davis spoke to the legislature on November 16, 1858, warning his audience of the dangers ahead.

It seems now to be probable that the Abolitionists and their allies will have control of the next House of Representatives, and it may be well inferred from their past course that they will attempt legislation both injurious and offensive to the south. I have an abiding faith that any law which violates our constitutional rights, will be met with a veto by the present Executive.—But should the next House of Representatives be such as would elect an Abolition President, we may expect that the election will be so conducted as probably to defeat a choice by the people and devolve the election upon the House.

Whether by the House or by the people, if an Abolitionist be chosen President of the United States, you will have presented to you the question of whether you will permit the government to pass into the hands of your avowed and implacable enemies. Without pausing for your answer, I will state my own position to be that such a result would be a species of revolution by which the purposes of the Government would be destroyed and the observance of its mere forms entitled to no respect.

In that event, in such manner as should be most expedient, I should deem it your duty to provide for your safety outside of a Union with those who have already shown the will, and would have acquired the power, to deprive you of your birthright and to reduce you to worse than the colonial dependence of your fathers. . . .

As when I had the privilege of addressing the Legislature a year ago, so now do I urge you to the needful preparation to meet whatever contingency may befall us. The maintenance of our rights against a hostile power is a physical problem and cannot be solved by mere resolutions. Not doubtful of what the heart will prompt, it is not the less proper that due provision should be made for physical necessities. Why should not the State have an armory for the repair of arms, for the alteration of old models so as to make them conform to the improved weapons of the present day, and for the manufacture on a limited scale of new arms, including cannon and their carriages; the casting of shot and shells, and the preparation of fixed ammunition?

Such preparation will not precipitate us upon the trial of secession, for I hold now, as in 1850, that Mississippi's patriotism will hold her to the Union as long as it is constitutional, but it will give to our conduct the character of earnestness of which mere paper declarations have somewhat deprived us; it will strengthen the hands of our friends at the North, and in the event that separation shall be forced upon us, we shall be prepared to meet the contingency with whatever remote consequences may follow it, and give to manly hearts the happy assurance that manly arms will not fail to protect the gentle beauty which blesses our land and graces the present occasion.

Augustus Benners

In the fall of 1857, Benners found the economic situation discouraging. The financial panic of 1857 proved to be short-lived but intense. A sharp increase in interest rates dried up the usual sources of credit.

Oct 22nd 1857 Cotton has declined from 16 to 8 cts and in fact is reported dull of sale at that—this in consequence of the financial embarrassments which have put a stop to almost all kinds of business and the end of which no man can tell—all the Banks in New York have suspended—all in the N. East & the N. West and many in the South, the Central, the Commercial & Saving Bank in this state and Mobile, Southern are expected to follow. Negro men it is said have declined to $1600 and a great fall in all kinds of property is expected. I am determined not to sell my cotton until a change occurs—In fact we cannot get it to Mobile—the river being as low as it ever gets. A strange exemplification this present state of affairs of the treacherous character of outward appearances—but a short time since everything was inflated and every kind of property was commanding the most extravagant prices—negro men selling at 1600 and women at 12 and 1500—cotton at 16 cts and every outward appearance indicated a long continuance of this seeming prosperity—the sea which but a short time since was unruffled even by a ripple has been swept by a storm & many a tall craft foundered by its violence—and still it rages—and still Bank after Bank suspends and firm after firm is proving infirm and much distrust and fear for the future have taken the place of confidence & hope I do not think that the Banks can speedily resume. I do not think they can act with sufficient concert & without this none can safely resume—but I do think cotton will improve and for a guess I will venture that it will sell for 10 cts by July next . . .

In November, Benners traveled to Montgomery for the annual Alabama state fair. He met old friends and had a pleasant time.

Nov 27th Friday—on Wednesday the 18th Nov I left home with Mr Charles Stickney in his buggy for Montgomery—got to Marion at 9 o clock—took cars at 15 minutes to 8 next morning, Selma to Montg'y which we reached to breakfast on friday morning. the day was cold and windy—Col Croom invited me to share his room or I must have slept on the floor—the city was very crowded—the cold and wind was very disagreeable on the fair grounds. Saw a great many people whom I knew, members of Legislature &c—Saturday was much pleasanter the trotting matches and tournament came off this day. The time was very good considering the heaviness of the track being at the rate of 2.56. The riding was quite interesting and was very good except Mr Posey

who did not succeed in even touching the ring—Mr Wm Knox was
the victor and presented the jewels to Miss Octavia Levert of Mobile.
I heard a splendid sermon on Sunday from bishop [James H.] Otey—
text "if the Lord be God serve him, but if Baal then serve him." Senator [Clement Claiborne] Clay was elected for 6 years from 1st March
1859 as senator to U. States senate. Mrs Clay made herself very agreeable when I saw her. The Bishops of Ala. Miss. Tenn. and Louisiana
were in Montg'y their business being to locate a Southern University.
The great question which was exciting the public mind in Montg'y
was the course which should be pursued towards the suspended banks.
Many persons are of the opinion they should be wound up and a majority I think are of opinion that suspension should not be legalised.

*In August 1858 he attended the wedding of a cousin in New Bern, North Caro-
lina, and then traveled to Washington, DC, where he met President Buchanan.
Benners was "much pleased with him."*

August 25, 1858 . . . In Newbern to which I returned on tuesday
the 10 August I attended the wedding of cousin Mary McKinley Daves
to Judge Ellis, the Governor elect of that State. The marriage took
place in the Church. And I waited on Cousin Betsy Daves. After the
marriage we had a very pleasant party at Cousin Betseys—we stopped
during our stay in Newbern at the Easton House and on friday the 13
August at 8-1/2 left in the cars for Old Point Comfort via Goldsboro—
we paid from Goldsboro to Newbern $2.00 from Newbern to
Goldsboro $2.25. We went to Welden to Dinner; on Saturday: (fare
2.75) by the Seaboard & Roanoke Rail Road to Portsmouth fare $4.00
to Old Point. 50 cts which we reached Saturday night to supper Aug
14th. Staid at Old Point Sunday & Monday & left Monday evening at
7 o clock for Washington City—at Old Point we were much pleased
with the fine bathing &c it is a beautiful place tho not so accessible to
breezes as Beaufort. the bathing is fine. We reached Washington to
Dinner. on tuesday morning visited the Capitol & Presidents home
same evening. Next morning visited patent office & Smithsonian institute and Presidents house. Called on the President Mr Buchanan—
were much pleased with him and with our visit—Alfred was particularly
so—We left Washington City on our way home on Wednesday evening
by the upper route as it is called. from Washington City we took a thro
ticket to Montgomery for which we each paid $32.

7

John Brown's Raid, Party Conventions, the Election of 1860, and Secession

NORTHERNERS

Abraham Lincoln

At the conclusion of a speech at Leavenworth, Kansas, on December 3, 1859, Lincoln referred to John Brown while arguing that the election of a Republican president was not a sufficient reason for Southern states to secede.

But you are for the Union; and you greatly fear the success of the Republicans would destroy the Union. Why? Do the Republicans declare against the Union? Nothing like it. Your own statement of it is, that if the Black Republicans elect a President, you won't stand it. You will break up the Union. That will be your act, not ours. To justify it, you must show that our policy gives you just cause for such desperate action. Can you do that? When you attempt it, you will find that our policy is exactly the policy of the men who made the Union. Nothing more and nothing less. Do you really think you are justified to break up the government rather than have it administered by Washington, and other good and great men who made it, and first administered it? If you do you are very unreasonable; and more reasonable men cannot and will not submit to you. While you elect [the] President, we submit, neither breaking nor attempting to break up the Union. If we shall constitutionally elect a President, it will be our duty to see that you submit. Old John Brown has just been executed for treason against a state. We cannot object, even though he agreed with us in thinking slavery wrong. That cannot excuse violence, bloodshed, and treason. It could avail him nothing that he might think himself right. So, if constitutionally we elect a President, and therefore you undertake to destroy the Union, it will be our duty to deal with you as old John

181

Brown has been dealt with. We shall try to do our duty. We hope and believe that in no section will a majority so act as to render such extreme measures necessary.

On May 23, 1860, Lincoln was notified that he had been nominated by the Republican Party for the position of president of the United States. He accepted in a brief letter.

Hon: George Ashmun:
Springfield, Ills., May 23. 1860
President of the Republican National Convention.
Sir: I accept the nomination tendered me by the Convention over which you presided, and of which I am formally apprized in the letter of yourself and others, acting as a committee of the convention, for that purpose.

The declaration of principles and sentiments, which accompanies your letter, meets my approval; and it shall be my care not to violate, or disregard it, in any part. . . .

A. Lincoln

During the campaign, Lincoln did little traveling. Instead he remained home and wrote letters in an effort to keep the party focused on the main issues and win the election. By August 4, optimistic about the results, he wrote to a friend, Simeon Francis, the publisher of The Oregon Farmer.

When you wrote, you had not learned of the doings of the democratic convention at Baltimore; but you will be in possession of it all long before this reaches you. I hesitate to say it, but it really appears now, as if the success of the Republican ticket is inevitable. We have no reason to doubt any of the states which voted for Fremont. Add to these, Minnesota, Pennsylvania, and New-Jersey, and the thing is done. Minnesota is as sure as such a thing can be; while the democracy are so divided between Douglas and Breckenridge [*sic*] in Penn. & N.J. that they are scarcely less sure. Our friends are also confident in Indiana and Illinois. I should expect the same division would give us a fair chance in Oregon. Write me what you think on that point.

Numerous efforts were made to have Lincoln restate his conservative views in order to assure Southerners that he was not a threat to them. One week before the election, on October 29, he wrote such a letter but decided not to mail it.

Geo. D. Prentice, Esq
Private & confidential
Springfield, Ills. Oct. 29. 1860

My dear Sir: Yours of the 26th. is just received. Your suggestion that I, in a certain event, shall write a letter, setting forth my conservative views and intentions, is certainly a very worthy one. But would it do any good? If I were to labor a month, I could not express my conservative views and intentions more clearly and strongly, than they are expressed in our plat-form, and in my many speeches already in print, and before the public. And yet even you, who do occasionally speak of me in terms of personal kindness, give no prominence to these oft-repeated expressions of conservative views and intentions; but busy yourself with appeals to all conservative men, to vote for Douglas—to vote any way which can possibly defeat me—thus impressing your readers that you think, I am the very worst man living. If what I have already said has failed to convince you, no repetition of it would convince you. . . .

And, now my friend—for such I esteem you personally—do not misunderstand me. I have not decided that I will not do substantially what you suggest. I will not forbear doing so, merely on *punctilio* [social comformity] and pluck. If I do finally abstain, it will be because of apprehension that it would do harm. For the good men of the South—and I regard the majority of them as such—I have no objection to repeat seventy and seven times. But I have *bad* men also to deal with, both North and South—men who are eager for something new upon which to base new misrepresentations—men who would like to frighten me, or, at least, to fix upon me the character of timidity and cowardice. They would seize upon almost any letter I could write, as being an *"awful coming down."* I intend keeping my eye upon these gentlemen, and to not unnecessarily put any weapons in their hands.

Yours very truly

A. Lincoln

On November 6, Lincoln was elected to the presidency. In the following month he was reluctant to make further statements about his position on slavery. He did allow Senator Lyman Trumbull to make a quasi-statement in a speech delivered on November 21. However, Trumbull chose not to use the paragraph.

In Trumbull's speech as reported in the Illinois State Journal, November 21, 1860, the following passage is inserted at this point: "It should be a matter of rejoicing to all true Republicans, that they will now have an opportunity of demonstrating to their political adversaries and to the world, that they are not for interfering with the domestic institutions of any of the States, nor the advocates of negro-equality or amalgamation, with which political demagogues have so often charged them. When this is shown, a re-action will assuredly take place in favor of Republicanism, the Southern mind even will be satisfied, the rights of Northern men will be respected, and the fraternal feeling existing in olden times, when men from all parts of the country went forth together to battle for a common cause, against a common enemy, will be restored."

In December, in a letter to Elihu Washburne, Lincoln repeated his opposition to any kind of compromise on the extension of slavery.

Springfield, Ills. Dec. 13. 1860
Hon. E. B. Washburne
My dear Sir. Your long letter received. Prevent, as far as possible, any of our friends from demoralizing themselves, and our cause, by entertaining propositions for compromise of any sort, on "*slavery extention.*" There is no possible compromise upon it, but which puts us under again, and leaves all our work to do over again. Whether it be a Mo. line, or Eli Thayer's Pop. Sov. [popular sovereignty] it is all the same. Let either be done, & immediately filibustering and extending slavery recommences. On that point hold firm, as with a chain of steel.

Yours as ever

A. Lincoln

Lincoln said little about secession in the campaign. Afterward his position slowly became clearer.

Springfield, Ills—Dec. 17—1860
Hon. Thurlow Weed
My dear Sir . . .
I believe you can pretend to find but little, if any thing, in my speeches, about secession; but my opinion is that no state can, in any way lawfully, get out of the Union, without the consent of the others;

and that it is the duty of the President, and other government functionaries to run the machine as it is.

Yours very truly

A. Lincoln—

In mid-February he took a train to his inauguration in Washington, DC. Along the way, Lincoln stressed the need to preserve the Union. His speech at Cleveland was representative of many he gave before his arrival at the capital.

MR. CHAIRMAN AND FELLOW CITIZENS OF CLEVE-LAND: — . . .You have assembled to testify your respect to the Union, the constitution and the laws, and here let me say that it is with you, the people, to advance the great cause of the Union and the constitution, and not with any one man. It rests with you alone. This fact is strongly impressed on my mind at present. In a community like this, whose appearance testifies to their intelligence, I am convinced that the cause of liberty and the Union can never be in danger. Frequent allusion is made to the excitement at present existing in our national politics, and it is as well that I should also allude to it here. I think that there is no occasion for any excitement. The crisis, as it is called, is altogether an artificial crisis. In all parts of the nation there are differences of opinion and politics. There are differences of opinion even here. You did not all vote for the person who now addresses you. What is happening now will not hurt those who are farther away from here. Have they not all their rights now as they ever have had? Do they not have their fugitive slaves returned now as ever? Have they not the same constitution that they have lived under for seventy odd years? Have they not a position as citizens of this common country, and have we any power to change that position? (Cries of "No.") What then is the matter with them? Why all this excitement? Why all these complaints? As I said before, this crisis is all artificial. It has no foundation in facts. It was not argued up, as the saying is, and cannot, therefore, be argued down. Let it alone and it will go down of itself (Laughter).

Lincoln's installation on March 4 was followed by his Inaugural Address. He hoped to convince Southerners that there need not be a war.

My countrymen, one and all, think calmly and *well*, upon this whole subject. Nothing valuable can be lost by taking time. If there be an object to *hurry* any of you, in hot haste, to a step which you would never take *deliberately*, that object will be frustrated by taking time; but no good object can be frustrated by it. Such of you as are now dissatisfied, still have the old Constitution unimpaired, and, on the sensitive point, the laws of your own framing under it; while the new administration will have no immediate power, if it would, to change either. . . .

In *your* hands, my dissatisfied fellow countrymen, and not in *mine*, is the momentous issue of civil war. The government will not assail *you*. You can have no conflict, without being yourselves the aggressors. *You* have no oath registered in Heaven to destroy the government, while *I* shall have the most solemn one to "preserve, protect and defend" it.

I am loath to close. We are not enemies, but friends. We must not be enemies. Though passion may have strained, it must not break our bonds of affection. The mystic chords of memory, stretching from every battle-field, and patriot grave, to every living heart and hearthstone, all over this broad land, will yet swell the chorus of the Union, when again touched, as surely they will be, by the better angels of our nature.

For the next six weeks, President Lincoln was faced with the question of what to do about Fort Sumter in Charleston Harbor. He asked General Winfield Scott and his cabinet members for advice. Most thought it was difficult, if not impossible, to hold the fort. Finally, unwilling to surrender it to the Confederacy, Lincoln instructed Gideon Welles, the secretary of the navy, to send an expedition to supply Sumter.

To Gideon Welles and Simon Cameron
Executive Mansion
March 29, 1861
Honorable Secretary of the Navy [War],
  Sir: I desire that an expedition, to move by sea, be got ready to sail as early as the 6th. of April next, the whole according to memorandum attached; and that you co-operate with the Secretary of War [the Navy] for that object.

Your Obedient Servant
A. Lincoln.

It took six days to make ready the fleet. On April 4 a letter from Secretary of War Simon Cameron to Robert Anderson, the commander of Fort Sumter, informed Anderson of the situation.

To Robert Anderson
[War Department] Washington, April 4. 1861
Sir: Your letter of the 1st. inst. occasions some anxiety to the President.

On the information of Capt. Fox, he had supposed you could hold out till the 15th. inst. without any great inconvenience; and had prepared an expedition to relieve you before that period.

Hoping still that you will be able to sustain yourself till the 11th. or 12th. inst. the expedition will go forward; and, finding your flag flying, will attempt to provision you, and, in case the effort is resisted, will endeavor also to reinforce you.

You will therefore hold out if possible till the arrival of the expedition.

It is not, however, the intention of the President to subject your command to any danger or hardship beyond what, in your judgment, would be usual in military life; and he has entire confidence that you will act as becomes a patriot and a soldier, under all circumstances.

Whenever, if at all, in your judgment, to save yourself and command, a capitulation becomes a necessity, you are authorized to make it.

[Respectfully,
Simon Cameron]

Sumter was attacked by Confederates at 4:30 A.M. on April 12, 1861. The Northern Fleet arrived but was unable to supply the fort. Major Anderson surrendered at 1:30 P.M. on April 13.

Charles Sumner

Sumner recovered his health in late 1859 and resumed his seat in the Senate. The trial of John Brown was over. Like many other Northerners, Sumner was torn between admiration for Brown's courage and anger at his act of violence at Harpers Ferry. Writing to the Duchess of Argyll from Washington on December 20, he explained his position.

My voyage was long & disagreeable. Out of its 16 days I was seasick 12; so that I was most happy to touch the firm earth. I found conversation & the press much occupied by the recent inroad into Virginia [John Brown's raid], of which only a hint had reached England before I embarked. Every where the enterprize has been condemned, while it has seemed almost mad, but the singular courage & character shewn by its author have awakened very general admiration. People find in his conversation & letters since his imprisonment & in his death much of the Covenanter, the Puritan & even the early Xtian [Christian] martyr.

Of course his act must be deplored, & yet it was the pedestal which has shewn to the world a most remarkable character, whose courageous example is destined to influence powerfully our dreadful question.

In May the Republican Party met to choose a presidential candidate. William Seward led on the first two ballots, while Lincoln was nominated on the third. In another letter to the Duchess of Argyll, on May 22, 1860, Sumner explained the political process and his evaluation of the new Republican nominee and his actions.

You may remember that, while in England, I always expressed a doubt whether Seward could be nominated. Perhaps my position enabled me to appreciate better than the public generally something of the impediments. It is hard for a person, who is in the Senate, exposed to bitter opposition & also to jealousies & rivalries, to rally for himself the whole party, & perhaps the very brilliancy of his position is against him. He is too much known, & the neutral men, whose votes are wanted, cannot sustain him. Thus far in our history no man in the Senate has been chosen President.

We have recently seen an illustration of these ideas. Seward was the favorite of earnest Anti-Slavery men, but men representing the great middle states, declared that their voters were not far enough advanced in the Anti-Slavery cause to sustain him. After an active contest he has been defeated in the Convention. I had not expected it, for during the last few weeks I thought there were signs that this conservative interest would yield to the pressure for his nomination. I was mistaken.

This will be a bitter disappointment to Seward, who is now at his home in New York. During all this winter he has regarded himself as the candidate, &, I think, has allowed his mind to be much occupied by the thought.

Mr. Lincoln, who has been selected as the candidate, is a good honest Anti-Slavery man, who was never in the Senate, & has served two years only in the other House. He was brought forward, in order to make sure of carrying certain states at the North—West—Illinois & Indiana—& also Penn., which with Seward would have been doubtful. Those who know him speak of him as a person of positive ability, & of real goodness. But I think it is admitted that he has very little acquaintance with Govt., & is [uninformed?] on Foreign affairs. We think he will be the next President.

Meanwhile the Democratic party is split on the question of Slavery. Should this continue, it will make our victory more certain.

By September, Sumner was certain that Lincoln would be elected. He spoke on behalf of the Republican ticket throughout the fall. On September 3 he wrote again to the Duchess of Argyll.

Meanwhile our Presidential canvass goes on. The election is at the beginning of Nov. Till then newspapers & speakers will be constantly occupied. I do not doubt the result. Lincoln will be chosen. Then, however, will commence a new class of perils & anxieties. The threats of a dissolution of the Union have no force. But it remains to be seen how competent the new Presdt. will be to organize the govt. of a great country. Idealist as I am, I shall prepare myself in advance for many disappointments.—I have sent you in the papers another speech which I have recently made.

Sumner was delighted with the election of Abraham Lincoln but began to worry as Southern states met in conventions and talked of secession. He was willing to let the Cotton States go if that move would end secession. On December 18 he again wrote to the Duchess of Argyll.

The slave states seem as mad as ever. They even hope to enlist Virginia & Maryland before the 4th March so as to prevent the inauguration of the new President at the National Capital. The imbecility of Mr Buchanan is more apparent every day. A vigorous will on his part would have arrested this movement. . . .

One by one the President is losing his Cabinet. One has left him, in order to organize treason at home. Another, Genl. [Lewis] Cass— the oldest & most respectable—has just resigned, because he could not concur with the President in leaving the small garrison at Charleston, amidst the disunionists, without reinforcement. His Administration will end in shame.

The course of the press in Europe is now of vast importance. It may at once make the slave-holders feel the *moral blockade* in which they will be placed.

All that we hear of the new President—who lives 800 miles from Washington—is favorable. He is calm & decided. But before his term commences, dismemberment will have begun, & he will be obliged to meet this or the alternative of civil war.

For myself I know no better rule than to stand firmly by the great principles of justice & to meet the consequences.

A month later, on January 28, 1861, in a letter to his friend Francis W. Bird, Sumner believed that no compromise on slavery should be made: "The question is to be settled now."

I see the future clearly—all bright for Freedom, if the North will only keep its tranquility & firmness. If Mass. begins a retreat, I know not where it will stop. There is nothing of Freedom [at?] the North which will not be endangered. God guard her from any backward step! . . .

Freedom is about to have her greatest peril; —to be followed by results of unspeakable importance. Men will press compromise; but I am happy to believe *in vain. The question is to be settled now.*

Virginia will secede carrying with her all the rest, —except, perhaps, Maryland which will be retained by the national capital. There are some who think this cannot be done; but that the revolution which carries Maryland will seize the capital. Perhaps.

February will be an eventful month.

I have not spoken because I could say nothing which would not be perverted by the compromisers as an attempt to widen the breach. Meanwhile I insist upon an inflexible "No," to every proposition. "No"— "No"—"No"; let the North cry out to every compromise & to every retreat; Then will be days of glory.

After Lincoln's inauguration, Sumner was appointed chairman of the Senate Foreign Relations Committee. He was at the center of power in the making of appointments and was now defending the new administration. He wrote to the Duchess of Argyll on March 19, 1861.

I wish that I had something pleasant to write with regard to our affairs. There is a lull for the moment; but the future is uncertain. Thus far in a most remarkable way events have been so tempered & restrained, as to avoid bloodshed. Can this be always? I hope so; but I am not certain.

Our new Administration comes to power at a moment of unprecedented difficulty. But beyond this, it has an awkwardness, which is partly attributable to its inexperience. I trust, however, that it will shew itself able to deal with events as they occur.

On April 16, Sumner wrote to a fellow senator, William Fessenden: "At last the war has come." He was relieved. The time for action had arrived.

At last the war has come. The day of insincerity & duplicity is now passed, & *all* the cabinet is united in energetic action. It will be needed, for the Slave States will be united.

The Presdt speaks simply & plainly of the state of the country, & I think understands it. As I see more of him I like him better.

George Templeton Strong

In October 1859, John Brown's raid at Harpers Ferry, Virginia, captured Strong's and the nation's attention. Strong saw it first as a legal matter and then as an issue that threatened to split the Union.

October 18 . . . News from Harper's Ferry of a strange transaction. Some sort of insurrection, an armed gang getting possession of the United States Armory: railroad trains stopped, x+y hundred fugitive slaves under arms, government troops, marines, and other forces sent on. Seems to have been a fight this morning (and the rebellion quashed, of course), but the whole transaction is as yet most obscure, and our reports probably much exaggerated.

Six days later he had a better idea of the "insurrection."

October 24, Monday. . . . The Harper's Ferry insurrection (seventeen white men and five niggers) is suppressed (after conquering a town of two thousand inhabitants) by a combined movement of state and federal troops. State of Virginia was awfully frightened. The leader, old Ossowatamie John Brown of Kansas, seems cracked. . . . Insanity won't save him from the gallows. He will undoubtedly be hanged. Were I his jury, I could not acquit him, and twelve terrified Virginians will have little difficulty about a verdict. This insane transaction may possibly lead to grave results.

By early December, Strong, convinced that Brown would be hanged, began to worry that he might become a martyr.

December 2. . . . Old John Brown was hanged this morning; justly, say I, but his name may be a word of power for the next half-century. It was unwise to give fanaticism a martyr. . . . This man Brown's elements of popular available heroism and martyrdom are unhappily numerous.

He began to admire Brown's willingness to die for his convictions. His execution was a severe blow to slavery.

December 4, Sunday. . . . Old Brown's demeanor has undoubtedly made a great impression. Many heroes of the Newgate [Prison, in London] Calendar have died game, as he did; but his simplicity and consistency, the absence of fuss, parade and bravado, the strength and clearness of his letters, all indicate a depth of conviction that one does not expect in an Abolitionist (who is apt to be a mere talker and sophist), and that tends to dignify and to ennoble in popular repute the very questionable church of which he is protomartyr. Slavery has received no such blow in my time as his strangulation. There must be a revolution in feeling even in the terrified State of Virginia, unless fresh fuel be added to the flame, as it well may be, within the month. The supporters of any institution are apt to be staggered and startled when they find that any one man, wise or foolish, is so convicted of its wrong and injustices as to acquiesce in being hanged by way of protest against it. So did the first Christian martyrs wake up senators and landed gentlemen and patrician ladies, *tempore* [in the time of] Nero and Diocletian, and so on. One's faith in anything is terribly shaken by anybody who is ready to go to the gallows condemning and denouncing it.

In the spring of 1860 the Democratic convention met in Charleston, South Carolina, but failed to nominate a candidate. It met again in Baltimore in late June. Strong noted that the party was now in bad shape.

June 21. . . . The Democratic Baltimore Convention is still sitting, and none the easier for sitting. The great old Democratic Party is *in articulo mortis* [at the point of death]; its convention is abolishing of itself, and just on the eve of suicide by dismemberment and disintegration, after the manner of certain star-fishes *(vide* Gosse).* If Douglas be nominated, a Southern limb drops off. If any other man is nominated, a Northwestern ray or arm secedes. Southern swashbucklers demand an ultra-nigger platform that would cost the party every Northern state; unless it be adopted, they will depart to put on their war paint and whet their scalping knives. The worst temper prevails; delegates punch each other and produce revolvers. . . .

Whatever may be the result of this Convention, the Democracy has disgraced itself and damaged itself beyond cure. I half expect that Republicanism and Abe Lincoln will sweep every vestige of that party out of existence.

June 23. Mr. Ruggles came in this evening and reports that the rump of the Convention has nominated Douglas.

The Republican Party met in Chicago on May 16. Strong expected Seward to be the nominee. Instead there was a surprise.

May 19. Thy Nose, O W. H. Seward, is out of joint! The Chicago Convention nominates Lincoln and [Hannibal] Hamlin. They will be beat, unless the South perpetrate some special act of idiocy, arrogance, or brutality before next fall.

Strong was uncertain about the presidential candidates.

May 26. . . I don't know clearly on which side to count myself in. I've a leaning toward the Republicans. But I shall be sorry to see Seward and Thurlow Weed with their tail of profligate lobby men promoted from Albany to Washington. I do not like the tone of the Republican

---

*See Gosse. An English naturalist, Philip Henry Gosse had just published *A Manual of Marine Zoology* (1856).

papers and party in regard to the John Brown business of last fall, and I do not think railsplitting in early life a guarantee of fitness for the presidency.

I could vote for [John] Bell and Mr. Orator [Edward] Everett [on the Constitutional Union ticket]. But I can't support them in their partnership with Douglas, the little giant, for I hold the little giant to be a mere demagogue. As to Breckinridge, the ultra Southern candidate, I renounce and abhor him and his party. He represents the most cruel, blind, unreasoning, cowardly, absolute despotism that now disgraces the earth.

By late October he shifted toward the Republican Party.

October 22. . . . I've nearly made up my mind to deposit a lukewarm Republican vote next month. It is a choice of evils, but we may as well settle the question whether a President can or cannot be chosen without the advice and approval of the slaveholding interests; whether 300,000 owners of niggers have or have not a veto on the popular choice. The question must be settled sooner or later, and we may as well dispose of it now.

On November 2, Strong finally admitted: "I will vote the Republican ticket."

November 2. . . . Think I will vote the Republican ticket next Tuesday. One vote is insignificant, but I want to be able to remember that I voted right at this grave crisis. The North must assert its rights, now, and take the consequences.

On election night, crowds gathered to cheer as Lincoln's victory became certain. Strong was a happy man.

November 7. Lincoln elected. Hooray. Everybody seems glad of it. Even Democrats like Isaac Bell say there will be no disturbance, and that this will quiet slavery agitation at the North.

News from the South continued to be unsettling and the stock market began to sag. Strong hoped that the storm would blow over, although the chances of secession appeared more certain than ever.

November 15. . . . We are generally reconciling ourselves to the prospect of secession by South Carolina, Georgia, Alabama, little Florida, and perhaps Mississippi, too. We shall be well rid of them. Perhaps the prevalence of this feeling—the cordial consent of the North—will keep them from seceding. I think these porcine communities incline to run out of the Union merely because they think we want to keep them in. One should never pull a pig in the direction one wants it to travel. They have long governed us and controlled our votes by the threat of secession. They naturally think secession will be a crushing calamity to the North and the severest punishment they can inflict on us for electing Lincoln.

Nevertheless, Strong did not regret his vote.

December 13. . . . Things look black. But I don't repent of my vote for Lincoln. It contributed to an experiment that tests our Boiler, and it must have undergone that same test very soon had Lincoln been defeated. The question may as well be settled at once whether we have a national government that can sustain itself under pressure, or a mere sham government that must perish whenever a set of semi-barbarous Southerners pronounce against it, with or without reason.

By February 1, 1861, seven states had seceded and planned to meet in Montgomery, Alabama, to form a new "Confederation." Strong was ready to let them go.

January 31. . . . .
One's opinions change fast in revolutionary times. Three months ago, I thought with horror and incredulity of the chance that poor little South Carolina might be mad enough to "secede" alone. Now I am content to let her go, and carry all the Gulf States with her to chaos and the devil, if Maryland, Virginia, Kentucky, Tennessee, and Missouri will but be true to themselves and to the Union, or rather (it's the better word) to the *nation*. Let the barbarians of Mississippi and Alabama rebel if they like, and call it "secession." We can get on without them. The national councils are well rid of their representatives.

There were many differences of opinion about Lincoln's Inaugural Address, but Strong found it satisfactory. It had "a clank of metal in it."

March 5. . . . People differ about Lincoln's Inaugural, but favorable criticism preponderates, though stocks have gone down. At Trust Company Board this morning, Kernochan and other ultra "conservative" Southronizers approved and applauded it as pacific and likely to prevent collision. Maybe so, but I think there's a clank of metal in it. It's unlike any message or state paper of any class that has appeared in my time, to my knowledge. It is characterized by strong individuality and the absence of conventionalism of thought or diction. It doesn't run in the ruts of Public Documents, number one to number ten million and one, but seems to introduce one to *a man* and to dispose one to like him. . . .

March 6. . . . The Inaugural is generally approved by Democrats as well as by Republicans. I think it is going good even at the South, though Southern politicians denounce its "coercion" spirit and vapor horribly. Indications in Virginia and elsewhere are favorable today.

Strong's attention shifted to Fort Sumter in Charleston Harbor. He believed that it would be forced to surrender to the Confederates, which would be a national disgrace. "I'm tempted to emigrate."

March 12 . . . this is a time of sad humiliation for the country. Every citizen of what has heretofore been called the Great Republic of America, every man, woman, and child, from Maine to Texas, from Massachusetts to California, stands lower among the inhabitants of this earth tonight than in March, 1860. We are a weak, divided, disgraced people, unable to maintain our national existence. We are impotent even to *assert* our national life. The country of George Washington and Andrew Jackson (!!!) is decomposing, and its elements reforming into new and strange combinations. I shall never go abroad. That question is settled. I should be ashamed to show my nose in the meanest corner of Europe. Naples and Florence and Milan, now triumphantly asserting their national life and unity, are entitled to look down on Boston and New York. All my right, title, and interest in the Fourth of July and the American Eagle and the Model Republic can be bought at a "low figure."

I'm tempted to emigrate, to become a naturalized British subject and spend the rest of my days in some pleasant sea-side village in the southern counties of old Mother England. It's a pity we ever renounced our allegiance to the British Crown.

In early April there were signs of an effort to reinforce Fort Sumter in Charleston and Fort Pickens in Pensacola, Florida: "Great stir in army and navy."

April 5 . . . There are symptoms of a decisive move by the Administration. Great stir in army and navy. Governor's Island, Fort Hamilton, and Brooklyn Navy Yard full of business. Troops moving, no one knows whither. Ships getting ready for sea in hot haste and sailing with sealed orders, some say for Fort Pickens (Pensacola), and others for Fort Sumter. Abandonment of Fort Sumter is *not* determined on, according to present reports; and Pensacola is to be reinforced anyhow. Bellicose rumors abound today. Colonel Keese and Colonel Henry Scott were off early this morning, I hear. Curtis tells me they were very doleful and despondent half an hour or so at Dr. Van Buren's Thursday evening party. Forsyth, one of the "C.S.A." Commissioners, was expected, but was summoned to Washington by his colleagues yesterday afternoon. All this looks as if things were coming to a crisis. . . .

The sending of the fleet to Charleston meant that the Union would not end "without a struggle."

April 9. Great anxiety for news of our armada, by this time in Southern waters, and general gratification, even among the more moderate Democratic malcontents, at this vigorous move, the first sign of national self-assertion. Many believe the fleet destined for Charleston harbor, and that Fort Sumter is not to be given up after all. At the Law School tonight George Allen, Professors [Francis] Lieber and Bidwell, [Columbia College] President [Charles] King, and others were jubilant over this indication that our great Union, so bragged of for so many years, is not to perish without a struggle.

On April 12 the New York City newspapers announced the Confederate bombardment of Fort Sumter. Strong finally bought a paper.

April 12. . . . Walked uptown with Gouverneur Ogden and that wooden-headed Dunscomb. The streets were vocal with newsboys— "Extry—a *Herald*! Got the bombardment of *Fort Sumter*!!!" We concluded it was probably a sell and that we would not be sold, and declined all invitations to purchase for about four blocks. But we could not stand it longer. I sacrificed sixpence and read the news to Ogden and that galvanized pumpkin Mr. Dunscomb by the light of a corner gas lamp. The despatch is a column long, from Charleston, in substance to this effect. The rebel batteries opened on Sumter at "twenty-seven minutes after four" this morning. Major [Robert] Anderson replied only at long intervals till seven or eight o'clock when he began firing vigorously. At three P.M. (date of telegram) he had produced no serious effect. "No men hurt" in the rebel batteries. No impression made on the "floating battery." Fort Sumter suffering much. "Breaches, to all appearance, are being made." The *Harriet Lane* in the offing, but no other government ships on hand. "Troops are pouring in," and "within an area of fifty miles, where the thunder of the artillery can be heard, the scene is magnificently terrible." That magnificent and terrible sentence sounds as if it belonged to a genuine despatch from the South. Yet I doubt its genuineness vehemently. I can hardly hope that the rebels have been so foolish and thoughtless as to take the initiative in civil war and bring matters to a crisis. If so, they have put themselves in a horribly false position. The most frantic Virginian can hardly assert that this war is brought on by any attempt at "coercion."

Strong began a new chapter in his journal entitled "War" on the next day.

April 13. . . . So Civil War is inaugurated at last. God defend the Right.

Frederick Douglass

Douglass was surprised and disappointed by the nomination of Abraham Lincoln for president. Still he agreed that Lincoln was a radical Republican fully committed to the preservation of the Union.

Mr. Lincoln is a man of unblemished private character; a lawyer, standing near the front rank at the bar of his own State, has a cool, well balanced head; great firmness of will; is perseveringly industrious; and one of the most frank, honest men in political life. He cannot lay claim to any literary culture beyond the circle of his practical duties, or to any of the graces found at courts, or in diplomatic circles, but must rely upon his "good hard sense" and honesty of purpose, as capital for the campaign, and the qualities to give character to his administration.

His friends cannot as yet claim for him a place in the front rank of statesmanship, whatever may be their faith in his latent capacities. His political life is thus far to his credit, but it is a political life of fair promise rather than one of rich fruitage. . . .

There was no doubt in Douglass's mind who should be supported in the fall 1860 election.

. . . But as between the hosts of Slavery propagandism and the Republican party—incomplete as is its platform of principles—our preferences cannot hesitate.

While we should be glad to co-operate with a party fully committed to the doctrine of "All rights to all men," in the absence of all hope of rearing up the standard of such a party for the coming campaign, we can but desire the success of the Republican candidates. . . .

While the election of Lincoln pleased Douglass, he worried that it might mean the end of the abolition movement.

. . . Nevertheless, this very victory threatens and may be the death of the modern Abolition movement, and finally bring back the country to the same, or a worse state, than Benj. Lundy and Wm. Lloyd Garrison found it thirty years ago. The Republican party does not propose to abolish slavery anywhere, and is decidedly opposed to Abolition agitation. It is not even, by the confession of its President elect, in favor of the repeal of that thrice-accursed and flagrantly unconstitutional Fugitive Slave Bill of 1850. It is plain to see, that once in power, the policy of the party will be only to seem a little less yielding to the demands of slavery than the Democratic or Fusion party, and thus render ineffective and pointless the whole Abolition movement of the North. The safety of our movement will be found only by a return to all the agencies and appliances, such as writing, publishing, organizing, lecturing, holding meetings, with the earnest aim not to prevent the extension of slavery, but to abolish the system altogether.

Douglass' Monthly, December 1860

In a review of Lincoln's March 1861 Inaugural Address, Douglass found it a "double tongued document," "vastly below" what it should have been. And its position on slavery was too weak.

Mr. Lincoln opens his address by announcing his complete loyalty to slavery in the slave States, and quotes from the Chicago platform a resolution affirming the rights of property in slaves, in the slave States. He is not content with declaring that he has no lawful power to interfere with slavery in the States, but he also denies having the least "*inclination*" to interfere with slavery in the States. This denial of all feeling against slavery, at such a time and in such circumstances, is wholly discreditable to the head and heart of Mr. Lincoln. Aside from the inhuman coldness of the sentiment, it was a weak and inappropriate utterance to such an audience, since it could neither appease nor check the wild fury of the rebel Slave Power. Any but a blind man can see that the disunion sentiment of the South does not arise from any misapprehension of the disposition of the party represented by Mr. Lincoln. The very opposite is the fact. . . . Some thought we had in Mr. Lincoln the nerve and decision of an Oliver Cromwell; but the result shows that we merely have a continuation of the Pierces and Buchanans, and that the Republican President bends the knee to slavery as readily as any of his infamous predecessors. Not content with the broadest recognition of the right of property in the souls and bodies of men in the slave States, Mr. Lincoln next proceeds, with nerves of steel, to tell the slaveholders what an excellent slave hound he is, and how he regards the right to recapture fugitive slaves a constitutional duty; and lest the poor bondman should escape being returned to the hell of slavery by the application of certain well known rules of legal interpretation, which any and every white man may claim in his own case, Mr. Lincoln proceeds to cut off the poor, trembling Negro who had escaped from bondage from all advantages from such rules. . . .

Though supportive of the new president, Douglass had little hope for the future.

. . . The perusal of it has left no very hopeful impression upon our mind for the cause of our down-trodden and heart-broken countrymen. Mr. Lincoln has avowed himself ready to catch them if they run away, to shoot them down if they rise against their oppressors, and to prohibit the Federal Government *irrevocably* from interfering for their deliverance. With such declarations before them, coming from our first modern anti-slavery President, the Abolitionists must know what to expect during the next four years, (should Mr. Lincoln not be, as he is likely to be, driven out of Washington by his rival, Mr. Jeff. Davis, who has already given out that should Mr. Lincoln attempt to do, what he has sworn to do—namely, execute the laws, fifty thousand soldiers will march directly upon Washington!) This might be taken as an empty threat on the part of the President of the Confederate States, if we did not see with what steadiness, promptness and certainty the rebels have from the first executed all their designs and fulfilled all their promises. A thousand things are less probable than that Mr. Lincoln and his Cabinet will be driven out of Washington, and made to go out, as they came in, by the Underground Railroad. The game is completely in the hands of Mr. Jefferson Davis, and no doubt he will avail himself of every advantage.

Douglass' Monthly, April, 1861

SOUTHERNERS

The events of the eighteen months before the Civil War looked very different to Southerners. To them, John Brown's raid on Harpers Ferry was an attack upon the South by Northern abolitionists. Moreover, national political parties offered little hope that Southern interests would be protected, and the election of Abraham Lincoln as president was their worst nightmare—a black abolitionist president. Without guarantees of their states' rights and especially the protection of slavery, Southerners moved toward secession. There seemed to be no other way open to them.

John J. Crittenden

In January 1860, Crittenden, alarmed at the growing radicalism in the North and South, offered a resolution in the U.S. Senate to gather the views of citizens concerning ways to avoid an impending civil war.

Whereas, The Union is in danger, and, owing to the unhappy divisions existing in Congress, it would be difficult, if not impossible, for that body to concur in both its branches by the requisite majority, so as to enable it either to adopt such amendments to the Constitution as are deemed necessary and proper to avert that danger; and *whereas*, in so great an emergency the opinion and judgment of the people ought to be heard, and would be the best and surest guide to their representatives; therefore

Resolved, That provision ought to be made by law without delay for taking the sense of the people, and submitting to their vote the following resolutions as the basis for the final settlement of those disputes that now disturb the peace of the country and threaten the existence of the Union.

The views of thousands of citizens were gathered in the next year. In December 1860, Crittenden had many resolutions to cite for his peace efforts in early 1861.

Crittenden was one of the founders of the Constitutional Union Party, a faction of old conservatives—primarily former Whigs and members of the American Party. Its platform was "the Constitution and country, the Union of the States, and the enforcement of the laws." Edward Everett of Massachusetts referred to Crittenden as the acknowledged head of the party. The Southerner was urged to allow himself to be nominated for the presidency, but he declined, and Everett and John Bell of Tennessee were chosen for the two top places on the ticket.

Crittenden made numerous speeches and wrote many letters in support of the party. In a letter to several friends in late August 1860 he explained his position.

I agree with you that the state of our public affairs is gloomy, and that it is not easy to find the path of duty through that conflict of parties in which our country is now involved,—parties, some of which seem to be at war not only with themselves, but with the country and the Union. Two fatal symptoms mark the character of two of the presidential parties that now agitate the country,—sectionalism and disunion. The one indirectly, the other directly, endangering the dismemberment of the United States. I mean the Northern party, supporting Mr. Lincoln, and the Southern party, supporting Mr. Breckenridge [*sic*].

The party supporting Bell and Everett is fairly indicated by the name it bears,—the Constitutional Union party. It has arisen out of the troubles and dangers of the country, and for the protection and preservation of our institutions, shaken by the dangerous controversies of collisions of the North and South. This is, in my judgment, the party that is safest and most conservative; and I think its candidates, Bell and Everett, from their position, as well as from their high qualifications and characters, afford to the country the best prospect of security and peace. They will, therefore, have my support, though I admit that the party supporting Mr. Douglas is entitled to be regarded as national, and that he himself has shown a patriotic devotion to the Union.

The election of Lincoln in November alarmed Crittenden. Believing that it meant disunion and war, he began to search for a compromise that would avoid catastrophe. On December 4, 1860, he offered remarks on the imminent danger to the Union.

This Union was established by great sacrifices. The Union is worthy of great sacrifices and great concessions for its maintenance. I trust there is not a senator here who is not willing to yield and to compromise much, in order to preserve the government and the Union. I look forward with dismay and with something like despair to the condition of this country when the Union shall be stricken down and we shall be turned loose again to speculate on the policies and on the foundations upon which we are to establish governments. I look at it, sir, with a fear and trembling that predispose me to the most solemn considerations I am capable of feeling; to search out, if it be possible, some means for the reconciliation of all the different sections and members of this Union, and see if we cannot again restore that harmony, that fraternity, and that union which once existed in this country, and which gave so much of blessing and so much of benefit to all. . . .

Later in the same speech he indicated his view about the right to secede.

. . . I do not agree that there is no power in the President to preserve the Union. If we have a Union at all, and if, as the President thinks, there is no right to secede on the part of any State (and I agree with him in that), I think there is a right to employ our power to preserve the Union. I do not say *how* we should apply it; under what circumstances we should apply it,—I leave all that open. To say that no State has a right to secede, and that it is a wrong to the Union, and yet that the Union has no right to interpose any obstacles to its secession, seems to me to be altogether contradictory.

Two weeks later Crittenden introduced his Constitutional Amendments, which he believed could preserve the Union. His plans included an extension of the Missouri Compromise law, a guarantee of the preservation of slavery where it then existed, and the prohibition of the abolition of slavery in the District of Columbia. He insisted on reestablishing the Missouri Compromise line. In the next few months he asked for consideration of his proposals while presenting petitions from citizens across the country who favored his amendments. The Senate had some discussion of his proposals as well as those of the Peace Convention, which were reported back on March 1, 1861.

Despite these efforts the majority of the senators opposed any compromise that allowed the spread of slavery. Crittenden offered to accept the Peace Convention recommendations, but this move was not sufficient to convince enough senators. Slavery would not be allowed to expand beyond its present boundaries.

On March 2, Crittenden presented his successor, John C. Breckinridge, to the Senate. It was a bittersweet moment for him; he was running out of time to find a satisfactory compromise. In his farewell speech, Crittenden made a last plea for the Union.

Mr. President, it is an admitted fact that our Union, to some extent, has already been dismembered; and that further dismemberment is impending and threatened. It is a fact that the country is in danger. This is admitted on all hands. It is our duty, if we can, to provide a remedy for this. We are, under the Constitution and by the election of the people, the great guardians, as well as the administrators, of this government. To our wisdom they have trusted this great chart. Remedies have been proposed; resolutions have been offered, proposing for adoption measures which it was thought would satisfy the country, and preserve as much of the Union as remained to us at least, if they were not enough at once to recall the seceding States to the Union. We have passed none of these measures. The differences of opinion among senators have been such that we have not been able to concur in any of the measures which have been proposed, even by bare majorities, much less by that two-thirds majority which is necessary to carry into effect some of the pacific measures which have been proposed. We are about to adjourn. We have done nothing. Even the Senate of the United States, beholding this great ruin around them, beholding dismemberment and revolution going on, and civil war threatened as the result, have been able to do nothing; we have done absolutely nothing. . . .

He believed that the major point of disagreement revolved around the extension of slavery into the territory of New Mexico.

. . . All we ask, all that is necessary, I believe, to settle this great mischief that is now going on in the country is, that you shall agree that in that sterile country, where there never can be any number of slaves—you being in power, you having the power to change everything, even the Constitution itself—you having all power, shall now agree with us that the state of things there shall remain as it is—until when? Forever, the gentleman says. He says it establishes it there forever. It is very easy to make speeches in this round and unmeasured sort of language. Let it remain as it is—until when? Until this Territory of more than one hundred thousand square miles—twice as large as the State of New York—shall contain in its borders a hundred thousand, or a hundred and twenty, or a hundred and thirty thousand inhabitants. Will that require all time? For that short period let things remain as they are just now, that we may not be perplexed with the fear of change from your superior power. When it does come in, as it shall do when it has one hundred and thirty thousand inhabitants, then they will be entitled, and we will give them the right to form themselves into a State and be admitted into the Union; and when so admitted, they shall have the right to dispose of this question of slavery just as they please; only, for the sake of peace, let this question rest in silence for that short time. Give the country, who are now greatly alarmed and greatly agitated upon the subject, a little repose. Give them time for their confidence to be restored. Give them time for better feelings to take the place of the bad feelings which now prevail. Cease your action for a moment. Give to the nation breathing-time. . . .

This effort also failed, and Crittenden's last hope was for the Senate to pass a resolution from the House of Representatives to render the Constitution "unchangeable in its negation of power to this government to interfere with slavery in the states." It was less than he wanted, but it offered a ray of light for a better day.

Now, I want to see, at least, this amendment made. May we not agree that all of the amendments which are now offered to it shall, at this last moment, in a spirit of amity and of conciliation, be withdrawn, and that we now have a vote upon the resolution from the House of Representatives? It may not be worth much, but it will show the way to peace; it will show the way to reconciliation; it will show that there is no stern, unreasoning, and blind opposition to every sort of acquiescence in amendments that are desired to the Constitution. It may not be of much effect for the present, or it may be.

It failed, and Crittenden took his leave of the Senate. He moved to the House as a congressman, having been elected as a Unionist.

William Gilmore Simms

Despite the burning down of his Charleston house in the spring of 1860, Simms continued to observe the unfolding political process. In a letter to Congressman William Porcher Miles on July 15, 1860, he analyzed the current situation.

You will, I suppose, have no opposition to Congress; at all events during the term of Breckinridge; and the chances of his election, I hold to be good. The Abolitionists are such an odious tyranny, even among the Northern people themselves that I really believe nothing keeps them now in the ascendant but their own *momentum*. This will be greatly impaired by their rejection of their real leader, & the adoption of a substitute who has no prestige in the popular enthusiasm. There can be no compromise between the *leaders* of the two democratic sections; but there will be a comparative fusion of the masses. I think it probable that in none of the Southern States will an openly avowed Douglas ticket be run—not even in Georgia. They will disguise their support of him, if they give it, under the name of opposition, hoping thus to make a general haul of the discontents—Know Nothings, Old Line Whigs, our outsiders seeking seats inside. The truth is the general *instinct* of the Southern people has become a conviction, that Douglas is secretly if not openly their enemy. The suspicion generally fastened upon him now, to this effect, will not only drive the masses from him, but will serve to make the leaders timid in bringing him forward & urging his claims. I take for granted that Breckinridge will carry all the Southern States, not excepting Tennessee, for I suspect that as the election approaches, every body will see that the only effect of Bell's running will be to throw away the vote of the State or States that may happen to support him. . . . I had a long & earnest talk with [David F.] Jamison, begging him to see [Robert Barnwell] Rhett & urge strenuously upon him what I should say. I told J. that while I was anxious like himself, for the formation of a Southern Confederacy, I saw clearly, not only that such a declaration would drive our people from us (at this time—the fruit is not ripe) but that we should really retard the final day of deliverance. I showed him that no party, no confederacy can be held together by abstract principles simply. The great body of politicians & people require some symbols which they couple with principles, and which they finally receive as a substitute for it. These symbols are our candidates for office. It is absolutely impossible to teach our politicians the value of any sort of principles, separate from their candidates. Hence their willingness to take any platform, however self-stultifying—if you will give them the man for office. I counselled Jamison that whether we elect our candidates or not, the great point gained was to get the South acting together, in a *quasi* independent attitude. . . .

Simms had contempt for the Republican Party, or Black Republicans, as he called them. He expected them to "destroy the prestige of the Union" and prepare the way for Southern success.

Do you not see that this helps forward events wonderfully? Do you not see that before we could relieve the South from the usual subsidization, by National Parties, of their chief men, that we have to sectionalize the country? Do you not see that Black Repubn. has done us this great good in the North. That Providence (*Quos Deus vult perdere prius dementat*) [whom God would ruin he first deprives of reason] has made the brutal partisans of Douglas, absolutely insane, forcing the destruction of the only national (*soi disant*) [so-called] party which remained? Do you not see that these things bring us to the condition, when the South & North, standing asunder, & the former in a decided minority, in every trial of political strength, the latter has no longer motive to conciliate the former, becomes reckless, & in its very wantonness of strength forces final & practical issues upon us. The B.R's having no political sagacity, their fanatics being really in the ascendant, must, under the goading insistence of their conscious strength, tear every thing to tatters. No doubt they will split up & divide, in time, & new parties will form which will, one or other, affiliate with the South, or try to do so. But they will first have weaned us from them; they will have destroyed the prestige of the Union; they will have taught us to hate if not to fear them; and their very attempts at affiliation then, will teach us their dependence upon us, and how much we may do for ourselves, if independent. We shall learn a thousand things of our own strength in the meanwhile, & our politicians will see that their chances for place & power, will be even more numerous in a Southern than in a confederacy of the whole as before.

On October 16, 1860, in a letter to James Lawson, he predicted that Lincoln's election would spark Southern secession. One should quietly prepare for this possibility.

Our elections are just over, and our State has elected almost the whole Legislature, secession men. If Lincoln is elected, a convention will be immediately called, and South Carolina will secede from the Confederacy, even though she goes alone. But she will not go alone. She will be followed by Alabama, Mississippi, Georgia, Florida, Louisiana, & more slowly by North Carolina, Virginia, Tennessee, Kentucky, &c. You may rest assured that all this is going to happen just as I tell you. There is but one feeling at the South now, except among the Yankee agents & shopkeepers and they will need to keep shut mouths. Get in all the money (cash) you can, & keep it safe. Look quietly & cautiously to your investments. . . .

The day before the election, in a letter to James Lawson dated November 5, 1860, he predicted that South Carolina would not wait for an overt act but would secede alone.

In respect to the political future, our excitement grows rather than diminishes. Our Legislature meets this day to elect Electors. *They will probably continue in session in order to be prepared for Lincoln's election.* The moment he is known to be elected, they will call a convention of the people. The Legislature is almost wholly for secession & they are fresh from the people. I have been recently on a journey of 200 miles in our State, on its Northern border. The excitement is great & concentrated. The minute men are forming & arming in all directions. South Carolina is putting her house in order; and my impression is that she will secede *alone*, leaving to the other States to follow. She will await no overt act. Will not wait Mr. Lincoln's Inauguration. She will be out of the Union by the 1st. Jany. And I, too, counseled this very policy. So all my friends. Leading politicians of the other States counsel it, & say that the rest will follow. One word more. See to your stocks. *My opinion is that Rail Road stocks in the old states will be the best in all bad conjunctures.*

In the days after the election he predicted that "at least five states will secede before January." Two days before South Carolina's convention he was certain that it would secede. It did, by a vote of 169 to 0. In a letter to a friend he explained the future as he saw it.

. . . our policy is to shed no blood: To throw every thing of responsibility on the Black Republicans. We urge a legitimate right to secede & will secede. The blood upon their heads. We have 2,000,000 bales of Cotton, waiting England, who must have it, & will open all blockades for it. Georgia will follow S.C. & so will Alabama, & Mississippi, & Louisiana & all the Cotton States, & so will Virginia & Maryland & even New Jersey. We will precipitate no struggle if let alone. If vext, we shall discriminate against the North, in importations, and if blockaded, we will let loose a thousand privateers, under letters of Marque, and—England—must have our Cotton. Peace is the best policy for all parties. But we are prepared for war. Must have free ports—free from blockade.

For the next few months he wrote many of the editorials for the Charleston Mercury *on "public affairs." All were unsigned. Later, in November 1861, he admitted that he had written "nearly all the articles on public affairs" published in the newspaper for the last eight months.*

Simms was pleased with the preparations by Southern planters for the war and the willingness of so many men to volunteer to fight.

In the country, there is scarce a planter who has not meat & bread for himself, people & slaves, to last one year. I have, for example,—& my crop was a shorter one than that of most of my neighbours,—about 3000 bushels of Corn; 8000 lbs Bacon, 200 head of Hogs, 80 of Cattle; 25 Goats, 22 Sheep, 100 of poultry, besides rice, potatoes, & other *stores.*

And we are now planting corn which will be ready for use in the last of July or middle of August. I have 150 acres of rye & oats growing; have several tons of Fodder & Hay cured & put away. So much for starvation. . . .

Now, there has been no draft—not a man has been drafted. All are volunteers. We have more volunteers than we want or care to feed. More than 30,000 have volunteered in S.C. alone, & in the Confederacy, there are more than 200,000 ready to take the field & eager for a call . . . never were a people better satisfied than those of S.C.

In early April, Simms traveled to Charleston to see friends and observe the firing on Fort Sumter. His dream of secession began in the 1840s and now it was realized. It was a special time for him.

To Margaret Maxwell Martin
[c. April 15, 1861]

I have just returned from an eight days' absence in Charleston, where I witnessed the bombardment of Fort Sumter. I congratulate you on the expulsion of the enemy from the sacred soil of Carolina, now *doubly* sacred to you since your first-born was one of the first sacrifices in its redemption. May his memory blossom anew in your hearts with love, to mature hereafter to a glorious ripeness, while it remains enshrined in the tender regrets of his countrymen! God is surely with us, my dear friend, thus far, in our progress to independence. May we never, by any vain exultation leading to presumptuous confidence, forfeit the powerful favor of the mighty King of all nations who hath thus far been our shield and strength in the day of our trial. . . . Let us only feel how great are God's mercies to us, and so act as not to forfeit them, and the ordinary thought of our waking hours is prayer sublimed for heaven.

The Jones Family

Young Charles Jones was busy: "the duties of an attorney in full practice are very engrossing and demand uninterrupted attention." He was so occupied that he failed to mention the Dred Scott Decision or the Lincoln-Douglas debates in his correspondence. He continued, however, to advise his parents on a number of economic matters including the buying and selling of slaves. There was little mention of anything beyond their personal lives until John Brown's raid. Then everything changed.

The attack on Harpers Ferry greatly disturbed his father, and on November 7, 1859, the Reverend Charles Jones wrote an angry letter to his son about the "Harpers Ferry affair."

The Harpers Ferry affair proves to be more serious than at first it appeared to be—not in reference to the Negro population, for that had nothing to do with it; but in reference to the hostility of large numbers of men of all classes in the free states to the slaveholding states, even unto blood, and their readiness to aid and abet such attempts with counsels and money, and to employ reckless agents to carry them out. There is a covert, cowardly, assassin-like heart in these men. Why do they not arm and come to the field in open day? From the tone of the abolition press in the free states, both secular and religious, there is great sympathy for the prisoners at Harpers Ferry. Some go so far as to justify the act, and only condemn the time and manner of it! The whole abolition crusade which has been preached for thirty years *ends in the sword.* The volunteering of counsel for the prisoners from the free states is another proof of sympathy in their crime, and an insult to the justice of the South.

. . . There is no place left for forbearance—no ground for compromises. The magnanimity of the South must not be exercised towards public criminals of the deepest dye, but towards herself in all her greatest and best interests, and towards our common country. Such sparks as these, struck to produce a universal conflagration, should be stamped out immediately. Such enemies should be met and overwhelmed without quarter in a moment. A decision of this sort is demanded by our circumstances, and brings the free and the slave states to a perfect understanding on the whole subject.

These are my sentiments, and I believe they are the sentiments of every intelligent and truehearted citizen in the Southern states. And I am sure they will not only be entertained but acted upon whenever there may be occasion for it. If the conservative and loyal men of the free states, who we believe do now possess the power, are willing and ready to rule down this spirit of treasonable and violent aggression upon an unoffending and invaluable section of our country, we shall be most happy to see them do it. But if not, then let them know that the fortunes of the American republic are embarked in one vessel, and neither stem nor stern shall be broken up without damage and loss of the whole; and that they, secure as they may esteem themselves to be, will surely, and to their heart's content, come in for a full draught of the cup of political ruin!

In the fall of 1860, Charles was elected mayor of Savannah. It came as a surprise, but he accepted the honor.

My dear Father and Mother,

By today's papers you will see that I have been elected mayor of the city of Savannah. This appointment was on my part *wholly unsolicited*, the nomination having been made during my absence from the city. It was also a nomination and ratification by the citizens of Savannah irrespective of party. Under these circumstances I did not feel at liberty to decline, and must admit that the compliment of the election comes home with peculiar effect, conferred as it is by the city of my birth, of my choice—a city, too, whose soil covers the honored dust of Great-Grandfather. . . .

As the new mayor of Savannah he was concerned about the rapidly changing political scene and the upcoming presidential election.

October 18, 1860 . . . The doubt which attends any attempt to conjecture what another month may bring forth in the political and social status of our country exerts in all probability its depressing influence. The election of Lincoln seems now almost a fixed fact, in view of the recent advices received from Pennsylvania, Ohio, and Indiana. The Republicans claim New York by a clear majority of forty thousand. Should Lincoln be elected, the action of a single state, such as South Carolina or Alabama, may precipitate us into all the terrors of intestine war. I sincerely trust that a kind Providence, that has so long and so specially watched over the increasing glories of our common country, may so influence the minds of fanatical men and dispose of coming events as to avert so direful a calamity.

His father saw few problems with Lincoln's election. There should be no cause for violence since the Southern states had "the right of self-government."

October 27, 1860 . . . I do not apprehend any very serious disturbance in the event of Lincoln's election and a withdrawal of one or more Southern states, which will eventuate in the withdrawal of all. On what ground can the free states found a military crusade upon the South? Who are the violators of the Constitution? Will the conservatives in the free states make no opposition? If the attempt is made to subjugate the South, what prospect will there be of success? And what *benefit* will accrue to all the substantial interests of the free states? . . . Is not the right of self-government on the part of the people the cornerstone of the republic? Have not fifteen states a right to govern themselves and withdraw from a compact or constitution disregarded by the other states to their injury and (it may be) their ruin? But may God avert such a separation, for the consequences may in future be disastrous to both sections. Union if possible—but with it we must have *life, liberty, and equality.*

Ten days later Lincoln and Hannibal Hamlin were elected as president and vice president of the United States. Charles was uncertain about the future.

The telegrams announce the fact of Lincoln's election by a popular vote! South Carolina has today virtually seceded. Judge [Andrew G.] Magrath of the U.S. Circuit Court for the District of South Carolina, Hon. William F. Colcock, collector of the port of Charleston, and other government officers have resigned, and we learn that the [state's] Palmetto flag will be hoisted on the morrow. A meeting of the citizens here is called for tomorrow evening. We are on the verge of Heaven only knows what.

Mary Jones, in a letter to her son, expressed her conviction that the next step would be the formation of a "Southern confederacy."

It is a new era in our country's history, and I trust the wise and patriotic leaders of the people will soon devise some united course of action throughout the Southern states. I cannot see a shadow of reason for civil war in the event of a Southern confederacy; but even that, *if it must come*, would be preferable to submission to Black Republicanism, involving as it would all that is horrible, degrading, and ruinous. "Forbearance has ceased to be a virtue"; and I believe we could meet with no evils out of the Union that would compare to those we will finally suffer if we continue in it; for we can no longer doubt that the settled policy of the North is to crush the South.

Charles's father, however, wrote on November 15, 1860, that there would be a war, but the South would prevail "if the Southern states are united."

A nation to be born in a day, without a struggle, would be a wonder on earth. If the Southern states resolve on a separate confederacy, they must be prepared for any emergency, even that of war with the free states; as their arrogance and confidence in their power may urge them to attempt our subjugation—although I do not fear it if the Southern states are united. We have a heavy Northern element, and a Southern element Northernized, to contend with in our own borders, and may perhaps lead to some embarrassment; but the majority the other way is so decided that it cannot—at least it is so to be hoped—effect much. Certainly we do need "the prayers of the pious and the wisdom of the wise."

Mary Jones felt an "indescribable sadness" with the imminent dissolution of the Union, yet she wrote her son that she could see no alternative.

An indescribable sadness weighs down my soul as I think of our once glorious but now dissolving Union! Our children's children— what will constitute their national pride and glory? *We* have no alternative; and necessity demands that we now protect ourselves from entire destruction at the hands of those who have rent and torn and obliterated every national bond of union, of confidence and affection. When your brother and yourself were very little fellows, we took you into old Independence Hall [in Philadelphia]; and at the foot of Washington's statue I pledged you both to support and defend the Union. *That Union* has passed away, and you are free from your mother's vow.

After reading Lincoln's Inaugural Address carefully, Charles admitted to his father that he still remained uncertain about its meaning.

Lincoln's inaugural is before us, and a queer production it is. What does it mean? It means this, and it means that; and then it may mean neither. That sly fox Seward, I expect, has had the shaping of it.

For the next month, Mayor Charles Jones prepared the defenses at Savannah. He expected some type of hostilities to occur soon.

We are all busily engaged in getting our defenses in order, in anticipation of hostile demonstrations on the part of the United States. You have seen the telegrams of yesterday. Even at this date we are at a loss to know the purposes of Lincoln.

On April 12, 1861, the South fired on Fort Sumter, which surrendered the following day. Five days later Charles Jones worried about "the fanatical administration at Washington." He had no doubt about the Southern response.

Can you imagine a more suicidal, outrageous, and exasperating policy than that inaugurated by the fanatical administration at Washington? The Black Republicans may rave among the cold hills of their native states, and grow mad with entertainment of infidelity, heresies, and false conceptions of a "higher law"; but Heaven forbid that they ever attempt to set foot upon this land of sunshine, of high-souled honor, and of liberty. It puzzles the imagination to conceive the stupidity, the fanaticism, and the unmitigated rascality which impel them to the course which they are now pursuing. I much mistake the policy of this Confederacy and the purposes of our worthy President (at once soldier and statesman) if in the event of our pure rivers and harbors being blockaded by Northern fleets, a great Southern army is not put in motion, attracting to itself the good and true men of every section, whose object it shall be to redeem the tomb of [George] Washington from the dominion of this fanatical rule, and to plant the standard of this Confederacy even upon the dome of the capitol at Washington [DC]. This is a favorite scheme with President Davis, and he has brave men such as Major [Ben] McCulloch and General [Gideon J.] Pillow to sustain him in carrying the idea into practical effect.

Three days later the Reverend Charles Jones wrote to his son of his great distrust of the United States. He could also see God's hand controlling the events. God, of course, was on the Southern side.

The conduct of the government of the old United States towards the Confederate States is an outrage upon Christianity and the civilization of the age, and upon the great and just principles of popular sovereignty which we have contended for and embraced for near an hundred years, and brands it with a deserved and indelible infamy. We have nothing left us but to work out our independence, relying, as our good President instructs us, upon "A just and superintending Providence." . . . The Lord keep you, my dear son, and strengthen you to serve Him and to fear His great and holy name, and to discharge your various and responsible duties to your family and country with cheerfulness and self-possession, with purity and integrity, and with intelligence, decision, and kindness. Seek to do all things well, and everything in its proper time.

Augustus Benners

On May 29, 1860, Benners lost another child, James Marbury, at "1 year and nine months old."

June 4th 1860 Again it has pleased our Heavenly father to visit us with severe affliction by the death of our sweet little darling James Marbury Benners. He died at Arcola May 29 after a sickness of four weeks. He was taken on the 1st May with dysentery—and the Doctor was called in—. . . in vain were remedies applied—the darling child lay like a patient little sufferer ebbing his life away—and by his ineffable beauty & sweetness winding around our hearts if possible more strongly than ever. He was a great favorite with all—just beginning to talk and his little voice when he would say I, I Ride the last words he ever spoke—was melody itself. He was 1 year and nine months old at the time of his death—he was brought up from Arcola on Wednesday the 30th May & buried in my lot in the town burying ground south of his little brothers grave—there my two sweet little ones await the last trump when they shall come forth to be clothed with immortal bodies. His early death has removed him from a world of sin and sorrow to a safe home in Heaven—and to the eye of reason we should not weep for him—but oh! the pang of parting with our darling little one is bitter—his death has made a large void in our home circle—and a heavy sorrow on our hearts—may we have Gods grace to enable us so to live that when we come to die we may go to meet our dear departed children at Gods right hand—For Christ's sake Amen!

The election of Abraham Lincoln as president in the fall distressed him. Furthermore, "S. Carolina seceded on the 20th Dec."

Dec 29 1860 . . . The season is one of deep gloom—the election of Lincoln president of the U. States has produced such intense dissatisfaction in the Southern States that revolution is imminent. S. Carolina seceded on the 20th Dec and the news was rec'd by telegraph last night that the Fort Moultrie had been abandoned by [Major Robert] Anderson and the U States officers and set on fire we are on the eve of great events. How they will terminate God only knows. in war and anarchy I much fear. In God is our trust.

The news was even worse nine days later: "Civil war seems imminent."

Jany 7th 1861 The year has gone out & the new one been ushered in amidst the deepest excitement and gloom. The election of Lincoln by the Black Republicans of the North has been considered as the culminating of intended aggressions on the institutions of the Southern States. S. Carolina by her convention seceded from the Union on the 20th Dec. and to day the convention of Alabama meets to do as I believe the very same thing—Civil war seems imminent every mail comes freighted with exciting intelligence and mens minds are filled with gloomy apprehensions for the future—The forts at Charleston have been taken, fort Sumter is besieged by S. Carolina and the forts of Ala. have also been captured. Where it will end God only knows may he give us courage & wisdom to do our duty as men.

A few days later Benners noted that there was the firing of guns at Fort Sumter.

Jany 16th The U. States sent the Star of the West to reinforce Major Anderson at fort Sumter—on the 11th she was fired into by S. Carolina from Morris Island and hit 3 times trying to get in—she retired—The expectation is now that U. States will send more troops with larger ships of war and the battle will begin—It is hard to give any idea of the distressing gloom and sadness that pervades all classes. Alabama decided on the 11 Jany—Mississippi has also & Florida—our Company of L. A. Guards [Greensboro Guards, 5th Alabama Infantry Regiment] went last Sunday to Fort Morgan. it was a sad parting and many a brave spirit may be lost in battling for his countrys right

The next month, he tried unsuccessfully to attend the Southern Congress in Montgomery.

Feb 11th I started with Judge Moore on last Friday to Montgomery to attend Southern Congress which met on the 4th. We got left by Cars at Newbern and I went to my plantation and spent the night. They were reported all well, but had had a tremendous rain friday previous 1st Feb. Herrin was sowing oats on the land between the well and the house—had received 50 bushels from Mobile via Selma. The roads were in bad condition— next day took cars to Selma and having learned sessions of Southern Congress were secret and being pretty well worn out in Selma waiting for a boat we returned on Sunday— Mr Lyon from the legislature & Price were in the Cars.

Benners's last diary entry before the war was on March 7, 1861. The newspapers reported Lincoln's Inaugural Address.

March 7th Commenced planting corn at plantation on Monday March 4th. On Wednesday March 6th we had a white frost and again this morning—much uneasiness is felt lest the fruit has been killed by the cold. Tom brot up a load of fodder on yesterday—Lincolns inaugural was received last night and is considered very warlike. Probably before new hostilities have begun—perhaps at fort Sumter—he denies the right of secession and says that he must collect the revenues and possess the forts—The prospect of a war is very imminent—

There is no further mention of the events leading to the outbreak of war.

Tryphena Fox

On New Year's Day 1860, Tryphena wrote to her mother in Massachusetts of a happy Christmas on the plantation, a special gift from her husband, and the ongoing problem with Susan.

Last Sunday—Christmas—was one of the most lovely Sabbaths I ever spent—warm as many a June day is with you, with that peculiarly delicious hazy atmosphere known only during our Indian Summer. The day passed very happily to me for I spent it, trying to make the others happy—You know the negroes look upon it as their especial holiday and always expect a "Christmas gift" from Master & Mistress. Though I could neither go or send to town this year & was too sick the week before to make anything for them, I managed to please all. Old Reuben was delighted with a whole suit of his master's clothes—(quite good ones which I had been saving all the year for him) from me, a silver dollar, from his master & a dime from "Miss Fanny". I gave Susan a new pr. of shoes—($1.50)—and a paper box, containing needles, thread, tape, hooks & eyes & buttons and a worked linen collar which I made for myself but it did not fit me nicely. That blue basque of Emma's which you gave me & which I packed away last spring just fitted Adelaide & made her walk five times faster than ever I knew her to, when in the greatest haste; and it is really a very pretty little garment for her to wear as "dress up". Maria in one of her Miss Fannys *yellow* aprons of last summer & Buddy in a bonnet, strutted about the yard all the afternoon not only to their own amusement but very much to Dr. R's & mine. I gave Ann a good muslin dress & checked skirt for next summer with which she was quite delighted. . . .

For Christmas present, Dr. R—brot me this new portfolio on which I am writing my first letter—nicely gilded & well filled with paper, envelopes &c, &c. and a pretty 8 day clock which cost 7 dollars—an article I have *wanted & needed* ever since my marriage. I dont know that it will make any difference with my work, for the servants are just so slow anyhow but it will be company for me. This morning I had them all called at five & it is now after seven & yet Susan has not brot the breakfast in & the washing will be behind-hand all day. But it is freezing cold & I must take it easy. No use trying to get much out of a darkey on a frosty morning—They only know how to hover over the fire.

Two weeks later she had another baby boy, but he soon died. It was one of her saddest days: "I never, never loved anything as I did him."

Feb 1st 1860. This is the first day I have sat up. It is two weeks yesterday since my poor little baby was born—it struggled along until Tuesday morning the 30th when it breathed its last in my arms. It seemed very well until the ninth day when he began to grow poor & pale & when the nurse dressed it she found a large *boil* under its right jaw halfway between the chin & ear. Dr R— lanced it & about a tea-spoon-ful & a half of matter ran out. It continued to discharge until the day before he died. The poor little thing evidently suffered inexpressibly from the abscess & was wasted to skin & bones when it died. I could not have wished it to live under such circumstances, but it was hard for me to give him up. He was a beautiful child & I never, *never loved* anything as I did him. He was my summer's wish & all the dreary sick days of winter I was only consoled with the hope of soon having a boy baby to love & relieve the loneliness of my many solitary hours. But he is come & gone & life will resume the same old routine Friday & only the memory of his fleeting life will remain with its deep love & keen anguish to remind me that the monotony has been broken.

In need of rest after the loss of her child, Tryphena went to Washington, Mississippi, for two weeks of relaxation away from the "household chores, no servants to look after." When she returned, there were still difficulties with Susan.

March 17, 1860 . . . Susan managed to be quite smart the Tuesday after I left—she was to have done all the work for Sister E— & the Dr during my absence, but concluded she would *have a baby*—a fine mulatto boy. As a negress could not be hired to fill her place Emily had to do all the housework & nursing herself during the whole two weeks of my visit. I not hearing from home at all, knew nothing of it or I should have been very much worried & hurried back. When the child was a week old, Sister went to spend the day with Mrs Borland & Susan neglected the child & it took cold & died from the effect of it the day after my return in my arms—I feel badly about its death for it was a pretty baby & I took a fancy to it on account of its being so near the age mine would have been, but for its premature birth. We are getting along just as we can for the present—Maria does pretty well in the kitchen with my showing [her] & I do the housework. I think Maria is going to make me a most excellent servant. She is young & heedless but a little training & teaching will make her all I can want & save me many a step & hour's labor. She is very apt; her great fault is—want of order. Everything is left just where she last used it. . . .

I hope there are better & happier days in store for me—it seems as though there was never any true enjoyment of the present moment here at home; always something to deprive me of rest & peace. But is it not so with everybody?

After the election of Lincoln she was concerned about "Northern opinions or move-ments" but was not worried about the possibility of violence from slaves in her area.

Dec. 16th, 1860. . . . As a ride takes me by the P.O. this morning, I write you a few lines, though no answer has reached me to my last. Neither our Northern papers or letters have been received regularly since Lincoln's election—there has not been *one* number of the "Pittsfield Sun"—I do not think the subscription has run out: can you inquire about it for me? We know nothing of Northern opinions or movements; the Secessionists are strong in number & energetic in action here.

Father Fox, from whom we heard last night, says the same in regard to the Mississippi people & has had no doubt, but we shall soon be involved in a civil war. . . .

We do not consider ourselves in any danger from the negroes *alone*—A Free negro is to be hung at the Court-house of this Parish, this month for attempting to excite insurrection.—There has been nothing of the kind in this vicinity. I send you the Governor's message, that you may have some idea of what is going on here, and I will send you some of the pamphlets which are freely distributed throughout every Southern State.

Tryphena's last letter to her mother before the outbreak of the war on March 29, 1861, made no reference to the impending crisis. Rather, she wrote about her many family guests (Aunt Ellen and Cousin Mary) and hopes of visiting her mother in the summer and bringing her back home. However, most of the letter dealt with the burdens of owning slaves.

We shall probably sell [Maria] as soon as she is found—the great trouble with her being her fondness for *running out nights*; I regret losing my year's training for she had certainly improved in almost every respect, until she suited me very well indeed—as well as any black person I ever expected to find. I had taught her after a great deal of pains & many an hour's hard work on my part, to sweep & dust & arrange a room nicely, to wash & iron fine clothes, particularly shirts, to cook cakes & custards & jellies & cut out & make quite a variety of garments. She was one whom I could depend upon if I were sick or away from home & could feel that she would keep house & attend to everything just as I would myself; that is if she chose to do it & not run out nights & sleep all day as she was very fond of doing, too fond to suit me when I had a house full of company & was anxious to keep it in decent order & have the work done at a proper time. The Saturday morning that she left I sent her into the parlor to make a fire & arrange the room She was gone a long time & when I went to see if she was not most done & ready to make a fire in Aunt Ellen's room, not a thing was touched & she lay sprawled out on the hearth-rug *fast asleep*. I punished her for it, & she did tolerably well until night when after supper I ordered her to make haste & wash the supper dishes, she left them until within a few minutes of nine, when we began to talk of retiring & I went to the back door to see if everything was right & in good order for the night, all the buildings shut up & the keys brought in—what should I find but all the dirty dishes standing untouched & she in the kitchen very busy talking to Susan. I disliked to say any thing to her master he whips her so severely, so I punished her again myself—not very severely & she promised to do better for she had troubled me all the week. I thought no more about it but went to bed. She brought the key to the back door & made up her bed in the hall, but the next morning when called she was missing having got out through the Office window, the only place that was left unlocked. Some men helped her out, for we found their tracks under the window in the soft mud. We have had a good many different reports about her, but all attempts to find her have proved failures. . . .

I wish you could see us all or we you—but what plans do you think are laid for the future? Of course we can only *hope* they may be fulfilled, for many changes may occur before two summers shall have come & gone. Brother James graduates two years from this month, living with us when not attending lectures, & after graduating coming here to attend to Dr R—s practice while *we* take a trip & spend the summer North! It is a long time to look forward to but it will pass quickly & if nothing happens, the plan is a very good one & easily carried out. & Dr R— will help you until then & then you must all come back with us.

The war interrupted their plans. Mother and daughter would not see each other until 1877, when the Foxes finally traveled to Massachusetts.

Keziah Goodwyn Hopkins Brevard

Keziah Brevard in 1860 was a fifty-seven-year-old widow who owned and ran a plantation with over two hundred slaves. In the middle of September she was especially concerned about the possibility of a slave insurrection.

15th Saturday . . . This night, if reports are true, had been set apart to cut us off—Oh God, because we own slaves—Lord thou knowest our hearts—save us for a calmer end & let us never cease to think & to bless thee for thy loving kindness—Lord, save this our good country & make us *all* & *every one*, bond & free, to love thee & do thy will as good servants—*we* are *all* thy servants—all in thy hands—Oh save us.

Continuing frustration with her slaves, especially those serving her in her house, caused her constant annoyance. She was distressed by their "impudence."

18. . . . . Oh my God I have so many little things to unnerve me—I wish I was prepared to die & could go to my God. I wish to be kind to my negroes—but I receive little but impudence from Rosanna & Sylvia—it is a truth if I am compelled to speak harshly to them—after bearing every thing from them I get impudence—Oh my God give me fortitude to do what is right to these then give me firmness to go no farther—At my death it is my solemn desire that Tama—Sylvia— Mack—Maria & Rosanna be sold—I cannot think of imposing such servants on any one of my heirs.

A month later news of a political rally in Columbia inspired her indignation over Northerners' desire to free Southern slaves.

13th Saturday . . .—it is time for us to shew the rabble of the North we are not to be murdered in cold blood because we own slaves—there are no doubts but thousands would have prefered being born in this beautiful country without the encumbrance—but they have been transmitted down to us & what can we do with them?—free such a multitude of half barbarians in our midst—no—no—we must sooner give up our lives than submit to such a degradation—From the time I could reason with myself I wished there was a way to get rid of them—but not free them in our midst yet. They are not prepared for freedom, many of them set no higher value on themselves than the beasts of the field do—I know a family in five miles of me where there are six women who have & have had children for thirty years back & not one of them but have [been] bastards & only one ever had a husband. . . . That wretch John Brown—if he had come as one of christ's Apostles & preached down sin he might have been the instrument of good—but he come to cut our throats because we held property we could not do otherwise with—was preposterous—Did God set the children of Israel to cutting their masters' throats to flee [free] them from bondage—no—no—he brought them out of Egypt in his own peculiar way & he can send Africa's sons & daughters back when he knows they are ready for their exode. I own many slaves & many of the females are of the lowest cast—making miserable their own fellow servants by medling with the husbands of others— . . . This is a dirty subject—& had I not thought of those cruel abolitionists who wish to free such people in our midst I would not have spoken this truth here.

Brevard learned with horror of the election of Abraham Lincoln on November 9. She refused to even consider the freeing of slaves "in our midst."

Oh My God!!! This morning heard that Lincoln was elected—I had prayed that God would thwart his election in some way & I prayed

for my *Country*—Lord we know not what is to be the result of this—
but I do pray if there is to be a crisis—that we all lay down our lives
sooner than free our slaves in our midst—no soul on this earth is more
willing for justice than I am, but the idea of being mixed up with free
blacks is *horrid*!! I must trust in God that he will not forget us as unworthy as we are—Lord save us—*I would give my life to save my Country*.
I have never been opposed to giveing up slavery if we could send them
out of our Country— . . . but the die is cast—"Caesar has past the
Rubicon." We now have to act, God be with us is my prayer & let us all
be willing to die rather than free our slaves in their present uncivilized
state.

*By December she was certain that secession would indeed occur. Afterward, she
hoped, all the slaves could be returned to Africa.*

Monday 10th . . . I hope & trust in God as soon as Secession is
carried out—we of the South begin to find a way to get all the Negroes
sent back to Africa & let the generations to come after us live in more
peace than we do—I can't see how we are ever to be safe with them in
our midst-—I wish every soul of them were in Africa contented in
their own homes—let us begin on corn bread & live in peace & security—as long as they are here & number so many more than the whites
there is no safety any way—Men of the South—I fear our end is near
& the Yankeys will glory over their work. I do hate a Northern Abolitionist—Lord forgive me—but who can love those whose highest ambition is to cut our throats.

*Late in the month federal troops stationed at Fort Moultrie in Charleston were
sent to Fort Sumter. This move greatly alarmed her.*

28 Friday Mrs. James H. Adams with Janie, Laura, Carry, Ellen &
Jim spent the day with Goodwyn & myself—Randy's little Jane with
them. They brought this morning's paper with them, the "Guardian,"
from it we read that Ft. Moultrie had been evacuated on the 27th &
the Ft. was on fire at 5 O'clock thursday evening. God alone knows the
design of it—we are all in the dark as to the future—Oh that this strife
could be ended for the good of the whole country—I know not what
to think, certainly awful troubles seem hanging over us—

In early January 1861, President Buchanan sent the Star of the West, *an unarmed merchant ship, to reinforce the Union forces at Fort Sumter in Charleston Harbor. When fired upon, the vessel withdrew.*

Thursday 10 . . . Last night we received the news of the Star of the West—from Charleston—O God put it into the hearts of the Northern people to do right & let us once more shew to the world we can yield to all that is right in thy sight—We have never invaded Northern rights—all we want is *right* in its plainest sense.

The future looked very bleak to Brevard. It meant civil war and bloodshed.

Wednesday 30 Oh my God I see nothing ahead but trouble—Our country will pass from bad to worse—the South never would be united or it might have sent Douglass [Stephen Douglas] instead of Lincoln— if she could have been united 'twould have been far better for her—I do hope if we have Civil war—that God will take me before the first drop of blood is shed—O God canst thou, wilt thou not spare us—I do not say we deserve it—no—no—slavery ever will make trouble I care not where found—I wish I had been born without them with a sufficiency to keep me from want in as good a country as this with our liberal religion—

By late February, Brevard believed that the Lincoln administration "would be a dire one to the South." And the South was helpless to do anything about it.

February 28th . . . Now what of my country?—a few short days & we shall hear from Lincoln's lips what we may expect—if he makes war on us the whole body of men No. & So. should rise against him & make a blow at the man himself who would dare to bring such trouble on this land won by the blood of our fore fathers from British encroachments. If the N. should be let loose on us, the fanatics will run mad with joy & tongues cannot tell where the scene will end—if ever, until a dark age sinks the nation into brutes— . . . I thank the Heavenly Father I have never had a son to mix my blood with *negro blood*—Oh such a sin would [be] & is disheartening to Christian Mothers—

On the day that Lincoln became president, she wrote about "Northern fanatics" and "black Republicans."

Monday [March] 4th . . . I pray that Lincoln's administration may disappoint his friends & his opposers—his friends are black republicans, our enemies—they must have dreadful hearts to wish to cut our throats because we are sinners—as if they were pure & undefiled—no surer sign of what deceivers they are than to see how self conceited they are—God can punish every sinner & will do it—perhaps many of them may yet have their eyes opened to the enormity of *their own* sins—if not in this world [then] in the next. Blessed be the Lord God Almighty who will make each answer for their own sins—& this will be like millstones to many deceivers. Thankful I am that I have a just God to go before & not Northern fanatics nor black Republicans—Lord let me have right feelings towards them because it [is] thy will, we should forgive our enemies. 'Tis hard for us to feel right towards those who sent John Brown (that Devil) to cut our throats—

By April 2 she feared that all would be "leveled in ashes."

April 2nd. . . O Lord let me not murmur—I am sorry our once strong country is now severed & I believe forever—for I see no disposition in the stubborn North to yield any thing from advantage—& the South thought she would make the North succumb to her—*I* never thought it—& have ever thought we have began troubles for ourselves & cannot see how we are to be one tittle better off than we were—if all the South had gone united we might have maintained ourselves—but six states only—we are doomed I fear to be the division of the Old United States. O my God *help us*—*help us*—Let me not live to see these six states disagree & I fear it very much.

On the next day, Brevard struggled between loyalty to the old Union and the likely secession of the South.

April 3rd Wednesday . . . I still fear So. Ca. cannot be pleased—I do not love her disposition to cavil at every move—My heart has never been in this breaking up of the Union—but if we could be united lovingly & firmly, I will cling to my dear native land—for I love my country—but I hate contention:—too many are waiting for the loaves & fishes, South as well as North—

Still she held out hope that there would be a resolution of the crisis. On April 11 she wrote:

How thankful I am—my Country is still spared—Lord save us & make us better—I pray that all things will be ordered for peace. How changeable my feelings are—sometimes buoyed with a hope of good times (this is momentary), then I can see & hear nothing to hang my hopes on—Why are they stubborn about the forts if they have any thought of reconciliation?

Bad news came on April 13 with the fall of Fort Sumter. "Oh how desolate many are now," she grieved.

Spent Sunday at home—had two little negroes sick—sent for Dr Taylor—he came in the afternoon & gave me the news from Charleston—Said Ft. Sumpter had been taken—Col. Anderson surrendered—he lost 9 or ten men—So. Ca. not one—Oh my God I thank thee for spareing blood here—Lord 'twas hard the citizens of Charleston should be rendered so miserable by that Fort—I am thankful it is no longer there a terror, but Oh my God we may still tremble for we have enemies in our midst—Oh God send them away to a land they love better than ours & Oh devise a way for our peace & safety & let the praise be thine—for who can doubt but thou didst so order it. A few months ago & 'twas said man could not take Ft. Sumpter unless walking over five or ten thousand dead—it has been taken—& not *one* life lost of those who aided in taking it—My God the work is thine & if we serve the[e] truthfully thou wilt save us—Oh save us & make us still a united contented people—we wish no ill to the North—all we ask is that they leave us to ourselves or gra[n]t us privileges & laws that will protect us—My God be with all thy dear Children—Oh how desolate many are now—Husbands & sons gone to the scenes of war—to save their [country].

Her final diary entry was on April 15. It was a cold day. She did not want to see civil war begin: "My God, save this country & do not let me live to see misery in this once favored land." But she lived for another twenty-five years—through the outbreak and conclusion of war—and died in 1886.

Jefferson Davis

Davis's response to John Brown's raid on Harpers Ferry was to urge the U.S. Senate on December 8, 1859, to make a full inquiry into the incident.

I believe a conspiracy has been formed, extending not only over a portion of the United States, but also into England; that money has been contributed at both places; that it has been the work of years; that a military leader was sent from England here to participate, first in the Kansas trouble, and then in this raid upon Virginia. It was foretold in England long before occurred this treasonable act, that insurrection among the slaves of the South would happen, and the disappointment must be, that the only rebellion of the slaves was against the incendiaries who got possession of them, and from whom they escaped to return to the protection of their masters. If this is the fact, and there is surely enough to justify the suspicion of conspiracy, what Senator can decline to enter into the inquiry zealously, promptly, thoroughly; to seek whether such assault has been made upon our institutions or not?

By the summer of 1860, Davis was an active supporter of John C. Breckinridge for president. He had been chosen by the Southern wing of the Democratic Party.

To William B. Sloan
Washington, D.C., July 8, 1860
My Dear Sir: . . .
Believing the preservation of the government in its vigor and purity depend mainly on the Democracy, I hoped earnestly for its unity and harmony; but when it became manifest that the organization, and consequent power of the party could only be maintained by the surrender of constitutional duties, I rejoiced that Mississippi was represented at the Convention by men who were equal to the nobler part of vindicating her equality and honor, regardless alike of empty promises and emptier threats.

To admit that our property is not entitled to receive from the General Government such protection as it affords to the property of other sections, is to consent to be degraded below our fellows. Such a proposition needs no argument—to state it is to present its condemnation. Our party alone, of those now seeking popular support, recognizes the equality of the right of the South to the common territories and pledges there to give federal protection to the property of our citizens by all the constitutional powers of the Federal arm. Can a Southern man hesitate under such circumstances, as to which of the tickets he will adopt?

The political sky is daily growing brighter, and permits us to look with increasing hope for the triumph of the National, that is, the Constitutional Democracy. . . .

Davis campaigned for Breckinridge during the summer of 1860. His speeches were an enthusiastic endorsement of the candidate.

Our cause is onward. Our car is the Constitution; our fires are up; let all who would ride into the haven of a peaceful country come on board, and those who will not, I warn that the cow-catcher is down— let stragglers beware! (Cheers.) We have before us in this canvass the highest duty which can prompt the devoted patriot. Our country is in danger. Our Constitution is assailed by those who would escape from declaring their opinions—by those who seek to torture its meaning, and by those who would trample upon its obligations. What is our Union? A bond of fraternity, by the mutual agreement of sovereign States; it is to be preserved by good faith—by strictly adhering to the obligations which exist between its friendly and confederate States. Otherwise we should transmit to our children the very evil under which our fathers groaned—a government hostile to the rights of the people, not resting upon their consent, trampling upon their privileges, and calling for their resistance. But I place my trust in democracy—in that democracy which has borne this country on from its commencement, which has illustrated all its bright passages of history, which has contributed to it all which is grand and manly, all which has elevated and contributed to its progress—the democracy of Washington, of Jefferson, of Jackson, and of Buchanan (great applause) shall be the democracy of the next four years. (Renewed applause.) . . .

The national democracy present a ticket to the country which may well inspire the most lofty patriotism. The name of Breckinridge comes down by lineal descent from one who asserted the great principles of 1798, as reaffirmed at Baltimore; and as for [vice presidential nominee Joseph] Lane, he is too modest to boast of the deeds of his younger days. No doubt he has split a hundred rails to Lincoln's one! (Laughter and cheers.) Let us then be encouraged to go into the conflict, determined to succeed, and transmit to our children the rich inheritance we have received from our fathers unimpaired. (Applause.)

Despite Lincoln's election, Davis was not willing for Mississippi to secede unless other states did likewise. It was essential that more states join such an effort or there could be failure. In answer to Robert Barnwell Rhett of South Carolina, on November 10, 1860, he took a cautious approach.

The propriety of separate secession by So. Ca. depends so much upon collateral questions that I find it difficult to respond to your last enquiry, for the want of knowledge which would enable me to estimate the value of the elements involved in the issue, though exterior to your state. Georgia is necessary to connect you with Alabama and thus to make effectual the cooperation of Missi. If Georgia would be lost by immediate action, but could be gained by delay, it seems clear to me that you should wait. If the secession of So. Ca. should be followed by an attempt to coerce her back into the Union, that act of usurpation, folly and wickedness would enlist every true Southern man for her defence. If it were attempted to blockade her ports and destroy her trade, a like result would be produced, and the commercial world would probably be added to her allies. It is therefore probable that neither of those measures would be adopted by any administration, but that federal ships would be sent to collect the duties on imports outside of the bar; that the commercial nations would feel little interest in that; and the Southern States would have little power to counteract it. . . . My opinion is, therefore, as it has been, in favor of seeking to bring those states into cooperation before asking for a popular decision upon a new policy and relation to the nations of the earth. If So. Ca. should resolve to secede before that cooperation can be obtained, to go out leaving Georgia and Alabama and Louisiana in the Union, and without any reason to suppose they will follow her; there appears to me to be no advantage in waiting until the govt. has passed into hostile hands and men have become familiarized to that injurious and offensive perversion of the general government from the ends for which it was established.

By the following month, Davis had given up "all hope of relief in the Union."

To Our Constituents
Washington, Dec. 14, 1860.
The argument is exhausted. All hope of relief in the Union through the agency of committees, congressional legislation or constitutional

amendments, is extinguished, and we trust the South will not be deceived by appearances or the pretence of new guarantees. In our judgment, the Republicans are resolute in the purpose to grant nothing that will or ought to satisfy the South. We are satisfied the honor, safety, and independence of the Southern people require the organization of a Southern confederacy—a result to be obtained only by separate State secession—that the primary object of each slaveholding State ought to be its speedy and absolute separation from a Union with hostile States. . . .

Jefferson Davis,
U.S. Senator, Mississippi.

In his farewell address on January 21, 1861, given to an overflowing gallery in the Senate, he paid tribute to John C. Calhoun for his great love for the Union, which led him desperately to want to remain in it. However, Davis reminded his listeners, when the rights of a state are violated, that state has the right to secede.

It is known to Senators who have served with me here, that I have for many years advocated, as an essential attribute of State sovereignty, the right of a State to secede from the Union. Therefore, if I had not believed there was justifiable cause; if I had thought that Mississippi was acting without sufficient provocation, or without an existing necessity, I should still, under my theory of the Government, because of my allegiance to the State of which I am a citizen, have been bound by her action. I, however, may be permitted to say that I do think she has justifiable cause, and I approve of her act. I conferred with her people before that act was taken, counseled them then that if the state of things which they apprehended should exist when the convention met, they should take the action which they have now adopted. . . .

I find in myself, perhaps, a type of the general feeling of my constituents towards yours. I am sure I feel no hostility to you, Senators from the North. I am sure there is not one of you, whatever sharp discussion there may have been between us, to whom I cannot now say, in the presence of my God, I wish you well; and such, I am sure, is the feeling of the people whom I represent towards those whom you represent. I therefore feel that I but express their desire when I say I hope, and they hope, for peaceful relations with you, though we must part. They may be mutually beneficial to us in the future, as they have been in the past, if you so will it.

Davis remained in Washington for one more week before returning to Mississippi. He was met by Mississippi Governor John J. Pettus, who offered him a commission as major general in charge of the state's militia. Less than two weeks later Davis received a telegram that changed his life.

From Robert Toombs et al.
[received] Febry 11th 1861
By Telegraph from Montgomery 9th 1861
Sir
We are directed to inform You that You were this day unanimously elected President of the provisional Government of the Confederate States of America, and to request you to Come to Montgomery immediately, We Send also a Special Messenger do not wait for him.

R Toombs
Barnwell Rhett
Jackson Morton

Despite many reservations, Davis accepted the position and left immediately for Montgomery, Alabama, where the delegates from the Southern states were meeting. On February 18 he was installed as president of the Confederacy and gave his inaugural address.

GENTLEMEN OF THE CONGRESS OF THE CONFEDERATE STATES OF AMERICA, FRIENDS AND FELLOW-CITIZENS:
Called to the difficult and responsible station of Chief Executive of the Provisional Government which you have instituted, I approach the discharge of the duties assigned to me with an humble distrust of my abilities, but with a sustaining confidence in the wisdom of those who are to guide and to aid me in the administration of public affairs, and an abiding faith in the virtue and patriotism of the people. . . .

Sustained by the consciousness that the transition from the former Union to the present Confederacy has not proceeded from a disregard on our part of just obligations, or any failure to perform every constitutional duty, moved by no interest or passion to invade the rights of others, anxious to cultivate peace and commerce with all nations, if we may not hope to avoid war, we may at least expect that posterity will acquit us of having needlessly engaged in it. Doubly justified by the absence of wrong on our part, and by wanton aggression on the part of others, there can be no cause to doubt that the courage and patriotism of the people of the Confederate States will be found equal to any measures of defense which honor and security may require.

Davis, now president of the new Confederacy, contacted Governor Francis W. Pickens of South Carolina regarding arrangements to take Fort Sumter, held by Union forces, in Charleston Harbor. Both men worried about defending the South Carolina sea lane. They were in constant contact in the next month about preparations.

On April 3, John Campbell contacted Davis about his conversation with Secretary of State William Seward. Campbell, an Associate Justice of the Supreme Court, was trying to prevent an armed conflict. Three days later Davis responded to Campbell's message. Grateful for his efforts, he was suspicious of signs that Fort Sumter would not be surrendered but instead strengthened.

To John A. Campbell
Montgomery Alabama April 6th. 1861.
My Dear Sir,
Accept my thanks for your kind and valuable services to the cause of the Confederacy and of Peace between those who though seperated have many reasons to feel towards each other more than the friendship common among nations. Our policy is as you say, peace, it is our sentiment also, and surely it must be the interest of both the parties concerned. We have waited hopefully for the withdrawal of garrisons which irritate the people of these states and threaten the respective localities, and which can serve no purpose to the United States unless it be to injure us. So far from desiring to use force for the reduction of Fort Sumter we have avoided any measure to produce discomfort or to exhibit discourtesy, until recently when we were informed that the idea of evacuation had been abandoned and that supplies convoyed by an armed vessel under the command of Capt [Silas Horton] Stringham had been sent to Fort Sumter, and that Fort Pickens was to be reinforced. Troops have been drawn from the frontier of Texas where they might have been claimed to be necessary to restrain the mexicans and Indians, and have been placed at [Forts] Taylor & Jefferson where they could only be designed to act against the Confederate States. This is not the course of good will and does not tend to preserve the peace. It is not the preservation of the States, under any possible view of our relations.

... Were it possible for the U S Govt to look beyond the events of a war and to adopt now the terms which after Thousands of lives and Millions of Treasure have been lost they must be content to accept, it would be a triumph of reason over vanity which would in all time testify to the progressive civilization of our age. In any event I will gratefully remember your zealous labor in a sacred cause and hope your fellow citizens may at some time give you acceptable recognition of your service and appreciate the heroism with which you have encountered a hazard from which most men would have shrunk. With equal confidence in our power to meet the political danger of peace, and the physical danger of War I wait the determination of a problem which it belongs to the Govt of the United States to control. ...

Very faithfully yours

Jeff Davis

Once Davis was certain that supplies were being sent to Fort Sumter, he called a cabinet meeting to decide on the next step. All but one member (Secretary of State Robert Toombs) agreed that force must be used to take the fort before the federal expedition arrived. Davis agreed, believing that the North was now the aggressor.

Davis ordered General Beauregard to secure Sumter's surrender before the supply ships arrived. These efforts proved futile. During the night of April 11–12, three officers—Col. James Chesnut, Jr., Lt. Col. A. R. Chisolm, and Capt. Stephen D. Lee—visited the fort and informed Major Anderson that he would have to evacuate it. Anderson's response was that he would evacuate on April 15 at noon if he did not receive additional supplies or further orders from his government. These terms were considered unsatisfactory. At 3:30 AM the officers refused the proposal and served notice upon Anderson that General Beauregard would open fire in one hour. The firing commenced at 4:30 AM on April 12, 1861. The war had begun.

Sources

Augustus Benners: From unpublished journals, 1850–1885.

Keziah Goodwyn Hopkins Brevard: From *A Plantation Mistress on the Eve of the Civil War, the Diary of Keziah Goodwyn Hopkins Brevard, 1860–1861*, edited by John Hammond Moore, University of South Carolina Press, Columbia, 1993.

John J. Crittenden: From *The Life of John J. Crittenden with Selections from His Correspondence and Speeches*, Vols. 1 and 2, edited by Mrs. Chapman Coleman, J. B. Lippincott & Co., Philadelphia, 1871.

Jefferson Davis: From *The Papers of Jefferson Davis*, Vols. 3–7, edited by Lynda Lasswell Crist and Mary Seaton Dix, Louisiana State University Press, Baton Rouge and London, 1985, 1989. And from *Jefferson Davis, Constitutionalist*, Vols. 1 and 2, edited by Dunbar Rowland, Jackson, Mississippi, 1923.

Frederick Douglass: From *The Life and Writings of Frederick Douglass*, Vols. 1–3, edited by Philip S. Foner, International Publishers, New York, 1952. And from *The Frederick Douglass Papers*, Vols. 2 and 3, edited by John Blassingame et al., Yale University Press, 1982.

Tryphena Blanche Holder Fox: From *A Northern Woman in the Plantation South, Letters of Tryphena Blanche Holder Fox, 1856–1876*, edited by Wilma King, University of South Carolina Press, Columbia, 1993.

Charlotte Forten Grimké: From *The Journals of Charlotte Forten Grimké*, edited by Brenda Stevenson, Oxford University Press, New York, 1988. Copyright 1988 by Brenda Stevenson.

Jones Family: From *The Children of Pride*, edited by Robert Manson Myers, Yale University Press, 1972. Copyright 1972 by Yale University Press.

Abraham Lincoln: From *The Collected Works of Abraham Lincoln*, Vols. 1–3, edited by Roy Basler, Rutgers University Press, New Brunswick, New Jersey, 1953. Courtesy of the Abraham Lincoln Association.

HORACE MANN: From *Congressional Globe*, 31st and 32d Congress (1848–1853). And from *Slavery: Letters and Speeches of Horace Mann*, B. B. Mussey & Co., Boston, 1851.

WILLIAM GILMORE SIMMS: From *The Letters of William Gilmore Simms*, Vols. 2–4, edited by Mary C. Simms Oliphant and T. C. Duncan Eaves, University of South Carolina Press, Columbia, 1955.

HARRIET BEECHER STOWE: From *The Life and Letters of Harriet Beecher Stowe* by Annie Fields, Houghton Mifflin & Company, Boston, 1897. And from *Crusader in Crinoline: The Life of Harriet Beecher Stowe* by Forrest Wilson, J. B. Lippincott Company, Philadelphia, 1941. Copyright 1941 by Forrest Wilson, renewed 1969 by Mrs. Forrest Wilson. Reprinted by permission of HarperCollins Publishers, Inc.

GEORGE TEMPLETON STRONG: From *The Diary of George Templeton Strong*, Vols. 2 and 3, edited by Allen Nevins and Milton Halsey Thomas, Macmillan, New York, 1952. Reprinted with the permission of Scribner, a division of Simon & Schuster, Inc.

CHARLES SUMNER: From *The Selected Letters of Charles Sumner*, Vols. 1 and 2, edited by Beverly Wilson Palmer, Northeastern University Press, Boston, 1990.

SOJOURNER TRUTH: From *Sojourner Truth, A Life, A Symbol*, by Nell Irvin Painter, W. W. Norton, New York and London, 1996. Copyright 1996 by Nell Irvin Painter. Reprinted with the permission of W. W. Norton & Company, Inc. And from *Narrative of Sojourner Truth, A Bondswoman of Olden Time, Drawn from her "Book of Life,"* by Olive Gilbert, published by the author, Boston, 1875.